Gilliam on Gilliam

Ian Christie is a film historian, teacher and broadcaster. He has written and edited books on Powell and Pressburger, on Eisenstein, Tarkovsky and Russian cinema, on Scorsese, and on early cinema. While at the British Film Institute, he worked with Terry Gilliam on a BBC television series, *The Last Machine*, and the Hayward Gallery exhibition *Spellbound*. He is a Fellow of the British Academy and currently Professor of Film Studies at the University of Kent.

Gilliam on Gilliam

edited by Ian Christie

faber and faber
LONDON·NEW YORK

For Maggie, Amy, Holly and Harry who have had to put up
with much of the past and most of the present – TG
This is for Beatrice, Laura, Isabel and Edward
and the other spectators of the future – IC

First published in 1999
by Faber and Faber Limited
3 Queen Square London WC1N 3AU
This paperback edition first published in 1999
Published in the United States by Faber and Faber, Inc.,
a division of Farrar, Straus and Giroux, Inc. New York

Typeset by Faber and Faber Ltd
Printed in England by Clays Ltd, St Ives plc

A CIP record for this book
is available from the British Library

ISBN 0-571-20280-2

2 4 6 8 10 9 7 5 3 1

Contents

Introduction: Poems Unlimited

'tragical-comical-historical-pastoral,
scene individable, or poem unlimited'
Hamlet, ACT 2, SC 2.1

Terry Gilliam is a film-maker who inspires strong emotions. He probably has more fans, obsessed by both the iconoclastic sweep and the esoteric minutiae of his career, than any contemporary director or indeed most stars. Among the many web sites devoted to his life and work, one is called 'The Terry Gilliam Worship Page'. And a lavish laser-disc edition of *Brazil*, aimed accurately at completists with three different versions of the film, sold out its first pressing within weeks.

Emotions among fellow film-makers probably divide along professional lines. Studio executives, producers and marketeers have good reason to fear Gilliam's own ire, often directed against their efforts to contain or modify his single-minded creative drive. Two of his films, *Brazil* and *The Adventures of Baron Munchausen*, have become legendary as a result of the epic struggles involved in releasing and completing them in the face of studio hostility. Yet for all the suspicion he may arouse in executive suites, Gilliam seems to inspire equally strong loyalty among actors and even more among the myriad artists and craftspeople, generally invisible to audiences, who build these virtual cathedrals of our time.

Gilliam's reputation among critics and the assorted arbiters of taste in cinema is similarly polarised – and here we run into an intriguing cluster of prejudices. As a former animator, a graduate of television and an ex-Python, Gilliam is triply suspect to many cinema purists. Is he a 'real' film-maker, in the same league as the great directors, or merely a humorist and creator of admittedly superior spectacle? These prejudices should not be dismissed too quickly by his admirers, for although it's easy to point to the growing number of respected film-makers who started as animators or in television, the qualities of Gilliam's work that are often attributed to his background have also long been considered incompatible with 'great cinema'.

Such typical complaints as visual excess, unevenness of tone and weak narratives all stem from a prejudice in favour of realism, which is still widely assumed to be cinema's true vocation. Gilliam, however, is clearly no realist: indeed he is one of the few film-makers at work today who can legitimately claim kinship with the founder of film magic, Georges Méliès. But in a way this is only to shift the problem back since, for all the lip-service paid to Méliès, his elaborate and frankly artificial spectacles are often considered 'uncinematic'. Méliès's own career collapsed in 1913 largely because he failed to adapt to the new realist melodrama of Griffith and DeMille which was sweeping all before it and would soon usher in the era of the big stars and their vehicles.

Sixty years later, Terry Gilliam knew that he didn't want to continue making comedy sketches *à la* Python, but neither did he want to embrace any of the new forms of seventies realist melodrama. What he had to do was create a new form, suited to his own needs and talents, which he set about fashioning in the medieval burlesque of *Jabberwocky*.

This leads to the question of genre, which has equally bedevilled Gilliam's critical reputation. While it is easy enough to say that *Monty Python and the Holy Grail* and *Monty Python's Life of Brian* show a surprising, if erratic, interest in historical authenticity – definitely more Bergman than *Carry On* – to what genre do Gilliam's most personal and passionate films belong? Peopled by *Monty Python* regulars as well as 'real' actors, *Time Bandits*, *Brazil* and *Munchausen* mix elements of Python undergrad revue humour with an appeal to the mythopoeic that would normally be considered serious. Yet their tone is rarely that: it is scatological, surreal, symbolic – and often silly. But 'silly' isn't pejorative in the Gilliam universe: it invokes a tradition of playful nonsense that includes Disney, Carroll, Hoffmann and, for that matter, Shakespeare.

Likewise, his more recent films, *The Fisher King*, *Twelve Monkeys* and *Fear and Loathing in Las Vegas*, although all seeming to be rooted in a recognisable contemporary world, also veer disturbingly into the supernatural or the fantastic. But is this a failure to unify their tone, to resist the temptations of caricature and excess; or is it the creation of a distinct Gilliamesque world, in the sense that we speak of 'Carrollian' or 'Kafkaesque'? A world of tragedy mixed with absurdity, in which dreamers such as Sam Lowry and the Baron seek refuge in fantasy; in which heroes, as well as gods, turn out to be fallible, and often closer at hand than we think; and in which death, hovering like the vulture-witch of *Munchausen*, can only be kept at bay by a combination of innocence and invention.

One category in which Gilliam is routinely placed is that of cartoonists turned live-action film-makers, a transition that was common in the early days of moving pictures, and has since produced Eisenstein and Fellini. But while Gilliam's graphic fluency is not in question – as the storyboards reproduced here prove – and has clearly helped him to create complex and original (as well as economical) visual worlds, it may be necessary to insist that the films cannot be reduced to mere caricature. Rather, their visual fabric is something alive and dynamic, as important to him as characters or narrative; and this unusual quality may well be what defeats many literary-minded critics.

An older tradition is that of the fabulist: the creator of an imagined world, especially one in which the natural and supernatural touch. When Gilliam refers a satirical character detail in *Jabberwocky* to its source in a painting by Bosch, and the same film's title and monster to Lewis Carroll, he invokes an arc of the fantastic which has one root in medieval superstition and another in the English 'nonsense' tradition. And he does so knowingly. Instead of falling short of a mainstream ideal – let's call it the modern realist melodrama – why not place him squarely in the category to which he most obviously belongs? This is what the medievalist Tom Shippey recognised in a perceptive reading:

> The surprising claim that *The Fisher King* makes and, I think, proves is that the old motifs of myth and romance work, move and persuade audiences who have no previous knowledge of them, because they are, if not true, then in a deep way needed: if they are not present in the imaginative diet, then you will get scurvy of the soul, and all the sitcoms in the world won't cure you.
>
> (*Times Literary Supplement*, 22.11.1991)

For Shippey it is clear that this, even more than other Gilliam films, operates in the realm of the 'fantastic', which he defines, following Todorov, as 'a world where events have a rational explanation, but where an irrational explanation also fits the facts and seems in some respects more persuasive'. Gilliam's heroes – innocents all, from the time-travellers of *Time Bandits* and *Twelve Monkeys* to Hunter S. Thompson adrift in Vegas – are engaged in quests, which lead them into perilous worlds of illusion, poetry and nonsense. They are the latter-day descendants of the heroes of the Grail legend, and the other romances which Gilliam is reinventing. Little wonder that he feels a lonely kinship with Méliès and fellow exponents of this ancient tradition.

This is not a work of criticism, taking an external view of Gilliam's work. It is a first-person narrative, which speaks eloquently of the struggle to make bold and original films in the confusing landscape of contemporary cinema. It offers an extraordinary insight into the sheer physical and mental effort involved, and the courage needed to keep going in the face of disaster. Rarely has the drama of film-*making* been so honestly evoked.

What emerges from Terry Gilliam's own account of his life and early career is a consistent passion for cinema, which first found its outlet at an unexpected time and place – at the end of the sixties in Britain, when the UK's theatre and novel-inspired 'new wave' had more or less run its course, and television was enjoying a new prestige. Not only the television of *Z Cars* and the *Wednesday Play*, but that of satire and zany tomfoolery. Building on the prestige of *Python*, Gilliam was able to create a niche for himself in the emerging world of low-budget UK independent production. Since that breakthrough, he has attempted an even more precarious balancing act: taking Hollywood's money to make his own films. The price paid, in personal as well as career terms, has often been high. But the rewards are that Gilliam remains remarkably uncompromised among contemporary film-makers.

The figure of comparison Gilliam evokes is Welles, thinking of his struggle with Hollywood from *The Magnificent Ambersons* onwards, and perhaps also of his unfinished *Don Quixote*, another long-planned Gilliam project. Welles, of course, was also a magician, a fabulist, and in his own way an exponent of the quest theme. But if there is another illuminating comparison, it is surely with Sergei Eisenstein. Although Gilliam rejects the Eisenstein of 'audiovisual counterpoint', just as Tarkovsky scorned the Eisensteinian montage he had been taught, it is arguable that both of these film-makers are reacting more to a fusty image of Eisenstein than to the quicksilver, self-questioning reality of 'the little boy from Riga' behind the legend. There are striking parallels between Eisenstein's graphic understanding of cinema as an art of construction and combination and Gilliam's multi-layered, allusive works; and they share a mordant, self-deprecating cartoonist's wit. The anecdotal fact that, on a visit to Eisenstein's museum-apartment in Moscow, Gilliam dislodged a signed Disney cartoon while reaching for Eisenstein's own copy of *Munchausen* seems a sure sign of poetic kinship.

Ian Christie, 1999

Acknowledgements

Anyone writing about Terry Gilliam owes a debt to Jack Mathews for his meticulous chronicling of *The Battle of Brazil* (Crown Books, 1987; 2nd edition, Applause Books 1998), which sheds light on much more than the saga of that film. Another valuable source of information and inspiration is Jean-Marc Bouineau's excellent *Le Petit Livre de Terry Gilliam* (Spartorange, 1996). Karen Stetler deserves special thanks for encouraging this book after working with Gilliam on the Criterion edition of *Brazil*, and for kindly making available interviews recorded during that project. I am also grateful to my collaborators on three projects that involved Gilliam, *The Last Machine*, *Spellbound* and *The Director's Eye*, for making possible those contributions, especially John Wyver, Richard Curson Smith, Ed Buscombe, Lucy Darwin, Greg Hilty, David Elliott and Astrid Bowren.

The interviews which form the basis of this book took place in 1996 and 1998. Rebecca Smart and Bisi Williams skilfully produced a first transcription; and many others helped in various ways during the long process of turning this into a book, among whom I would like to thank Roger Adams, Jane Bisset, Brian Mills, Justine Willett and my long-suffering editor Walter Donohue. Maggie Weston facilitated the vast amount of communication involved with great patience and good humour; and Patsy Nightingale provided invaluable advice, support and a bedrock of family life without which it wouldn't have happened.

Photographs courtesy of BFI Posters, Stills and Design. Copyright for the photographs is held by the following: Python (Monty) Pictures (*Monty Python and the Holy Grail*); Umbrella Entertainment (*Jabberwocky*); Handmade Films (*Monty Python's Life of Brian, Time Bandits*); Celandine Films/The Monty Python Partnership (*Monty Python's Meaning of Life*); Prominent Features/Laura Films (*The Adventures of Baron Munchausen*); Universal Pictures (*Twelve Monkeys, Fear and Loathing in Las Vegas*). Other illustrations are from the collections of Terry Gilliam and Ian Christie.

Minnesota , Magic
and the Movies

What are your earliest memories?
Snow White is the first movie I can remember and *The Thief of Bagdad*
was the first film to give me nightmares.[1] But I also remember having
scarlet fever – one of the many fevers you could get in Minnesota – and
that was the first time I really hallucinated. I was in the bedroom, and I
could hear my parents in the kitchen and the refrigerator was blowing
up and killing them all. It's remained with me, as if I'm still in that
room. I still have certain dreams that cling, which I'd swear are real
because my senses and my whole body seem to have experienced them.
That's always been the problem, not knowing what's real and what
isn't. I've got this sense memory of dreams I remember clearly, yet other
things that really did happen I don't remember at all, so which is the
more valid? I only know that one has formed me more than the other:
that's been basic from the beginning.

As a kid, everything was very tangible, because we lived in the country. There was a swamp on the other side of the dirt road, woods behind
the house and cornfields down the road, with a lake just a quarter of a
mile away. One of my favourite places was the swamp, where they
dumped huge logs off the edge of the road, and they formed little caves
where children could climb in. I used to spend time down there and just
thought these were the most wonderful places – all that green moss car-
peting, soft and womb-like, except the womb wasn't human: it was the
earth, the world.

In the winter, the snow would be incredibly deep and we'd dig igloos.
I have a memory of an igloo that we carved out of a great snow bank –
my dad must have helped because I couldn't have done it all – and one
day a dog peed on the top and melted the snow. Unfortunately, I was
inside and it came crashing down on top of me, dog and all. I also
remember my dad putting a sled behind the car, and we'd hold on to it
and roar over the frozen lake. And my mother would make ice-cream

The junior carpenter, following his father's example.

out of snow, snow with cream on it. We had an outdoor toilet for years, and I still find it hard to believe that it was 40 degrees below zero; I'm sitting there on a wooden two-holer out in the back garden, and my arse doesn't feel frozen.

There was a tornado once, just like in *The Wizard of Oz*. It all seems very elemental. It goes quiet and there's this rush of rain, then it goes dark and it's like the end of the world. Suddenly I see the twister coming, and I'm running into the house. I remember grabbing all sorts of laundry and trying to drag it in as the wind really got cooking; luckily it passed some distance away.

I'm not sure about the order of these little bits and pieces, but I could probably edit them together and make a life out of them.

How did your family come to be in Minnesota?
I don't really know. My mother is from Wyoming, or maybe Montana, and my dad was originally from Tennessee. I think he was in Minnesota because he was part of the last mounted cavalry unit in the US army. He must have been a real fine-looking gent on his horse. They somehow converged up there. These are things I should know, but I only remember things that are important to me, and that's not important – they were there, so it doesn't matter how they got there. However, I did discover something disturbing when a friend was preparing a documentary about me and she interviewed my mother. I had never met my grandfather on my mother's side and he was never mentioned, so I always had the feeling that he was a bum, living on the streets and a disgrace to the family. In fact, it turns out that my grandfather had run a cinema in Bismark, North Dakota. It seems very strange that from that far back there was a connection with movies, except I didn't know about it. Then, apparently, he went bad – which is what people associate with the cinema.

My grandfather on my father's side became a Baptist preacher by doing a mail-order course. He was a minister down in Hot Springs, Arkansas, which is always intriguing because it's such a completely different world down there: you leap into a field of grass, and come out with ticks and chiggers burrowing into you; you jump into the water, and there are cottonmouth snakes; and there are black widow spiders hiding under every porch. It's a place full of bugs and animals that want to eat you.

But it was also a place – and this is before the civil-rights movement started – where everybody you would meet on the street – whether black or white – seemed incredibly friendly. That was as long as everybody knew their place and stayed in it. For many people – those who

3

weren't frustrated and just wanted a quiet life – it must have been very pleasant. Everybody in their place – not so different from how England used to be, with its class system. But nowadays America is totally structureless. For those with ambition and drive, everything's possible. But for anyone who wants a safe, secure life, it's a nightmare. And those of us who write or draw – the artistic ones – we're fucking it up for all those other people who just want a nice steady solid life. In my family, I was always the one who escaped and rebelled; now I'm always talking about community and family, yet I'm running from it all the time.

The other thing that was important to me as a kid was radio. I'm convinced it gave me half of my imagination, or at least exercised those muscles. Whole worlds existed in this little box, and you had to people them with faces, build the sets, do the costumes, do the lighting, everything. It certainly introduced me to much more than I was getting in Minnesota. There were two worlds: one was real, with trees and plants and snakes, which I loved and wallowed in; and the other was the exotic realm of *The Shadow*, *The Fat Man*, *Let's Pretend* and *Johnny Lujack, Catholic Quarterback from Notre Dame*. The stories were always dark – somehow radio is good for shadows – and they tended to be urban.

So I was living in the country, where it was all light and air and green, with this urban world constantly pouring in – shadowy footsteps going down dark or misty alleyways. *The Shadow* was really clever for a radio show, because you had a character who could cloud men's minds. You'd have people in a room planning a robbery or some other awful crime, and suddenly there would be a laugh, *HA, HA, HA*, then you'd hear a *POW! What was that? URGH . . . OW! Someone's in here!* and a lot of crashing around. It was perfect for radio and wouldn't have worked on film. . . and didn't when they finally did it.[2]

You have to leave space for people's imaginations to do the work. When I make a film, I lay things out but don't always show how they relate. I juxtapose things and the mind has to make the connections. It's not that I want to confuse the audience, like it's a puzzle to be solved. I try to make the audience work at it and *do their bit*, and if it succeeds then everyone comes out with their own film. I know the story I'm trying to tell, but the one they come away with may be a different one, which is fine and dandy because they've become part of the film-making process.

What about comic strips?
L'il Abner and *Dick Tracy* are the first ones I remember; they were in the funnies in the Sunday newspapers in Minnesota.[3] I also loved *Terry and*

the Pirates.[4] As for comic books, there was *Captain Marvel*, whom nobody seems to remember any more.[5] One moment he was just Billy Batson, then he'd say the word 'Shazam' and *whoosh* . . . My son loves all that, and of course we all want to be a superhero so we can escape from everything we're bad at. I also bought the *Superman* and *Batman* comic books, but I was never a great collector.[6]

From when I was a little kid, I always drew cartoons. The first contest I won, when I was about ten, I won by cheating – and so my career began. We'd gone to the zoo and we were supposed to draw an animal that we'd remembered. I'd slipped a book in under my desk and I copied a bear, which won me a box of crayons. So from the beginning I was cheating and stealing! I think my mother has kept some early drawings I did of domestic things, such as a Hoover, that become Martians. Instead of anthropomorphizing, I was alienizing them. The other very important element was that we were serious churchgoers and I read the Bible all the way through . . . twice. You can't beat those stories for scale and drama and passion, and I grew up with all of that.

Were books important to you as a child?
Books were and are really important. As a kid I read Albert Payson Terhune, who I thought was probably one of the greatest British novelists of all time. He wrote books about collies.[7] I was reading collie dog stories as a kid, and Hardy Boys detective stories, like *The Short Wave Mystery*. Then there was *Misty of Chincoteague*. Chincoteague is a little island in Chesapeake Bay, like the Camargue, and Misty was one of those wild horses. When I think of all these books, including the Bible, it's what movies were like, especially in the fifties and early sixties – dog or horse stories, adventure stories. I think I read a lot of Walter Scott and Robert Louis Stevenson, always adventure stories, with all the elements of nature crashing around Scotland! You've got those rigid social structures and nature to fight against.

I remember all the Disney films – the cartoons were crucial. When you look at the artwork of *Pinocchio*, the world is so beautifully, carefully and lovingly rendered.[8] You really could enter that world and get totally lost in it because all the detail was there. Ten million things you couldn't even see at first were waiting for you on the next viewing, if you could see it again.

Did you go to the movies much?
It's really weird, but I just don't have any memory of going. I can't even remember walking into a cinema in Minnesota, though I obviously did. It was black, cinema is a black place, that's all I know. Perhaps because

it wasn't special? But it must have been special. I remember when television first came in. Just before we left Minnesota in the fifties, somebody up the road had a black and white television and I remember we were watching Sid Caesar's *The Show of Shows*.[9] It was brilliant. The writing was by the likes of Mel Brooks and Woody Allen. I also remember seeing Ernie Kovacs.[10] He was a surrealist and I'd never really come across surrealism before, so it was the funniest thing I'd ever seen. It freed me, because up to that point everything had been so literal, and suddenly there were these incredible leaps showing that a thing didn't have to be what it was. That's the key to surrealism for me: it's a moment when you make that leap and realize that nothing is just what it seems. I would have thought that religious studies would have understood this. Protestantism really took the fun out of it, throwing away all the graven images. That's why I feel so great walking into churches in Rome.

Thanks to all the church stuff when I was a kid, and with my father a carpenter and my mother clearly a virgin, I knew who *I* was, and my desire for martyrdom was considerable. A few years ago, my wife Maggie said she'd never really thought about mortality, and I found myself saying that every day since I was a kid I've thought about my own death. I always felt I was chosen and that I had something special – which is easy to translate into the wrong things if you're not careful. That's where humour has been my saving grace. When I look at other directors – all of whom are clearly mad and think they're God – the question is: how to combat the feeling that you're the Messiah with all the answers. I had a sense of what the truth of things was and I wanted to clear the world out a bit and do good, and yet my sense of humour always undercut these impulses. 'I fight not for me but for the gift that I've got' – this idea comes from a religious background. Well, I'm not the Messiah, but I've got a lot of stuff here which has to be protected from all those other people who are trying to destroy it.

Which church did your family belong to?
Presbyterian. Actually, I think we were Episcopalian in Minnesota, then we became Presbyterian when we moved to LA, because out there you could either be Lutheran or Presbyterian. What you didn't do was go down the road that extra block and become a Catholic – one of those papists and slaves of Rome! I think you just automatically went to church; it was part of the life of the community. And community is what I think of when I think back to Minnesota. It was Scandinavian, basically – the Hansons, the Johnsons, the Stensons – collectively known as the 'Scandahoovians' by us non-Scandinavians. Garrison Keillor writes

6

about the world I grew up in.[11] I think that world had changed a bit by the time the Coen brothers came along, but *Fargo* has very much a sense of the place.[12] I remember fairs where everyone would get together to cook pies. I miss that sense of community and yet, at the same time, I've always run from it as fast as I could. Maybe the point is that community was better than family, because in a family you don't get to choose your relatives, but with community you had a little more say in who you went around with.

I always ran from my family because I wanted relatives who were exotic and interesting, and I just had ordinary run-of-the-mill American relatives. So, as kids, we'd just run in the woods the whole time; we were always building. My dad and I managed to build a three-storey tree-house that became a great centre of activity. Three interior floors and then the terrace on the roof. It was probably quite small, but in the winter we would jump off the top into the huge snow banks and try to grab on to the electricity wires on the way down.

Making magic: an early desire 'to surprise, astound and even confound'.

7

Magic was another thing I did as a kid, and I remember my dad built a little booth out of wood, painted it red with all sorts of signs on it, and I would give magic shows. They were always really bad, and from early on I was known as a clown because I was either very silly or I would make a fool of myself by trying so hard to do well and failing. I remember the second floor of the tree-house had a ladder going up to the door, and the first nasty trick I did was to put a needle sticking out with a cork on it next to the door, so if you pushed the cork the needle would prick you. There was a sign there saying 'Don't Push', so of course one smart kid who was trying to invade our area came up the ladder and not only pushed, he went *wham*, to say 'fuck you'. The needle went into his hand and he toppled off the ladder and crashed to the ground, and there was a lot of running around, with him wanting to kill me. I think I've always stated my case and never been devious about what I'm trying to do – but nobody ever believes me.

There's always been that side of me that wants to see what happens when you do something bad, or you push things a bit further just to see what happens. At junior high school I was head of the ground patrol – like prefects in Britain – wearing a little sash, and I was supposed to make sure it was safe for kids around the school. One day somebody came tearing down the corridor at full tilt as I was walking with a friend, so I just pushed my friend in front of him to see what would happen. Of course, I was taken to the headmaster, who was shocked by my behaviour, being in a position of great responsibility and acting like a hooligan. We used to get swatted with a paddle then – bend over, here we go, then *thwack*. It was such a shock that I could do anything like that, and yet I think just because you're the head of the police doesn't mean you're perfect, or that you don't want to have some fun. There's clearly some kind of devil inside that just has to do these things.

But the Bible and the church did set up a whole way of viewing the world that has stayed with me, so there's always been good and evil, and responsibility or sin or punishment. I really like the Bible stories, because you're in this green, cold land and reading about desert people living in huge hot expanses, with camels and great armies running round the place. When I first started watching epic movies, I loved them because all those stories were suddenly there. Tens of thousands of people participating in these epic events. And, on another level, all the biblical imagery and symbolism is there as well; it accumulates and I find I'm constantly using it in different ways. Do you know Manly Hall? His *The Secret Teachings of All Ages* contains all this esoteric, arcane knowledge; it's just full of imagery of triangles and pentangles and I've always loved that.[13] My dad was a Mason, and he had a ring with the rays, and the triangle, and a 'G' – Gilliam or God? – on it, which I thought was great. I think there was one point when, although he never proselytized, he would have liked me to become a Mason, but I wasn't interested. Arcane imagery is something that Masons have always taken seriously, but I never did because I've always been more interested in what I take to be the real world around me . . . OK, and in stories of knights.

But these have also become quite 'real' since movies came along.
I think that's the problem. What I'm trying to do is rediscover the mystery. As a kid it's just there, floating around, and you don't have to think about it. I used to be very literal about the Bible but as I got older I became less so, because it is always a bit laughable if you take it too literally. I like movies because they are so tangible, which is fine for a certain phase, but in my late teens I was trying to escape from the trap of being so literal and missing the point. I was trying to escape, but if I hadn't had this background there would have been nothing to escape from.

Religion has always been around me and I've reacted against it because I've seen the hypocrisy that goes with it. In fact, I was going to be a missionary at one point: I had a scholarship to Occidental College, which is heavily funded by the Presbyterian Church, even though it's a totally liberal, non-religious place.

You were serious about becoming a missionary?
Oh yes. The Presbyterian Church, particularly in America, is very communal. I was head of the youth group in the local church, I would go to summer camps and my best friends were the minister's sons. But, in the end, I couldn't stand the fact that nobody felt able to laugh at God. Hold on a minute, I said, what kind of God is this that can't take my feeble jokes? It was the sanctimoniousness and, ultimately, the narrow-mindedness of the people who were protecting this deity that I never thought needed any protection. Their God was a much smaller God than I was thinking of – less powerful – and he needed them to protect him. I just got fed up with it because I thought: this is getting dull now and there's a whole world out there that's been off-limits. That was when I was about seventeen.

Once I was in college, I was away from it all. I had their money – just like making a movie – and I was off. It's terrible, because I was such a straight kid on one level and I did all the right things to graduate from high school – valedictorian, king of the senior prom, student-body president, whatever it was. Others might have wanted to get laid, I did as well, but I was too busy doing things. I floated through it all, because I found school was easy. But the curious thing with all this was I never felt I was there; I was always somewhere slightly different, and always surprised when I achieved these things. When they voted me student-body president, it wasn't as if I'd worked my way up through student politics, it was just that one day the group of girls who were the king-makers came and said, 'We'd like to run you for student president.' I said, 'What?' They said, 'We think you'd make a great president.' I'd been in my own little dream world doing whatever I was doing and was totally stunned by this. Then I got the job and didn't know how to run anything. I knew nothing about parliamentary procedure, I didn't even know how to chair a meeting. Utter madness. I was head cheerleader as well.

Did you feel like a provincial going to college in California?
No, it was different. Coming from Minnesota to Panorama City in the Valley was a shock, because I thought I was going out to the Wild West. I was going to *Red River* country, where there would be cowboys and Indians. Instead, it was houses built by Kaiser Aluminum.[14] The San Fernando valley had been orange groves and sheep farms up to the beginning of the fifties. Those had gone when the houses were built, but there were still some bits left. There was an old movie ranch out in Chatsworth, where lots of cowboy films – and especially TV serials – had been shot. That's why you see the same trees and rocks all the time. There was a place called Stony Point, which the movie Indians are always climbing, and we used to go and play there on weekend outings. Movies were all around us and one of my great disappointments was that my father never got a job in the studios, though he could have as he was an excellent carpenter. Nevertheless, he taught me the joy of making things. My sense of craftsmanship comes from him.

There's a weird religion that's kind of floating round the edge of my family. My mother's version was just this solid belief in something, and in morals and the right way to live. I remember as a kid we used to say grace. There were these tight groups of people working together, with the church as the focus, and out of that came summer camps and good works, and that's always been what I've really liked. At college you're in this protected environment for four years where you can do almost anything. Python was a group, and making films is the same, which is what I like about it. In a sense, I've got the best of both worlds: between films I don't even have a secretary and I can go back to my own little insular existence. Then, when a film starts, I gather the community together and we all focus and work. It feels good, and I think it all comes from Minnesota and that world.

In the end, I decided that religion is about making people feel comfortable – providing explanations and giving answers – while magic is about accepting the mystery and living with question marks. Mystery intrigued me more than answers. The difference between *Close Encounters of the Third Kind* and *2001: A Space Odyssey* is that the end of Kubrick's film is a question, while the end of *Close Encounters* is an answer – and it's a really silly answer – little kids in latex suits.[15] So for me what's important has always been the questioning and searching. You could say it's the Sagittarian side of my nature. I'm on the cusp between Sagittarius and Scorpio. Sagittarians are hunters and Scorpios have a sting in the tail, and I know I'm both of these. Sagittarians can be pretty nice when they're out there hunting and searching for things, but Scorpios are killers. Having these two sides can be useful in movies – maybe it's the only way to survive – and that's why I've worked hard on my schizophrenia.

When I was a kid, I always thought everyone else was so interesting, but I was just incredibly *normal*. It used to drive me crazy. I felt I had to suffer if I was ever going to be an artist. Maybe it was the religious side again, feeling you had to go through a lot of pain and strip away the outside to lay bare the soul. Anyway, other people seemed to have it, but I was just *nice*, good company. I'd entered college as the golden boy with a lot of scholarships and in the end I barely graduated.

What did you study at college?
I started as a physics major, because that was what America was about in the fifties. It was the technological leap forward and anybody with brains went into science. Germans, like Werner von Braun, were running the space programme, so it was important for Americans to study science. I did all the right things because I came from a family that did the right things. We weren't questioning in that sense: my table manners were brilliant and I did what smart kids were supposed to do. So I did science all through high school, but after six weeks at college I knew physics wasn't for me. Then I moved into art, but I didn't like the art-history professor. He was so tedious and I just wanted to paint and draw. But art history was a required course, so I pulled out of art and became a political-science major. There were only four required courses; the rest were electives – drama, oriental philosophy, even some art classes could apply. It was a fantastic opportunity to devise my own liberal education, and my generation was probably the last to have it.

Occidental College used to be known as the Princeton of the West. There were a lot of wealthy kids, it was liberal, and it was a smart school – even the dumb people were smart. This meant that there was a smart audience, and this was the end of the era of really good practical jokes. A serious practical joke is a very complex business which involves the joker doing much more work than the person it's played on. So at Occidental, for example, they would take a car apart and reassemble it in someone's dorm room while he was away. The occupant would return to find a car – with the engine running – occupying his room. That's clever stuff. The joke really was about how much work was involved in doing it. Other things you'd do were to fill a room completely with crumpled paper so nobody could get into it; or take the pins out of a door hinge, then run a rope from the inside handle across to the window and hang a bed outside on the end of it – when you turned a key in the lock, the door just flew across the room and smashed against the window. I don't think anyone does that kind of thing today. It came from an era of privilege, the world of Scott Fitzgerald, and the kids from wealthy families who came to our school had been to private schools where it still continued.[16] I'd got in on merit, but it was great to meet people like that who had time on their hands and were serious about having fun.

The high school I went to was the biggest in LA. It had been a Second World War hospital, and it had a real mix of kids. There were Mexicans from San Fernando and – my mother hates me saying poor white trash – we were lower middle class or upper working class; anyway, we had a proud clean house. And then there were kids from Encino whose parents worked in films – as editors, writers and musicians – and these were the ones I gravitated towards, and used to use their pools sometimes. It was a fantastic time to be young, with the Peace Corps starting up and a lot of altruism around.[17] Maybe it was too aggressive in trying to impose America on the world, but it was well meant and there really was a feeling that if you were privileged you also had responsibilities.

Did you want to join the Peace Corps?
I tried to go to Hong Kong for the church, but I never got past the selection board. Getting away from home meant that I was suddenly released, I could start being different without effort. They wanted clear and focused people for things like the Peace Corps, and I was beginning to get sillier and less willing to put up with the kind of crap they expected. What I really did at college was the humour magazine, which was copied from *Help!*[18] We photographed and wrote and cartooned, and had a captive audience at the college. We bought endless rolls of butcher paper and I'd paint posters and banners to cover the walls of the student union. So every morning people would come down and find

a new show. The college authorities didn't like us much because we were messy, but it was entertaining.

Before that, I was the head of the Bengal Board. Because our football team was the Occidental Tigers, the Bengal Board was in charge of the cheerleaders and boosting school spirit. Now, I knew that this could mean anything at all – Goebbels was head of the Bengal Board in Germany, except they didn't call it that. There was a Greek amphitheatre up on a hill behind the college and we organized midnight torchlight processions, almost like Nazi rallies, where all the freshmen had to come and be initiated. We invented all these traditions as a joke and what amazed me was that everyone bought it. By the end of the year, even the seniors believed these traditions had been around for ever. It was a scary moment: I suddenly realized the power of this kind of thing and how much people want to be led. Ever since feeling that first taste of power at college, I've been worried about responsibility, because half of what I want to do is stir things up and you never know how far it might go.

I think most artists are driven by a feeling of frustration, and so for the first part of your career you're railing against the establishment because you don't belong. Then, if you become successful, you're in a tricky situation: do you continue railing even though you're living in a nice house with a nice family and everything? I mean, what have *I* got to complain about? Not a thing, so what am I railing about? Yet I'm still angry and still frustrated. So what am I looking for? Trying to clear all the shit away to find out what truth is and what reality is.

But there are clear patterns that run through all your work, even when you're trying to do something different.
If you look at everything I've done, they're all search films, they're all trying to discover the truth, what the solution is to the problem. Perhaps they're really trying to find out what the question is. I used to think I had the questions and it was just the answers I was searching for. But the older I get, the more lost I feel, which stimulates more questioning.

1 *Snow White and the Seven Dwarfs* (Disney, 1937, US); *The Thief of Bagdad* (Berger/Powell/Korda/Whelan, 1940, GB).
2 *The Shadow* was filmed by Russell Mulcahy in 1994.
3 The classic newspaper strips *L'il Abner* by Al Capp started in 1935 and *Dick Tracy* by Chester Gould in 1931.
4 *Terry and the Pirates*, by Milton Caniff, started in 1934.
5 *Captain Marvel* starred in one of the new comic book magazines which first appeared in the 1940s.
6 *Superman* (Joe Siegel and Joe Shuster, from 1938) and *Batman* (Bob Kane, from 1939) were the pioneer comic-strip super heroes, also in comic books from 1940.
7 Albert Payson Terhune (1872–1942), writer of popular dog stories, including *Lad: a dog* (1914).
8 *Pinocchio* (Sharpsteen/Luske, 1940), Disney's second animated feature, made extensive use of the multiplane camera and its rich detail has been admired even by those resistant to its characters.
9 Sid Caesar (b. 1922) was a popular US television comedian who starred in *Your Show of Shows* (1950–54), with Carl Reiner as his foil, and Howard Morris as co-writer. Reiner went on to create the *Dick Van Dyck Show* and to direct many early Steve Martin films.
10 Ernie Kovacs (1919–62) is widely considered to be one of the most original and eccentric figures in the late fifties television comedy. He made brief appearance in a handful of films before his premature death in a car accident.
11 Garrison Keillor, former host of US National Public Radio's *Prairie Home Companion* created the mythic Minnesota-Scandinavian back water Lake Wobegon.
12 Joel and Ethan Coen's *Fargo* (1995, US) is set in remote Minnesota.
13 Manly P. Hall, *The Secret Teachings of All Ages: an Encyclopedic Outline of Masonic, Hermetic, Quabbalistic and Rosicrucian Symbolical Philosiphy,* The Philosophical Research Society, 1977.
14 On Henry Kaiser's post-war venture into prefabricated housing, see Peter Wollen's essay on Gilliam in the catalogue, *Spellbound: Art and Film*, edited by Philip Dodd and Ian Christie, South Bank Centre, 1996, p. 61
15 *2001: A Space Odyssey* was directed by Stanley Kubrick in 1968 and *Close Encounters of the Third Kind* by Steven Spielberg in 1977.
16 Minnesota-born F. Scott Fitzgerald's novels *This Side of Paradise* (1920), *The Beautiful and the Dammed* (1922) and *Tender is the Night* (1934) chronicle the glamorous, dissipated life that he lived and many aspired to.

17 The Peace Corps, modelled on Britain's Voluntary Service Overseas, was launched by President Kennedy in 1961.

18 *Help!* magazine was created by Harvey Kurtzman, who had previously worked on *Mad* (from 1952) and would co-create *Little Annie Fanny* for *Playboy* in 1962. See also Chapter 2.

2

Alice and the assembly line; *Mad* at the Algonquin and filming Joyce; army life, escape to Europe and disillusion in Disneyland

Which films did you start to take seriously? You've often mentioned Kubrick's Paths of Glory *as a watershed experience, but what else impressed you as a teenager?*
Movies were like trees or rocks, they were just there as part of the landscape. I'm often shocked by how *un*analytical I am at times, just accepting some things while I'm busy analysing others and thinking I've got to the heart of reality. I was a big Jerry Lewis fan and I loved comedies and detective films. Of course I only knew the stars: directors didn't mean anything to me yet, except Walt Disney and Cecil B. DeMille, which were like brandnames. More than anything, I loved epics like *Ben-Hur* and *The Ten Commandments*, with all those tens of thousands of people running around. They might have been terrible films, but they made those ancient worlds believable.

The first movie that really got me was *Paths of Glory*, which I saw when I was sixteen at a Saturday matinée in Panorama City, with kids running up and down the aisle.[1] What's weird to me now is that I'd be watching a movie on Saturday afternoon: apparently movies were more important to me than I remember – I'm beginning to think that I suppress the good things and only linger on the bad. Anyway, what I never did was go to drive-in theatres. I hated the fact that you were there for everything but movies. So clearly I respected movies, and they were not to be trivialized by sitting there with your hands on a girl's tit and concentrating on that. Suddenly, with *Paths of Glory* there was a movie that was *about* something – about injustice – with themes and ideas, and the good guys didn't win in the end. That film completely changed me and I went around trying to get everybody I knew to see it.

There was one I remember before that. I used to think it was *The Incident at Owl Creek*, which came out in the early sixties and did the round of colleges.[2] But I'm pretty sure it was actually *The Ox-Bow Incident*, with Dana Andrews.[3] Then there was *High Noon*: injustice, standing up to mob rule – these are the things that really started making an impression on me.[4] I had grown up accepting America at face value, and clearly the Right had a point about trying to stop these films, because they made people like me think that maybe everything wasn't right in Mudville. I couldn't put my finger on it, but I knew they touched on something that nobody else was talking about. *The Ox-Bow Incident* is a wonderful film – I can't think why more people don't know it. They find the real rustlers at the end, but the mob has already strung up the wrong guys. Was that written by a commie as well, trying to undermine everything that we'd worked so hard for?

Lamar Trotti, who wrote and produced it, died in 1952. He wasn't one of the Hollywood Ten, but there were a lot of liberal westerns in the forties and fifties, and it was in these – as well as in science fiction – that politics got debated.

The War of the Worlds is the one I remember best, and also the giant ants in *Them*.[5] I rushed out to see all those movies because I liked the special effects and outrageous creatures in them, but I thought that most of them were pretty bad films.

I was also a great fan of the Ealing comedies, and loved all those British actors like Ian Carmichael, Alistair Sim, Terry Thomas, Margaret Rutherford, Alec Guinness and later Peter Sellers.[6] In fact, I became a real anglophile, and then *The Goon Show* started turning up occasionally on radio.[7] When I first heard it, I was astounded. So England began to have a very strong appeal for me, mainly through its sense of comedy. By then I'd forgotten Jerry Lewis, and started moving towards what seemed to be a much more sophisticated taste in comedy. It might not be so sophisticated if you're English, but it was to an American in the late fifties and early sixties, when I was going through college.

Another thing that only struck me recently, when I was at Sundance and Stanley Donen had an evening with clips from all his films, was what an influence he'd had on me – films like *On the Town, Funny Face, The Pyjama Game* and *Charade*.[8] I said I wished that I'd dedicated *The Fisher King* to him. The truth is that I was watching films all the time, but they were just part of the landscape. It's like the French being really bad at identifying all the trees and weeds when they're out in the country: I often can't pick out the detail from the mass.

Real life always used to surprise me when it interrupted my reveries, like when I was asked to be student body president at high school. I remember we were doing a Camelot theme for the senior prom, with knights, the round table, and a castle – I always used to do the sets for the dances: very important for a future film-maker – and I'm there with paint on my hands as people are arriving in their DJs, putting on the last touches and planning to rush home and get cleaned up before collecting my date. Suddenly, I'm elected king of the senior prom. Shock. Horror. It was supposed to be my best friend, who I was certain was the most popular guy in the school. Once again, I discovered that my clear understanding of the world was wrong.

I spent a lot of my time at college on drama, acting and doing sets for everything from *The Three Sisters* to revues, instead of academic work. In fact, I still have occasional nightmares about being at some college which I'm never going to graduate from because I'm missing all my classes. It's weird to have nightmares about it thirty-odd years after the event, but I must still feel guilty about spending so much time on entertaining the troops.

Did your parents have high expectations of you?
There was never any pressure from them, because they knew I always did well. I was the first-born and flying. What confused them was how the straight and narrow path started meandering at college, and I barely graduated. In fact, I wouldn't have if I hadn't begged my sculpture teacher to give me a D grade rather than fail me. So, in academic terms, I was a failure. But I'd learned everything I needed to know.

I had two favourite professors. One was in art: he did all the drawing classes and was really supportive, and he started making me look at things analytically – at shape and form and colour. He was putting into words a way of looking at the world, and that was really important for me. My political science professor – this was supposed to be my major – was great too, because he knew I was doing all these other things and not concentrating on my studies. But he also knew I was doing real politics as opposed to theoretical politics. I remember seminars with people arguing about how you couldn't do this or that, and I would go and do it – right outside the window – just to show them. 'Don't give me your theories – I'm *doing* it – just watch.' That's been fairly consistent: doing things just to spite people. If they're all going one way, I want to go the other, out of curiosity or because there's less competition and a little patch I can carve for myself.

Outside college – I think it was my sophomore year – I worked through the summer at the Chevrolet assembly plant on the night shift from eight until five in the morning. Even with the scholarships, I still needed to earn money. And because I failed the colour-blindness test, they didn't give me anything that required colour recognition, so I'm stuck washing all the glass on the right-hand side of the cars, inside and out, with ammonia. In the Californian summer, this has got to be one of the worst jobs. In 1960 they had those steeply raked windscreens, so there was a lot of this [*mimes vigorous wiping*] with ammonia dripping in your face, and I hated it. I think fifty-four cars an hour was the pace of this line, and I would always get behind and have to try to catch up during the breaks. It's still my ultimate nightmare: in my cartoons and in a lot of the animations for *Python* there are treadmills and machinery.

One day I wandered down the line in this vast factory to see where the cars that I'd polished to perfection went. I followed them and discovered they were covered with grease pencil marks again. I was just cleaning them for someone else to mark up, so I said, 'That's it, I'm out of here. I'm never going to work just for money again in my life.'

I made a rule that summer: I was only going to do things I could control. So I went and worked in a children's theatre for the rest of the summer, building castles again and painting myself green and playing the ogre, and that was the end of my proper work. In the summer between junior and senior years, I counselled at a summer camp up in the mountains above Palm Springs, where all the kids came from Beverly Hills. There was Danny Kaye's daughter, Hedy Lamarr's son and William Wyler's son – and I was the drama coach.[9] I didn't know anything about drama, except what I'd picked up from making a fool of myself and doing plays. So I decided to put on a very ambitious *Alice in Wonderland*[10] and got everybody involved with it. It was an eight-week camp, but we were working towards parents' day in the sixth week, and it soon became clear that I'd bitten off more than I could chew. So, at the last minute, with only a week to go, I said, 'No, it's a mess, we're not going ahead' – and cancelled the whole thing. This caused consternation all round since it was supposed to be the centrepiece of the whole event – and that was another nightmare that came back to haunt me on *Baron Munchausen*, when I was convinced I'd once again bitten off more than I could chew and it was never going to get finished.

Why did you choose Alice in Wonderland *in the first place?*
Because I loved it, and Ernie Kovacs did a wonderful nonsensical *Alice*, but in general America tends to be afraid of nonsense. That's what I liked about English comedies – they weren't afraid to be nonsensical – but America's always been too busy being earnest, moulding itself, wanting everything to be educational.

Maybe comic strips were America's special way of being nonsensical and fantastic. Which ones did you first get into?

I think the one I loved most was *Little Nemo* by Winsor McCay, and *The Katzenjammer Kids*.[11] Both of these were nonsensical in a way, but then they came from a European tradition. McCay looks as if he was classically trained and his sense of architecture seems definitely European. Of course I loved George Herriman's *Krazy Kat* and I grew up with *Mad* magazine, which was satirical but also playfully nonsensical.[12] That had a lot to do with Willy Elder's drawings, because he just couldn't stop himself putting a million gags in every frame.[13] It was silly beyond belief, and wonderful because it was so smart. *Mad* became the Bible for me and for my whole generation; all the guys who did underground comics in the sixties were raised on *Mad*, which had started in 1955. It was a combination of nonsense, satire and lampoon, but above all it was precise, because the editor, Harvey Kurtzman, was a real taskmaster. A lampoon had to look exactly like the real thing, and he insisted on real craftsmanship. This is what we ended up with on *Python*: when we made *Monty Python and the Holy Grail* we did it seriously, with the sets, costumes and lighting. Whether we achieved that is something else, but at least we set out to be as serious as Pasolini or Visconti or Cecil B. DeMille. Money – the lack of it – changed things sometimes, but the intent was always there.

In my last year at college, a group of us, with me as editor, took over *Fang*, the literary magazine – poetry, fine art and quality stuff – and turned it onto . . . shock, horror . . . a humour magazine. We did six issues and it got very silly: nobody had ever done that many before; at best they managed three or four. The magazine we were emulating whenever possible was *Help!*, which Harvey Kurtzman was editing with Gloria Steinem as his assistant.

One thing that *Help!* was alone in doing at that time was a version of the *fumetti* – photo comic strips as seen in Fellini's *The White Sheikh*.[14] Harvey got the idea from Italian romance magazines, but his were very funny pieces, written by comic writers and performed by actors like Dick Van Dyke and Steve Allen.[15] Ernie Kovacs was even on the cover of *Help!* Gloria was really good at hustling male actors to be in these things and Harvey's name was known to everyone in comedy. So I did a couple of *fumetti* in our magazine and sent copies to New York to my hero, and Harvey wrote back saying it was great.

Then I graduated with no idea of what I was going to do next. Everyone else joined multinationals and I ended up counselling at another summer camp. This time it's up in the High Sierra – with Burt Lancaster's daughters as campers. Once again I was a kind of art and drama coach. At the time I was reading Moss Hart's autobiography, *Act One*, which is about this kid, whose great hero is the playwright George Kaufman, who makes his way to New York – and just bumps into George Kaufman and becomes his partner in success after success.[16] So I wrote a letter to Harvey Kurtzman announcing, 'I'm coming to New York,' and he wrote back saying, 'Don't bother, there's 10 million kids here and they're all failing. It's an impossible city, don't do it.' Anyway, I packed my bags and went to New York and wangled an appointment with him. And where does this take place? After reading in Moss Hart's book all about the Algonquin Hotel and the Round Table – round tables seem to keep turning up in some form or other – naturally it's at the Algonquin.[17] *I'm meeting Harvey at the Algonquin!* So I go upstairs, since he'd rented a suite, and it all seemed a bit odd. Why is he asking a young lad from the West Coast up to his hotel room? All my fears of sodomy in New York were rearing their ugly head as I pushed the button, opened the door, and suddenly in that room are all of my heroes – Arnold Roth, Willy Elder, Al Jaffe, all these cartoonists from *Mad* and *Help!* – and they were working on the first instalment of *Little Annie Fannie*.[18]

So I walk in there and there they are . . . these gods! Harvey appears a bit later. It turns out that Chuck Alverson, who was then assistant editor of *Help!* and would later co-write *Jabberwocky*, was quitting and they were looking for someone to take his place. And who's standing there bright-eyed and bushy-tailed? Just like Moss Hart met George Kaufman and teamed up with him, I got the job.

It's strange how the things that have worked out for me have often been other people's stories that I go into, believing them so strongly that they happen. Anyway, I was hired at $50 a week – the dole was $52 a week – but it was Harvey and me, which was all that mattered. So I got to work with my hero for three years, doing cartoons, editing, and organizing the *fumetti*, which was like making movies. I'd have to get actors and find locations, then we'd get the costumes. When I was in LA, I was desperate to make films and I had all these semi-connections – I could go swimming at Danny Kaye's house, and there was Danny walking around – yet I was still outside all of this and I couldn't see how to get in. I certainly didn't want to work my way up – I've never been good at that – and I didn't like the films that were being made at that time. Although it all seemed so close, I had to go in the opposite direction, staying true to my idea of being in control of what I do and not working just for money.

So I was in New York, in my little eight-by-eight room with my pet cockroach who turned up in cartoons later. It was a really rough existence. It was bitterly cold when the first winter hit and I was still wearing my California clothes, which was all I could afford; I'm walking around in tennis shoes and the wind's howling. But I did buy my first Bogart mac and thought I looked cool wandering the streets of New York, even if I was freezing.

The editorial staff was just two of us. There was Harry Chester, the production man, and the publisher, Jim Warren, who was also doing horror comics at the time – he turns up in *Brazil* as Mr Warrenn, played by Ian Richardson; Ian Holm plays Mr Kurtzmann.[19] And there was Gloria Steinem, who was now working her way up in the world, wrapping useful and important men around her little finger.[20] She put together an extravagant, but ultimately silly book, *The Beach Book*, which I was briefly an assistant on, with J.K. Galbraith writing the introduction – that was Gloria. So I was running around meeting people too, like Harold Hayes, the editor of *Esquire*, and René Goscinny, the creator of *Asterix*, who was there because all the cartoonists of the world came to Harvey. In fact, the Kurtzman–Goscinny bridge was really important for American cartooning. Since *Help!* was the only national humour magazine at that time, we had guys like Robert Crumb and Gilbert Shelton – who started the underground comics of the late sixties – coming to us as the only outlet for their work.[21]

The business of getting actors for the *fumetti* eventually took me down to Greenwich Village. This was the year after *Beyond the Fringe* had conquered New York. So there were John Cleese, Graham Chapman, Bill Oddie, David Hatch and Tim Brooke-Taylor in *Cambridge Circus*, the Cambridge Footlights revue, doing material by themselves and also by Mike Palin and Terry Jones and Eric Idle. I got John to be in one of the *fumetti*, playing a man who falls in love with his daughter's Barbie doll and, as far as we can tell, has actual congress. Anyway, I became friends with John and he got the princely sum of $15 for a day's work. Then there was the guy who was the boyfriend of a brilliant folk singer, Judy Henske. She was about six foot one and she asked if she could bring her boyfriend, who turned out to be Woody Allen. He played a gangster boss in one of our *fumetti*, although Harvey had no idea who he was.

Harvey lived in his own little bubble and so did I. We were doing what were virtually mini-movies for the magazine, and I decided to go to film school at night, at the City College of New York. That lasted one month, because I just didn't have that pushy New York ambition. This was the time when Stan Brakhage and Andy Warhol and John Cassavetes were all in New York: everything was very experimental and we were all excited by these new ideas.[22] And Buster Keaton's stuff was being rediscovered. I started to see Fellini and Kurosawa and Bergman's work sometime towards the end of college and then New York really opened my eyes to European movies. Suddenly English movies weren't quite European movies; these others were art. They were serious and wonderful.

And you were more influenced by the European films?
Totally, because that's what all the people I knew were watching. Nobody was paying any attention to Hollywood movies. However, I did go and see *One-Eyed Jacks* in one of the 42nd Street dollar-fifty cinemas, and then stayed all afternoon to see it again and again. I was a huge Brando fan and I loved it. In fact, I still say it's a wonderful movie and I still love it, yet Brando was pilloried for doing what David Lean would get away with.[23] There's a scene where they ride along past those great crashing breakers, and he kept the crew waiting for the right sea – which David Lean did on *Ryan's Daughter* – but Marlon just got ripped apart because he waited for the waves.

Lean was riding high in 1962 with Lawrence of Arabia, *and certainly Brando was much mocked and criticized at that time, because* One-Eyed Jacks *is a truly ambitious as well as egocentric film.*
In any case, I only lasted a month at film school. Then Jim Hampton – a friend of Henry Jaglom,[24] who was working in a stop-motion studio where they did dancing cigarette packs for ads – said that they might need some help. So I quit film school after a month of misery, because it was all politics and jockeying for position, which I never liked. They didn't have a job for me, but I said I'd work for free. I still had the magazine, which was only coming out every two months, so there was always time in between to do other things, like submitting cartoons to other magazines and doing odd jobs for Gloria.

At first I was moving lights around, sweeping up, doing anything just to be near this stuff. It was great because I learned a lot about the physical side of the business, which has no magic in it. Eventually, I quit because the wife of the man who ran the studio, Mary Ellen Bute, had started making *Passages from Finnegans Wake*.[25] It was very shambolic, with everybody working for nothing. And one day they were trying to set up a shot and I said, 'You can't do that,' even though I was only a runner. There was a table with chairs upturned on it and somebody either behind the table or in front of it, and they were trying to keep the person and the table in line and do a circular track around it. I knew the only way to do this was to put it on a turntable, and I kept saying,

'Please, sir, please, sir.' In the end, I thought, 'This is ridiculous. I do understand spatial relationships. I've told them why it won't work and they're so grand they won't listen to me.' So I walked out, and that was the end of my film career for a while.

You wouldn't have realized that among the army of unpaid people working on Finnegans Wake *was a certain Thelma Schoonmaker, who was just starting as an editor, and she didn't know you'd worked on it until I told her.*[26] *But it was a time when all kinds of barriers were coming down and anything seemed possible.*

It was a great time to be in New York, but magazines were very much on the periphery. *Esquire* wasn't cool then, but the art director was Robert Benton, who was part of that great wave of energy and talent that came out of the Texas universities in the late fifties.[27] What I would do was phone to say that 'Mr Gilliam, the assistant editor of *Help!* needed something or other, and would be sending someone round.' Then I would turn up to collect whatever it was 'for Mr Gilliam'. I was twenty-two, but I looked more like seventeen, with this baby face. So I played a *Wizard of Oz* game as both the editor and the delivery boy.

From my $50 a week I was managing to live on $25 and saving the rest, writing down all my living expenses in a little notebook and not even buying gum because it cost five cents. By being that tight I saved enough to buy my first Bolex camera and my first tape recorder. Bingo! I had a camera and a recorder. I could make movies!

At this time I was rooming with another cartoonist and a writer, and I was also doing cheap children's fun-and-games books. We had already started drawing directly on to film, because it was easy to get blank film and spacing leader from trim bins. We went out on Sundays to make live-action films. We'd look at the weather and, depending on whether it was snowing or bright, we'd write ourselves a little movie, get funny clothes and just do it as an exercise: one three-minute roll of film per movie. I wasn't going to film classes and there was nothing academic in my approach. It was just a practical interest in making something. The one book I had was Eisenstein's *The Film Sense*, but basically we were just doing silly comedies, using stop-motion pixilation techniques.[28]

In my four short weeks at film school, I'd met a few people who were really interested in film. But I couldn't imagine being anywhere near the cool film-makers of that time, like Warhol. They were so sophisticated, so New York, and I was just doing gags. Occasionally, I was involved with *The Realist*, which was edited by Paul Krasner, the great political satirist of the sixties. Vietnam had just started and all the cartoons I was doing related to it – like Madame Nu going off to a Buddhist monk's self-immolation with a petrol can – but I'd also had to join the National Guard to avoid being drafted.

This meant doing Basic Training like the regular army for six months, then going to weekly meetings and summer camp for ten years. It was full of guys like me who had no desire to be in the army, but this was when they started sending volunteers over to Vietnam and it was frightening to see how all the excitement of war works wonders. Soon the guys in Basic couldn't wait to get out there. Of course, the training sergeants and officers were dying to get away from these idiot kids to go and kill some real people, which was scary to watch.

But any talent in the army gets you somewhere and I missed the worst parts of Basic Training because I could draw. I was in hospital with mumps when I developed an abscessed wisdom tooth. Since I didn't have any money, I asked the dentist if he'd take out the other wisdom teeth at the same time. Nothing wrong with them, he said. So I went back to my bed and spent an evening grinding my teeth so that my whole face was swollen up. The result was that I got 'em out for free, on the principle of using the army to get done everything medical that I'm going to need in life.

Just after I got out of hospital, I ran into my senior officer, a lieutenant, who must have been all of eighteen, while I was twenty-three or so. He was a little martinet and I found it hard to salute him without turning into a Jerry Lewis kind of character. No doubt he thought I was an absolute fool, but now and again it's useful to be a fool. So he greets me as I'm signing back in: 'Ah, Gilliam, what have you been up to (meaning *obviously something stupid*)?' 'Drawing,' I answer, and out comes the portfolio. He produces a photograph of his fiancée and asks if I can do a drawing of her as a wedding present.

Now, this is the last two weeks of Basic Training, when everybody is down in the mud under barbed wire and a hail of machine-gun bullets, and I'm sitting in the barracks, stretching out over two weeks something I could do in a day. Actually, the first one took a week, but he liked it so much that he wanted one of himself to make a pair. I hated the guy so much that I started performing to the rest of the men, putting Mickey Mouse ears on him and doing Napoleon gags, and one night he snuck into the barracks up the fire escape to see what I was doing. He walked right in on the show and he was just destroyed. He wanted to kill me, but he couldn't because I hadn't finished the drawing he wanted so desperately.

Later I was assigned to the Post newspaper, and again drawing came in useful. The colonel's wife had raised money for a new chapel and I had to go and sketch it, which allowed me to spend time in the library reading books. The colonel hated my guts, but he wanted the stuff. Because I was taking so long, he kept telling me it was good enough. Then he gave me some very serious advice. 'This stuff only has to be good, Gilliam, not great. The great is the enemy of the good.' That's how he went through life. 'Just do everything good enough.' Back comes Gilliam: 'No, sir, I'm sorry, sir. It's got to be great, sir.' What a fool I was . . . and am. This attitude has made my life much more tortuous than it needed to have been. What the army taught me most was how to malinger, something I'd never really done before – and it was depressing. It took a long time to get creative again. Anyway, Basic Training is normally six months, but I got out in four months and two days. *Help!* magazine had been getting weaker and finally closed, but Harvey wrote to the National Guard on letterhead notepaper that I was being sent abroad as head of the European division, so off I went to Europe for six months with $1,000 in my pocket. I hitch-hiked my way all over the continent until I reached Rhodes, where one of my former room-mates was now living. I wrote back to the National Guard that the magazine had now stationed me permanently there, and I was assigned to a control group based in Germany so that in time of war I could be called upon. However, I went to Istanbul and spent what little money I had on a foxskin coat and a little Turkish rug.

I arrived back in Paris with no money, and got some work from *Asterix*'s creator, René Goscinny, who was now editing *Pilote* magazine.[29] There I was in my little 8-franc-a-day Left Bank hotel, drawing in my garret in the middle of winter, making jokes about snowmen to earn enough to get me back to New York. That's the advantage of being a cartoonist: it's more immediate and people love it. My art professor wanted me to be a more serious artist, but the feedback from cartooning was instant, which was why I slid into it. I'm a sucker for feeling good and people liking me – it's very bad, but there it is.

After six months in Europe, I had developed a real fascination with it. Strangely enough, I think this had something to do with my weekly visits to Disneyland when I was growing up in LA. It used to fascinate me because it was so beautiful. There was no craftsmanship to match it in America at that time, unless you were a millionaire like Vanderbilt or Hearst and could build your own castle. But this was popular entertainment, beautifully done, and I loved it and went constantly.

Later I became disillusioned when they began taking advertising and sponsorship. You could legitimately have Beacon's Vans in the Old American Town, but to have Bank of America in Fantasyland seemed blasphemy. I felt there were very precise rules about what could and couldn't be done, and when it became more commercial in the later sixties, I was deeply disillusioned. But to a kid with a fantastic imagination, it was concrete and real, clearly done with a loving hand and real passion, not just to make money.

Europe was like Disneyland, only real and more surprising. And, as I travelled around Europe, it became clear to me how many things were wrong with America. I was very much against the Vietnam War and racial inequality was still a major problem. But although I was very critical of the country, it was another matter to hear Europeans doing America down. I had come to Europe and found all these Europeans who agreed with me. Yet I spent all my time defending America: 'Hold on, this is my country you're talking about.' Then I would catch myself doing this and realize something was wrong.

I began to feel the responsibility of being American and to realize what damage we were doing to the world by interfering everywhere. Even when Kennedy came up with the Peace Corps to try to make it a better place, we were still making a mess by walking into other people's worlds and trying to apply our values without understanding theirs.

One of the connections I tried to make when I was in Europe was with *Private Eye*.[30] Their whole technique of captioning photographs with speech bubbles was taken from *Help!* magazine, where Harvey did it first. But I didn't get very far with them. People forget nowadays just how hostile the English were towards Americans at that time. I remember when I went to a Lyons tea house and tried to order; they didn't understand me, and I couldn't understand them, so I got all the wrong things. An American accent got you nowhere fast. I used to sit on buses and try to hide when I heard loud American voices: I was trying to be a quiet American.

I'd landed in Southampton and travelled up to London. After that I went to Paris and down through Spain into Morocco; then back up across the Côte d'Azure into Italy and through Rome to the tip; from Brindisi to Athens, then to Rhodes, Izmir and Istanbul, heading for Paris and back to New York. It had been like going out into the real world after Disneyland and finding it was much better, more interesting, and that there was a lot more of it. I went back to the United States reluctantly, really wanting to stay in Europe, but being rather cautious I thought I'd better go back and make sure I wasn't mistaken.

In New York I stayed in Harvey's attic for a few months, doing some freelance cartoons. I've always liked fabrics, so I'd bought Turkish rugs, a little prayer mat and a huge foxskin coat without sleeves or lining, and I made a kind of Ali Baba's cave up there among the air-conditioning fans. Then I went to LA and continued cartooning for the best part of a year. I also illustrated some books; Joel Siegel and I did a book together called *The Cocktail People*. Somewhere along the line I hooked up with an English girl, Glenys Roberts, who was a correspondent for the London *Evening Standard* and was writing for *LA Magazine*, she moved in with me and I became her photographer.

Eventually, the money was all gone and I got a job through Joel Siegel, who was now working as a copywriter at the Carson-Roberts ad agency – the one that gave us the line, 'Have a Happy Day.' By this time my hair was long enough for me to be branded a 'long-hair'. I was hired as an art director, copywriter and resident freak. I did print ads and radio commercials, and quickly became disillusioned with the place. The desk I was given was an ex-secretary's desk: it had been Gayle Hunnicut's, before she was discovered. Meanwhile, Joel and I were put in charge of doing ads for Universal Studios, and they were making the worst movies imaginable. MCA, the parent company, was heavily into television and the films were only slightly elevated TV: B-movies with Doug McClure. One of the few decent ones was Don Siegel's *Madigan*, which I did a campaign for.[31] 'Once he was happy, but now he's mad-again' – Joel and I hated the job so much we used to sit there and hand in things like that, just waiting to get fired.

The other account we had was Mattel Toys, with the Barbie and Ken dolls. These were the actual names of the Handler children, whose parents had started it all. At this point, everyone wanted to be a pop star, Kenny Handler invited me up to his mansion one evening, and it turned out he was trying to model himself on Brian Epstein and Andrew Loog Oldham.[32] He started talking about the group that he managed, The Oranges of Hieronymus Bosch, who hadn't been clicking. Then, one night he realized what was missing, and before they went on he said, 'Listen, boys, I want you to go on without your underwear.' So they did and it was great. Kenny had told me his wife was upstairs putting the children to bed but, as the evening goes on, I begin to suspect that Kenny might be gay and he's after more than my career. Gay groups have talked a lot about the Ken doll since then, never guessing how close they were to reality.

Yes, it's 1966 and everything's starting to happen. It was before the word 'hippie' had been coined, before anything had been labelled – like the Garden of Eden before the naming. Drugs and girls were all over the place, there was Ken Kesey and, biggest of all, the Beatles.[33] I was in New York in 1964 when the Beatles first came to America, and I'd gone up Park Avenue on the back of my room-mate's motorbike. The place was stiff with police, and I'd taken shots of the Regency Hotel with my Bolex camera. When a window curtain moved an inch it set off a riot. Who knows if the Beatles were really at that particular window, but the crowd went wild and I managed to get that on film. I was also in Washington for the first big civil-rights march, as a photographer for *Help!* It was weird to be at all these major events, like a kind of Forrest Gump.[34]

I met Sandy Mackendrick in LA, through the girl who took over my job on *Help!* [35] Her husband was big in game shows and they had some idea about me being in a film, with Tony Curtis. But I wouldn't get a haircut. Up to that point I'd spent most of my life with a crew-cut: when I went into the army I was the only one who didn't need a haircut. However, once I'd made the leap to long hair, I wasn't going to cut it off, even to be in a movie with Tony Curtis.

This would have been the last film that Mackendrick directed, Don't Make Waves *(1967).*
Yes. Mackendrick seemed rather lost out there; he struck me as very dispirited, although I didn't know much about him at the time. But that's what Hollywood is still all about. Even now I see people there who have done great things, but they get dragged down and treated with no respect. The past – your past – limits you in the studios' mind.

When Ridley Scott was doing *Alien*, I remember asking Sandy Lieberson what was going on; why were they throwing all this money at him when the film was way over budget – something they wouldn't do for me.[36] He said the difference was that I was now a finite object: 'They know what you are, you're worth that much, that's the kind of audience you get, and that's the end of it.' Ridley, however, was still an unknown quantity and so was *Alien*. So they threw money at it because it could become anything. In some ways, it's probably better not to be successful at first in Hollywood, because if you're out on a limb you can still be anything. The worst thing to be is in film's budgetry middle class. You want to be in either the expensive upper or the cheap lower class, but not trapped in the reasonably budgeted middle class.

I was getting more and more disillusioned, and Glenys was keen to return to England. Then several things happened. The first was Lyndon Johnson coming to Century City, which in those days was just a hotel surrounded by a vast tract of land. Protests against the Vietnam War had already started, but this was one of the first in LA that turned really nasty. We were on our way to a party but, as a reporter, Glenys thought she should check out the protest. So we made our way to the front, where there was a line of blue and the crowd were putting flowers on the cops. Helicopters were hovering overhead and there were snipers on the rooftops. It was an extraordinary scene, with a very mixed, mainly middle-class crowd, all in friendly mood. Then a group sat down and started to chant: 'We shall not be moved.' It was like a signal, as if the cops were waiting for it, and they drove into them on their big Harley-Davidsons.

The demonstrators started shouting and people began to get hurt, and then it happened – behind the front row of cops there was a second row, who charged through, and I remember being grabbed by the hair and hit. When I got up, it was in the middle of no man's land, with people running in every direction across this huge empty space and the cops going berserk. It was a police riot: they were hitting people in wheelchairs and on crutches. As we tried to get away, the helicopters came in low with their searchlights – it was like *Apocalypse Now* before the movie existed. Eventually we got away: in fact, we even got to the party in time to see ourselves being beaten up on the television news.

The *LA Free Press* put out a special edition next day because the *LA Times* printed a pack of lies – the Forrest Gump version of the affair, all about communists and anarchists rioting. So the *Free Press* became a real free press for several days, giving out first-hand accounts of what had really happened. Then the *LA Times* reporters revolted and by the end of the week the paper had to publish the other side of the affair, which was an impressive victory. I did a poster about it, which was on sale in all the head shops, along with posters by Ron Cobb – he designed *Conan the Barbarian* and *The Last Starfighter* – who was the *Free Press* cartoonist at the time and did some brilliant work.[37] Michael Douglas was putting money into the paper, and it was a fascinating period when many people believed that everything was possible. But when I saw how quickly our words and images were picked up by Madison Avenue, how any word from the street could be used to sell something, I became even more disillusioned.

We went to the Monterey Festival that same year. It was the first of the modern pop festivals; it was where Janis Joplin was discovered by a big audience. We were in the press enclosure, with Pete Townsend and The Who on stage. I had never seen such decadence – Brian Jones and Nico looking so androgynous, and Pete in his eighteenth-century gear with antique lace – none of this had happened yet when I was in England.[38] Amidst all this, the Beach Boys looked so sad. Country Joe and the Fish, the Grateful Dead, Tiny Tim and Jimi Hendrix were all there. When Pete started smashing his guitar into the speakers and Keith Moon began breaking up the drum kit, the stage crew came rushing out to try and stop them: they didn't know it was part of the act. It was a really great, unique event.

Shortly afterwards I went to Disneyland to review the new rides, and this became the moment when I knew I had to leave America. The press office had arranged our visit: Glenys was writing for the *Evening Standard* and some friends of ours were reporters for *Newsweek*. All four of us were well dressed, but we had longer-than-normal hair. We went to the special gate and were met by security guards – all looking like CIA agents, completely shorn – who said we couldn't come in: 'We have a grooming policy here.' It didn't matter that we were wearing coats and jackets, while inside there were slovenly, bloated people in Bermuda shorts and with their hair in curlers. It was all about the length of our hair. We got on to the very embarrassed PR lady, who went to the head of security, but he held firm, arguing that if he overruled the men on the gate they'd lose respect for him. Then they explained that we weren't the problem: it was the short-hairs who would be offended by our appearance and they might even attack us. So it was for our own safety that we were being refused entrance.

This was the beginning of madness: the lowest man at the gate was stopping a bunch of reporters because two of them had long hair. Then I noticed the barbed wire along the top of the fence – Disneyland had become a kind of concentration camp. Truth, justice and the American/Disney way were getting confused. Some of this, along with the ad-agency experience, would eventually feed into *Brazil*. I had become one totally disillusioned American.

1 In Stanley Kubrick's *Paths of Glory* (1957), Kirk Douglas plays an officer who faces court-martial after leading his men on a suicide attack in the World War One Battle of Verdun.

2 *La Rivière du hibou/Incident at Owl Creek* (1961), directed by Robert Enrico, won both a Cannes Festival and an Academy award, and was widely distributed. A fiction short based on an American Civil War story by Ambrose Bierce, it expands a prisoner's fantasy of escape in the moment before his death by hanging.

3 William Wellman's *The Ox-Bow Incident* (1943) was a highly regarded 'serious' anti-lynching western.

4 *High Noon* (1952), directed by Fred Zinnemann and starring Gary Cooper, is a western about a retiring sheriff who tries to rally a timid town against outlaws' intimidation, and was widely understood as a parable about anti-communist witch-hunts and McCarthyism.

5 Byron Haskin's *The War of the Worlds* (1953), translated H. G. Wells's 1898 story of alien invasion to a contemporary Californian setting, and inevitably acquired political significance in Cold War America. *Them* (Gordon Douglas, 1954, US) is an apocalyptic tale of giant ants produced by an atomic test in New Mexico.

6 In the fifties, Ealing comedies – such as *Whisky Galore!*, *Kind Hearts and Coronets* and *The Lavender Hill Mob* – began to be shown widely in the United States.

7 *The Goon Show*, written by and starring Spike Milligan, with Peter Sellers and Harry Secombe, ran on BBC radio from 1952–9, and was briefly revived for television by Thames in 1958, with John Cleese as a guest.

8 Stanley Donen (b. 1924) was a dancer and choreographer before establishing himself as a director with *On the Town* (1949) and *Singin' in the Rain* (1952), both co-directed with Gene Kelly.

9 Singer and comedian Danny Kaye shot to fame with *The Secret Life of Walter Mitty* (1947) and remained a big star throughout the fifties. The much-married Hedy Lamarr came from Europe to the US in 1938 with a reputation as a sex siren and appeared in many glamorous roles during the forties, culminating in *Samson and Delilah* (1949). Director William Wyler made westerns, melodramas and epics with equal distinction, winning the Academy Award as best director three times. Ernest Gold was a Viennese-born composer of many famous Hollywood soundtracks in the fifties and sixties, including *Exodus* (1960) and *Judgement at Nuremberg* (1961), and his wife Marni Nixon sang invisibly for Deborah Kerr in *The King and I* (1956) for Natalie Wood in *West Side Story* (1961) and many others.

10 The White Rabbit, who first leads Alice into her *Adventures in Wonderland*, provided the title of one of the most famous songs by San Francisco

psychedelic band Jefferson Airplane. The song is heard in *Fear and Loathing in Las Vegas*.

11 *The Katzenjammer Kids*, created by P. Dirks in 1897, was part of the first wave of American newspaper comicstrips launched in the wake of Outcault's *The Yellow Kid*. *Little Nemo*, graced by Winsor McCay's remarkable draughtsmanship, started in 1905.

12 Herriman's inspired, surreal *Krazy Kat* started in 1911. Harvey Kurtzman's *Mad* began as a parody on comic strips and books in 1952 – 'humour in a jugular vein' – and launched a new satirical trend, but had to become a magazine in 1955 to circumvent Comics Code guidelines.

13 Will Elder was responsible for the brilliant parody and often subversive detail of *Mad*'s visual style.

14 Federico Fellini's first feature *The White Sheikh* (*Lo Sciecco Bianco*, 1951) contrasts seductive photo-*fumetti* with their makeshift conditions of production. The romantic *photoroman* (photo-story), later known as *cinéroman*, became popular in post-World War II France, Italy and Latin America.

15 Comedian and singer Dick Van Dyke was on the verge of success in 1962–3 with *Bye Bye Birdie*, *Mary Poppins* and his network television show. Steve Allen has appeared in occasional films, and took the title role in *The Benny Goodman Story* (1956), but was best known as a writer and radio and television entertainer.

16 Stagestruck Moss Hart (1904–61) collaborated with his idol George Kaufman (1889–1961) on many successful plays in the thirties and forties, including *The Man Who Came to Dinner*. Hart's autobiography, *Act One*, was filmed in 1963 by Dore Schary.

17 Other writers who met regularly at the Algonquin Round Table included James Thurber and Dorothy Parker.

18 *Little Annie Fannie* was a tongue-in-cheek erotic comic strip created by Kurtzman and Elder for *Playboy* in 1962.

19 Gilliam was advised to disguise 'real' names used for characters in *Brazil* by adding extra an 'n'.

20 Gloria Steinem (b. 1934) would emerge as a leading feminist campaigner and journalist in the late sixties, co-founding the Women's Action Alliance and *Ms* magazine.

21 Robert Crumb's *True Meat Tales* and especially *Fritz the Cat*, animated by Ralph Bakshi in 1971, became the best known of 'underground comics'.

22 Stan Brakhage (b. 1933) is the pioneer and poet of post-World War Two American experimental film, prolific from the early fifties. Andy Warhol (1927–87) started making films in 1963 as an extension of his other Pop Art activities. John Cassavetes (1929–89) was a rising television actor when he made the first of his influential low-budget features, *Shadows*, in 1961.

23 Brando's only film as a director, *One-Eyed Jacks* (1961), was widely criticized for self-indulgence; while David Lean was similarly accused by many of extravagance on his 1970 epic *Ryan's Daughter*.

24 Henry Jaglom (b. 1943), formerly an off-Broadway and television actor, has been making idiosyncratic independent films since 1971.

25 Texas-born Mary Ellen Bute's (c. 1904–83) first films in the late thirties were semi-abstract images synchronized to music, which she often managed to place in large cinemas. In the fifties she turned to electronically generated images, then embarked on a feature-length 'reaction' to James Joyce's last work, entitled *Passages from Finnegans Wake*, which premiered at the Cannes Festival in 1965. See David Curtis, *Experimental Cinema* (1971) and Jayne Pilling, ed. *Women and Animation* (1992).

26 Thelma Schoonmaker-Powell, the editor of Martin Scorsese's first feature, *Who's That Knocking at My Door?* (1969) and all his films since *Raging Bull* (1980), and the widow of Michael Powell, also worked on *Passages from Finnegans Wake*.

27 Robert Benton (b. 1932) had trained as an artist before becoming art director of *Esquire* from 1958–64, while working on various novelty books. In 1967, he and David Newman wrote the script of *Bonnie and Clyde*, which took him into cinema.

28 Sergei Eisenstein's *The Film Sense*, a selection of articles edited by Jay Leyda, first appeared in 1943, and became one of the very few books of film theory widely available.

29 The 'adult' graphic magazine *Pilote*, founded in Paris at the end of the fifties, promoted the French alliance between Surrealism and an appreciation of – especially American – popular culture. René Goscinny was the co-creator of *Asterix* with Uderzo.

30 The satirist Peter Cook took over *Private Eye* in 1963.

31 *Madigan* (1968) starred Richard Widmark as the forerunner of many movie policemen prepared to play rough in the interests of justice.

32 Brian Epstein 'discovered' and managed The Beatles; Andrew Loog Oldham was manager of The Rolling Stones in the sixties.

33 Ken Kesey, now best known for his novel *One Flew Over the Cuckoo's Nest,* filmed by Milos Forman in 1975, led a countercultural group in the mid-sixties known as The Merry Pranksters, whose antics were chronicled by Tom Wolfe in *The Electric Kool-aid Acid Test* (1968)

34 The eponymous hero of Robert Zemeckis's *Forrest Gump* (1994) miraculously witnesses most landmarks in recent American history, from Kennedy to the late eighties.

35 Alexander Mackendrick (1912–93) was one of Ealing's best writer-directors, with *Whisky Galore!* (1949), *The Man in the White Suit* (1951) and *The Ladykillers* (1955), before turning his satirical attention to America in *Sweet Smell of Success* (1957) and, a decade later, *Don't Make Waves*, after which he confined his activities to teaching.

36 Former music agent Sanford (Sandy) Lieberson was David Puttnam's partner in producing *Melody* (1971) and *That'll Be the Day* (1973), before going on to head 20th Century-Fox's UK operation at the time they backed *Alien* in 1979.

37 *Conan the Barbarian* (1981) directed by John Milius; *The Last Starfighter* (1984) directed by Nick Castle.
38 Brian Jones, a founder member of The Rolling Stones, died in 1969. German-born Nico sang on the first Velvet Underground album in 1967.

3

Late Swinging London; animation as stream of consciousness; a programme called *Monty Python*; and the *Holy Grail* on a shoestring

Hair seems to have been the final straw, so to speak, in your falling out with America and you've kept it long ever since. Why was long hair such a big issue?

I don't think kids today can have any idea what hair meant in the sixties. That was what the musical *Hair* was all about: if you had your hair cut in a funny way or too long, you were pulled up by the cops.[1] This would happen to me as I drove around LA in my little Hillman Minx convertible – an Anglophile already. You would see a cop car following and eventually you'd be pulled over and stood against the wall and have to listen to this monologue as they accused you of being a drug-dealing, out-of-work musician living off some middle-class girl. 'No, no,' you protest, 'I'm a copywriter and art director working in an advertising agency and making more money than cops do' – not a politic thing to say to a policemen when you're up against a wall, but I've never been good at this kind of thing.

When hair became such an issue, I decided I was going to keep it like this. In fact, it's an *Alice Through the Looking Glass* moment, because I can remember doing it.[2] I went to a girlfriend's house with a Beatles album cover and my hair was a fairly normal length, but I pulled it forward and cut it into bangs, and literally from that moment on I was shouted at in the street and attacked by old women in drug-stores. Now, it's just an embarrassment to my children: an old man walking around with long hair.

When we decided to travel across North America on our way to London, we discovered the depth of the hatred for long hair. It was a pre-*Easy Rider* experience, as we were attacked in small towns in Montana and elsewhere. As well as Glenys and myself, there was Harry Shearer – who's the bass player in Spinal Tap and provides lots of voices in *The Simpsons* and has a big radio show.[3]

There was one small town, Rawlins, Wyoming, where we were in a café, and this rather moon-faced, inbred-looking character, who'd been following us around and trying to taunt us, appeared with a dozen of his redneck friends. They sat in the booth next to us and kept up a steady stream of insults, like, 'Who do you think you are, Jesus? Maybe we should have Easter early this year.' The threats were getting worse, but what was outrageously ironic was that the Beatles' 'All You Need Is Love' was playing on the jukebox, and in a nearby booth a black couple were getting no harassment. A couple of years earlier it would have been them; now it was the long-hairs' turn. It was getting so bad that I asked the waitress to call the cops, so the sheriff came with his deputy but they didn't intervene – just made their presence known. We went to pay and so did the guys. Stepping outside, we found ourselves surrounded by more rednecks, pushing and shoving, forming a gauntlet of abuse. We managed to get to the car. Then there was a furious chase through the town. Somehow we were able to lose them and get back to the motel, where we hid the car and barricaded the doors with all the furniture. When I saw *Easy Rider* a couple of years later, I just howled because it's the same old thing that's always been going on: the victims change, but the business remains the same.

We visited Expo '67 in Montreal, where there were some wonderful film presentations, including Francis Thompson's six-screen *We Are Young*. The Czech pavilion had a film in which you could vote on which way the story should go at the end of each scene. When we were making *Twelve Monkeys*, Bob Gale, who co-wrote *Back to the Future* with Robert Zemeckis, made a film where every member of the audience was able to vote at key moments, and it was terrible. My daughters went to see it with me and it was us against two men behind us: we were outvoting them on every point. My daughters thought it might be a good game at home, but it's not why we go to the movies. Movies aren't about that kind of interactivity: the moment you do it you're pulled right out of the experience. My daughters understood that film is about storytelling, like sitting around a campfire at night, giving yourself over to the storyteller – he's the guide, not you.

Then I got to England, this time by plane. After staying with friends of Glenys for a few weeks, we ended up getting a little studio flat in Knightsbridge. I was still just doing cartoons, for *Pilote* in Paris and for some terrible magazines in the States. There was one called *CarToons*, a West Coast comic book all about cars; I used to do these stories based on *Faust* and *The Picture of Dorian Gray*, but all involving cars. At the same time I was running around London as a freelance illustrator.

37

It was a good time to be doing that, with the explosion of new maga-
zines all trying to outdo each other in layout and style.

Yes, there was Jocelyn Stevens with *Queen* and I think the *Sunday*
Times Magazine started during that first year I was in London. I remember Janet Street-Porter did something for a magazine that Audrey
Slaughter was editing – *Her* or *She*; I did the cartoons but Janet's name
was emblazoned while mine was very small. *Nova* was great, because it
had a really good art director, and I just loved working for them. Most
of what I was doing then was airbrush and watercolours. The collages
came later, around the time I started doing animation.

Then Glenys got a job as editor of the *Londoner* magazine, which
was backed by William Pigott Brown, who was throwing money at this
venture, and I became the art director. We were the first weekly colour
news magazine in London; it was early days, so we all pitched in
together. I would take all the artwork up to Darlington every week to
the printer's, then I'd come back on the train next morning with the first
copies and we'd distribute them by hand to all the editors in London.
We were busy kids running around making magazines.

Glenys's friends all came from Cambridge or were successful hacks
hanging around El Vino's.[4] The one person I already knew in London
was John Cleese, who by this time was working on *The Frost Report*. He
used to do sketches with Ronnie Barker and Ronnie Corbett. I asked if
there was any chance he could introduce me to some TV producers,
since I was desperate to escape from magazine work, and he gave me a
couple of names. One of these was Humphrey Barclay, who at that time
was producing *Do Not Adjust Your Set*, a kids' show that Mike Palin,
Terry Jones and Eric Idle were writing and performing in, along with
David Jason, Denise Coffee and the Bonzo Dog Doo-Dah Band. It took
me three months to reach Humphrey, because he never returned my
calls. Around this time I also tried to get into animation by taking all my
drawings round to Bob Godfrey, but he didn't know what to do with my
material and turned me down.[5] I was trying ad agencies, anything.

Finally, one day Humphrey accidentally answered one of my calls and
that was it – I was in. I brought him written sketches as well as cartoons.
He really liked the cartoons, and I think he took pity on me and bought
a couple of sketches as well – which he then forced on the group, much
to their chagrin. Who was this pushy American with his big sheepskin
coat? Eric liked the coat and befriended me – he's always been the one
who embraces the flash outsider – while Mike and Terry sat at the back
of the bar – this was at the Thames Television studios in Teddington –
being territorial and disapproving.

Later when London Weekend Television started, Humphrey got a job there producing *We Have Ways of Making You Laugh*, a show hosted by Frank Muir with a panel of regulars that included Jenny Hanley, Katherine Whitehorn, Benny Green, Dick Vosborough, Eric Idle and me. They were all the witty ones, while I would sit and draw cartoons of the guests, and the camera would track over my shoulder as I finished, then mix through to whoever it was. I used to wear transparent plastic sandals – I think I had the first pair in England – and I used to get a lot of close-ups on the show, because they became obsessed with those silly shoes. The show was live, but on the first night, after we had done what we thought was a terrific show, somebody came out and told us that the engineers had gone on strike and had blacked out the whole show. Imagine, my very first TV show and nobody saw it!

How did you start doing animation for television?
Dick Vosborough had spent months collecting the worst of Jimmy Young, the disc jockey: all the terrible little punning connections, but without the actual records. He didn't know what to do with it and I said, 'Why not an animated film?' And they let me do it, just like that. I think I had £400 and two weeks to make it. Remembering Stan Vanderbeek's Nixon film, I decided to use cut-outs.[6] I got lots of photographs of Young, drew funny things and stuck them together, and everyone thought it was wonderful because they'd never seen anything like it before.

No one could have seen any of Vanderbeek's work in Britain at that time, so presumably you'd discovered him back in the US. What other animation had impressed you?
In New York there was a cinema called the Thalia near where I was living, and I went there a lot, mainly because my social life was pretty miserable. The Thalia was in a bad area, just up from Needle Park, and I used to love it because you'd get the art crowd as well as local people who were hooting and making a lot of noise while the art people would be shouting, 'SHUT UP NOW!' I'd already seen Bob Godfrey's *Do It Yourself Animation Kit* in the States, but didn't realize he'd made it when I called on him in London. But I think the main influence was Borowczyk, whose shorts I first saw at the Thalia.[7] *Jeux des anges* was just extraordinary: the sense that you're on a train with the walls of the city going past, and then the sound of angels' wings – incredible. By the time I got to London, his first feature, *Goto, Island of Love*, had appeared and then *Blanche*. Terry Jones and I went crazy over Borowczyk because his films were so much about atmosphere and texture.

I came from a world where Doris Day and Rock Hudson films used to drive me crazy, because everyone in them was so clean and well scrubbed and shiny, with perfect white teeth and hair always in place. The world isn't like that, yet it was depicted this way in the cinema and people seemed to believe it, which really bothered me. Years later in New York when we previewed *Jabberwocky* – which is very much about textures and filth and smells – the audience reacted well to it. Then I read the reaction cards and they were negative. It was one of those shocking moments when you realize that how they're responding and what they write down are two completely different things. There was a kid – a fat, acned, awful creature – who went on about how ugly the people were in the film, how smelly and rotten it all was. He was living in New York – a far worse place than anything we put on film – and yet he couldn't see it. He looked into the mirror and saw Rock Hudson's perfect teeth and slicked-back hair.

In the late fifties and early sixties there was a glut of clean, bouncy films, like the beach-party movies. That was why I responded so strongly to *Paths of Glory*: I felt I was *there*, in the trenches, smelling them and experiencing everything through those tracking shots. I think that was why I moved to New York, to get away from all the cleanliness and neatness, which felt artificial, and to live instead in squalor, which felt honest and real.

And this revulsion against tidiness and perfection erupted in your first animations?

The piece that accompanied Jimmy Young's voice had a head coming in and doing stupid things, such as having a foot in its mouth. There were heads and bodies all coming apart. The extraordinary thing was that it went out on television, to however many million people, and, suddenly, I was an animator. I'd already done a lot of the things animation involved – like drawing and making children's flip books – and now this was just like another instrument I found I could play. The first time I picked up an airbrush, I understood immediately how to do it; and it was the same with animation. I'd watched enough films, had read about it and grasped the principles. I have to say that the one bit of reading that is absolute bullshit is what Eisenstein wrote about his music scores – composition of the picture goes left, right, rising, so the music's got to rise in the same shape.[8] Rubbish. For years I believed this because the guy was a genius; in fact, I think a lot of my life has been spent believing in geniuses and their godlike stature – especially their total control over what they do, their complete understanding of everything that they do. But I've never experienced that: it's always been after the event.

I think that was Eisenstein's experience too. A lot of his writing, including that fold-out chart of the picture-music graph in Alexander Nevsky, *is really an attempt to understand what he'd done intuitively in his films. As he said, more than once, 'No one ever asks if I follow my own principles.' But it's true that it can look as if he's completely in control.*

Did I tell you about my one trip to Moscow, when we showed *Brazil*? I went to the Eisenstein Museum with David Robinson, and I was already working on *Munchausen*.[9] Suddenly I saw a copy of *Munchausen* on the bookshelf, but when I reached up for it, I knocked a framed drawing on to the ground, which was a cartoon that Walt Disney had done for Eisenstein. My plan all along was to make *Munchausen* as a Disney cartoon, but in live action. Wasn't that wonderful? I forgive Sergei all the bullshit. In fact, I've always loved his appearance, with that great beaming face and *Eraserhead* hair.

Eisenstein would have loved that coincidence too, since he thought of Ivan the Terrible *as directly inspired by Disney's* Willie the Whale – *not an association that has struck many people, but an obvious one for Eisenstein who, of course, was also a cartoonist and often extraordinarily ribald in his private drawings.*

That reminds me of a cartoon I did which had Adam lying asleep naked and from his groin grows a tree with fruit on it, and there's Eve coming along intrigued, ready to have her first pluck. Around the time of the Jimmy Young film, I did another animated film of a guy walking along past a sign that says 'Beware of the Elephants', and of course an elephant does fall out of the sky, but it's a very elaborate stream-of-consciousness thing. I was also doing illustrations for Ronnie Barker's television show and Ronnie had a great collection of Victorian saucy pictures. They weren't hardcore porn; they were round and squidgy, like Ronnie himself, and naughty in an innocent sort of way. Ronnie gave them to me, for which I have to thank him, and they started turning up in my cartoons.

Dennis Main Wilson got me to do some animated cartoons for Marty Feldman's television show and then Eric Idle asked me to be part of the next series of *Do Not Adjust Your Set*.[10] One of the animations I did for that was *The Christmas Card*, which I made by raiding the Tate Gallery's huge collection of Victorian Christmas cards. It still gets screened and I think it's really good. The early ones could be good because they were complete in themselves, and not made as connecting tissue. So I was becoming an animator.

Where were you doing all this?

By this time I was living in flat near Putney Bridge, and everything was done in a tiny room there. The early stuff was shot on 16mm, though *The Christmas Card* might have been the first one on 35mm. I was shooting on Bob Godfrey's camera; so in one giant leap I'd become a famous TV animator using his facilities – that'll teach him not to hire me when I needed a job! But I was also still doing illustrations for magazines, and doing it all on my own without any kind of assistance. Cutting out images was such a freeing experience. Before, I'd had to draw everything and I'd get so precious about my own work. Now I could cut out other people's things and chop and change them. Why should I spend time learning to draw like Albrecht Dürer when I could just cut out his best stuff and make it do what I wanted? This eclecticism really fuelled me: I could use airbrush, engravings, photographs, anything. It was a huge leap, like going through the looking glass.

Right from the first, it was the limitations of time and money that dictated the style of the animation and, in a sense, I've used that as my excuse ever since. That's why deadlines are useful. I'm trapped by the terrible burden of wanting to do great or perfect work and constantly failing, so I need limitations to lift the onus of responsibility.

Marty Feldman took off very fast. The first time anybody saw him was in 1967 in *At Last the 1948 Show*, with John Cleese, Graham Chapman and Tim Brooke-Taylor. Marty and Barry Took had been writing together for years, then suddenly Marty was out there and his oddness definitely appealed. He was given his own show. His problem was that he thought he looked like Buster Keaton, so he tried to do physical stunts, but he just wasn't an acrobat. The rest of us were more or less content to stay in our own world, but Marty moved faster. When he started doing *Marty*, in 1968, everybody was writing material for him – Terry Jones, Mike Palin, John and Graham. Later he teamed up with Larry Gelbart and did *The Marty Feldman Comedy Machine* for ABC in America. I did the opening titles for that and had a contract to do twenty-five minutes of animation.

Anyway, when *Do Not Adjust Your Set* finished, Mike, Terry, Eric and I were part of a gang waiting to do something else. John Cleese and Graham Chapman had been working on many of the same shows and we began discussing working together. John had a long-standing invitation from the BBC to do any programme he wanted, and Barry Took had the unbelievable job of Head of Comedy and was keen to support us. So the six of us charged in. As far as the BBC was concerned, it was Cleese and Co. For us, it was a *Goon*-influenced show, but we were determined to find our own form and style. At that time Spike Milligan was doing his *Q* series which we thought was fantastic and ground-breaking.[11]

Terry Jones has always claimed that my cartoon *Beware the Elephants* was the inspiration for the continuous stream-of-consciousness approach in *Monty Python*; in other words, we weren't constantly stopping and starting. Much of our thinking about the show was based on watching what other people were doing that wasn't working. You'd see Pete and Dud doing brilliant sketches which had to end with a punchline, but the punchlines were seldom as good as the sketches.[12] So we got rid of punchlines and, when something ran out of steam, we moved on. And if one sketch didn't lead to another, I would come in with a cartoon. I think we altered the form by being able to flow on to any idea – or refer back to one if we wanted to. It was completely free in that sense.

That also meant we could work in different combinations and produce different forms of sketches. We did it by connecting ideas, and if a sketch didn't quite work one of us would take over and rewrite it until it blended in. And when the others got really stuck, they'd say: 'Gilliam takes over from here and gets us to there.' So I was pleased to be working within the parameters of A to B, even if they were totally unconnected. That freed me because I just seize up when I have the possibility of total freedom – the choices become infinite and I go round in circles not knowing where to begin. Apart from that, I do think the animations distinguished *Python* from other comedy shows at that time because suddenly there was this new visual aspect.

You must be tired of questions about Python *and what made it special. How did you actually work as part of the team?*
I don't know what to say about *Python* any more: it was just a great time. The others were usually off filming or in rehearsal while I was doing my stuff, so I was always slightly outside a lot of it. In the beginning, on the days in the studio, when they were recording the sketches, I would come in with my film and sit around. They'd leave parts open for me – the kind of parts that involved wearing silly costumes or awful make-up. No one else wanted to do them, but I was very happy to disguise myself. In LA, as a kid, I was obsessed with make-up: Lon Chaney – the man of a thousand faces – was my big hero.[13]

Come Hallowe'en every year, I would do serious make-up. One year I was the Phantom of the Opera and that took four hours of make-up, using all the techniques that Lon Chaney did, and the next year I was an Old Testament prophet, which took about twelve hours. And nobody ever knew who I was. It was fantastic to be able to walk into a party and no one have a clue. So some of that hung over when we did *Python*: I still dabbled in make-up and I ended up marrying the make-up girl . . . Maggie Weston!

If I had to be on the screen, I was always more comfortable not being me. Me wasn't interesting, but being those other creatures was. *Python* was incredibly hard work: it took about two weeks to do the animation for each show and by the later series I'd usually have an assistant working with me. But it was madness, working seven days a week.

The late-night sessions were the ones I found most liberating. With the phone not ringing and blackness all around, the pieces of paper on my desk would start arranging themselves very nicely for me. I'd find juxtapositions and connections that I didn't expect. That's why I keep so many books around me in my studio. There's a serendipity involved: as I'm reading one book, I notice another – oh, that's interesting – then another, and so on. If I put them all away neatly, I'd probably never look at them again, and the world would just stay neat and orderly. My desk was always covered with bits of paper that I wrestled with until eventually they'd form themselves into a story, a pattern, an idea or a character. And the constant pressure meant there was never time to think: 'Is this great? . . . No, it's good enough.' We just had to fill the space.

Working on the Marty Feldman series a bit later, in 1971, brought me up against censorship, because it was made for ABC. Larry Gelbart was really smart and charming and funny; he kept me going, but he didn't always protect me. There was a piece of animation I was doing on fat and I wanted to use a Rubenesque nude, but everyone said, 'Oh, I don't know if you can do that, this is for US television.' I said, 'But these are classical paintings.' So they referred it to the Standards and Practices lady and it was duly censored. It turned out that she was amazingly overweight and very unhappy. It was like belling the cat: we used to say that what she needed was a good tupping, but who was going to do it?

The Marty Feldman Comedy Machine, which was being made at Lew Grade's ATV set-up in Elstree, originally had most of the good British comedy writers involved, but because it was American-produced they wanted the writers to work nine to five in an office. Well, British comedy writers do *not* do that – 'we work at home' – and everybody just walked. So they had to bring in blacklegs from the States, like Pat McCormack and Barry Levinson, who was then part of a stand-up comedy duo.[14] That's how I first met Barry, as a blackleg writer for Marty, before he went on to write for Mel Brooks and then become what he is now – somewhat less funny, but much more successful.

Bits of bodies on the assembly line for *The Marty Feldman Comedy Machine* (1971).

Back with the fat – after they turned down the Rubens nude, I hunted around and found a rear view of a Boucher reclining nude. And it came back with a half-crown circle around the offending area, the crack in her bum: if you can cover this up we can do it. Well, I wasn't going to do that, and by now I was really pissed off, so I got one of Ronnie's nudes – it was a naked lady sitting with her legs crossed – and I cut out her breasts and then a fan shape out of her groin, and put her against a background. You could see through all the naughty bits. The Standards and Practices lady still said no. 'So I can't show the naughty bits, and I can't *not* show the naughty bits?' I went berserk: 'That's it! I'm finished.' The answer came back: 'But you've got a contract.'

So I started doing cartoons as revenge. One animation had a full minute of no movement. This guy is talking to a friend about his dog, a terrific animal who does fantastic tricks, then the dog comes on screen and stands still. So what's he going to do? 'OK, roll over and play dead.' The dog flips over and for a full minute nothing moves. The friend says, 'That's fantastic – oh, wait, his ear moved – no it didn't, you're right . . . hey, that back leg . . .' And so it goes on for a minute. I did another one in which someone rushes into a room, turns the light off and everything goes black. The scene is played with sound effects – animated radio. This was my response to their ridiculous censorship, and I have to admit it produced some interesting cartoons: when the blood starts boiling some of the best ideas come pouring out. Also, it was a chance to do some pieces that stood on their own, like *The Miracle of Flight*, which was five minutes and subsequently went around as a short.

What techniques of animation were you using?
With normal animation you'd record the voice first and work around it, but I never had the chance to do this on any of the animation for Marty Feldman or *Monty Python*. I'd prepare all the material myself, then there would be a day or so to do the actual filming, and I would over-shoot everything so that I had the latitude to wiggle it around to achieve lip-synch. Then we'd fix it later, as best we could, in the editing room with Ray Millichope, who cut all *Python*'s stuff. As for the sound effects, a lot of them were just me with a microphone under a blanket, using kitchen utensils or my mouth. And if I needed dialogue, I would catch the other guys in the corridor where it was quiet or in the dressing room on the day we were recording next week's show, and I'd ask them to say whatever lines I needed.

When it came to music, I usually had a record in advance so I could do a beat and be pretty accurate – although I'd let the pauses be slightly long so that I'd have a little room to manoeuvre and get synch if necessary. I always started with a rough little storyboard, then I would discover things and change it. Sometimes I had an idea for something I wanted to do in advance and I'd describe it so that the guys could include it in the script, then we'd find sketches that related and put them around it. At other times, it was only after the scripts were finished that I decided what I was going to do.

I discovered early on that it was very hard for me to describe what I was doing. I'd tell the others the story or idea and they'd shake their heads in bewilderment, then say, 'Just go and do it.' So I had the most freedom of anyone on the show. We'd have script meetings when the sketches were read out, and they'd be voted on as good, medium or reject. So I could vote on their material, but they couldn't vote on mine, because it was a *fait accompli* – I would just turn up on the Saturday and there it was. Most of the time it worked, it just flowed, and, as the programme developed, the sketches sometimes began to look like animation. We were all influencing each other, and yet we all had our specific talents and skills. With some sketches I couldn't tell you now who wrote them, because sometimes Mike and Terry were writing more like John and Graham. Eric was the great chameleon: he may have been less original than the others, but he was slicker and could take other people's ideas and find new ways of doing them. He was also by far the best wordsmith. Mike and Terry were often more conceptual in what they were doing, and John and Graham's were invariably about confrontational situations.

I chose the theme music. Roger Last at the BBC kept bringing in different music, and there was an album of Souza marches, which I've always loved. When I heard *Liberty Bell*, I knew that was it: it made a great start, just bouncing along. When we were making *Twelve Monkeys* in Philadelphia, we shot in a big department store called Wanamakers which has a huge atrium with an organ and, just as I walked in for the first time, it started playing the *Liberty Bell March*. Of course, I thought someone had set it up knowing I was coming; but no, because the actual Liberty Bell is in Philadelphia, they play that piece every day.

During the sixties, animation became very stylized, using all sorts of found imagery and allusions to graphic and painterly styles. Were you consciously part of this movement?
Because of the way I worked, I built up a cabinet of pieces; so, for instance, backgrounds would be in one drawer, skies in another, and buildings over there. It was a kit of parts that I could reassemble over

and over again in different combinations, adding new things to it. There was a photography studio off Regent Street where I would send books and magazines every day, all marked up with detailed instructions to be rephotographed to the size I wanted them.

So you didn't just cut them out?
Destroy a book? Never! I was working on a thirty-inch field, which is much wider than most animators use, so I was using as wide a glass platen as you could get. It had to be as big as possible to get rid of the shadows caused by all these bits of paper on top of each other. I became obsessed with shadows and edges and, when I had assistants, the least artistic, yet most important job they had to do was blacken the edges, to make it look as 3-D as possible. The technical quality of the work I did then wasn't bad and when we started doing the films it was on 35mm, which looked even better. Then, for the book, *Animations of Mortality*, we rephotographed all this stuff on a three-by-five-inch big format, so it looks terrific.[15]

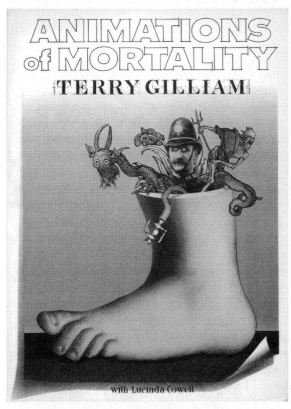

How did Python *make the transition from television to film?*
We always had the idea of trying to break into North America –
although no one was as ambitious as Marty Feldman. But we just
couldn't get the shows on to American television, so we made *And Now
for Something Completely Different* with money from Vic Lowndes and
Playboy in an attempt to break into the American market. Unfortunately, Columbia, who were distributing the film, had no idea what to
do with it. I remember they wanted the 'Twit of the Year' sketch cut out,
because no one *ever* ends a film like that. So we said, it doesn't matter,
it's funny. Then came our first brush with Hollywood mentality. They
wrote back, saying if we didn't cut out the sketch, they couldn't guarantee the success of the film. But the truth was that they didn't know
how to distribute it, and it basically bombed in the States. It did very big
business in Britain, which is rather depressing, because it was the same
old material that the public were going out to see again. We were so
determined to be original all the time, but our audience seemed to want
the same thing again and again.

*At this time you also went on the road, doing a live show. How did this
work?*
Tony Smith and Harvey Goldsmith had the idea of putting on a *Python*
stage show around the time we did the film. During the show we used a
screen and projected the animation, and some of the sketches, just to
give ourselves time to change – and it worked. We began in Southampton before travelling all round England. Then we went right across
Canada, doing one-night stands, because the show had been on CBC
and they knew us. Remember, this was the seventies, and we all wanted
to be rock 'n' roll stars – comedy rock stars – so it was great to be on
the road; and when we arrived at Toronto airport, getting our luggage,
we were mobbed by a cheering crowd, just like real rock stars.

We finished in Vancouver, then went down to LA to play *The Johnny
Carson Show*, only to discover that Johnny was on holiday and Joey
Bishop was hosting the show. He gave us a great introduction: 'I'm told
these guys are funny, but let's see.' So on we came, and it sounded like 500
jaws dropping, one after another. John and Graham were in drag doing
one of the pepper-pot sketches, and there was the wrestling match where
Graham wrestled with himself. Neither the audience nor Joey Bishop had
a clue what was going on – and that was our début in America!

We took a lot of pleasure from the fact that people were confused: we
were dividing them, making them think. When we were doing the first
Python show, my former boss Harvey Kurtzman came to London, but

he just didn't know what to make of it. I had an idea that during one sketch, we should turn the volume down very slowly so that the people at home would turn their volume up – until it was at maximum, then we were going to make the biggest noise known to man and blow out every television set in the nation. The BBC wisely wouldn't let us do it. But, in general, we had no pressure from anyone telling us we had to appeal to a particular audience: the six of us were left alone to do just what we wanted. If it made us laugh, in it went. Now that's really rare; I don't know many people who have ever been in that position. We knew we were getting between 4 and 6 million viewers – which wasn't as good as some other programmes – but there was no panic over ratings in the BBC at that time.

At the beginning, the BBC certainly didn't know what to make of us and they kept changing the time we went out: it was like 'Hide and Seek *Python*' And, after the fourth show, they actually pulled us off and put some international horse show in our slot, but in the middle of it there was a dressage performed to *The Liberty Bell* – our theme – they couldn't keep us out! There was so much critical response that they put us back on. There's nothing quite like the effect of everybody talking about it on a Monday morning after the Sunday transmission. It was like there was a critical mass who had all experienced the same thing, and were bubbling over with it and doing the jokes. You don't get that kind of feedback with movies. After the first series, I remember being in Greece with my wife, Maggie, on a campsite outside Athens, and waking up to hear someone singing 'Spam, spam, spam'. That was the first time I realized we were everywhere. We were interviewed on *Late Night Line-Up* by Joan Bakewell, and I thought that this was such heavy stuff – being asked serious questions on television – that I got my backpack and disappeared to Morocco for weeks, just to escape from the success that I feared would corrupt me. I knew how tempting it feels to be successful. It scares me so much that I run from it.

*You worked on other non-*Python *projects at this time, like the horror movie* Cry of the Banshee *(1970).*
That was for Samuel Z. Arkoff. I kept getting offers all the time and this film came along. The film, with Vincent Price, was made for almost nothing – they got all the costumes from *Anne of the Thousand Days* – so I just did a title sequence using Dürer woodcuts.[16] Around this time I also did a title sequence for a CBS show about Shakespeare called *William*. All the Pythons were being approached to do things for other people – John was doing films, and writing *The Magic Christian* with

Graham – but we stayed together, even though we were being pulled in different directions.[17] The strength of the group was that we were ambitious in a different way: we wanted to stay in control and not be forced to compromise.

So where did the impulse to launch out into Python *films come from?*
Terry Jones and I were the main voices. In the shows, we were constantly pushing for scenes where we could have shadows and dramatic lighting. In comedy – or light entertainment as it was called – they didn't use dramatic lighting. We were also in the editing room, dealing with how the show was put together. Ian Macnaughton produced and directed it, but we were always back-seat driving – 'Ian, why is the camera there?' – with increasingly clear ideas about how things should or shouldn't be. Terry really handled the editing, though the rest of us, in different combinations, were involved as well. By the time we reached *And Now for Something Completely Different*, I was pissed off by the way certain things were being shot; this was no longer television, but it was still being shot like television. So when the offer came to do *Holy Grail*, Terry and I said we wanted to direct it – not Ian – to show what we could do after all our moaning.

Was this controversial with the rest of the group?
Not really, because the others had misgivings about Ian and knew his limitations. Terry and I were the know-it-alls, always making the most noise about how things should be done. So we said we'd do it and off the two of us went. Mark Forstater was the producer, Julian Doyle was Mr Everything Else and he got Terry Bedford to light it – he had been trained by Ridley Scott in the school of smoke and backlight. This was the time when the top income-tax bracket was 90 per cent, so all the successful pop people wanted to get rid of their money and get tax relief. Michael White put together the package with Pink Floyd, Led Zeppelin, Elton John, Island Records, Chrysalis Records – *Python* was always very popular with the pop world – so there was a pile of money and off we went to make a movie.

How did you and Terry Jones split the responsibilities?
I started storyboarding and designing with Roy Smith, and Hazel Pethig did the costumes. With great energy, Terry and I ran around the nation looking for castles and locations, and then we went off and shot it in less than five weeks for £460,000. But, of course, everything went wrong. On the very first day of our very first film, the camera broke down on the very first shot. We were up in Glencoe, miles away from

Grail gags: from cartooning to storyboarding.

Woman Ted
Long Knights

56

any replacement, so what were we to do? I was in make-up as a bridge-keeper and we've all got our gear on. Did we shoot the wide shot? No, we panicked and did close-ups which could have been done anywhere in the world. It seemed like chaos but, in fact, we were working fast and learning on the job.

Terry and I had always been very close and seemed to see eye to eye. But when we started working together in this way, the differences soon became apparent. My obsession about the look of things used to irritate the others, because they just wanted to get on with doing the comedy and not have to squat in odd positions to get the angles right. I began to realize this was not as much fun as it was supposed to be. And, of course, there were two voices – Terry's and mine – shouting slightly different orders; so we decided to combine our voices in the first assistant, Gerry Harrison. But it turned out that Gerry wanted to be a director too, so though he was the only voice shouting, he wasn't saying what we wanted him to say. We shut him up and divided the responsibility so that, basically, Terry was with the guys and I was with the camera. I'd say to him, 'Let's set up here, and do this,' then he would tell the others to do this and that, and it worked surprisingly well.

Looking back now, I don't know how we did it in the time and for the money, but we didn't know any better and just worked flat out. By the time we reached the editing room, Terry and I were not seeing eye to eye. There was one last sequence with the Black Knight: Graham and I

When knights were told: *Holy Grail* required swordfighting lessons.

were in the wood, so it was dark behind us. We cut to the Black Knight, and it's light behind him; then the reverse shot back to me and Graham, and it's black behind us. Terry insisted that it looked like two separate places and demanded we reshoot. I got completely pissed off by this and just got on a boat and left, because they couldn't reshoot it if I wasn't there. Terry's very forceful – he likes fighting even more than I do – and sometimes I would just back down because it wasn't worth the fight. Then I'd go back late at night and recut what had been done during the day, and he wouldn't notice what I'd done. It was very silly at times, but in the end we were both happy and it worked well.

'Mud and shit, which you certainly hadn't seen in comedy before.'

What was striking at the time, and seems even clearer now, is how much Monty Python and the Holy Grail *is really quite a serious medieval movie disguised as a spoof. Even Leslie Halliwell couldn't resist praising its 'remarkable visual sense of the Middle Ages'.*
We admired Borowczyk's *Goto* and *Blanche*, as well as the Pasolini films, so we approached it as seriously as either of those film-makers. We were doing comedy, but we didn't want it to look like light entertainment. I'm not sure how many film-makers before us had taken the sense of place so seriously in comedy – even Mel Brooks was always very pas-

The ride of the coconut shells: saved from mediocrity by poverty in *Holy Grail*.

tiche. But, for me, it was important that the settings were as believable as possible, so that we could be completely off the wall. We were all excited about films; we wanted to make an epic, except we didn't have the money to do it properly. I think the restrictions made the film better, because if we'd had the money for real horses there would have been no coconut shells, which are far funnier. So we were saved by poverty from the mediocrity to which we aspired!

A Samuel Bronston-style epic, like El Cid *or* The Fall of the Roman Empire – *not that there isn't a lot to be said for those.*
Yes, we really wanted it to look as rich as that, but there was also a lot of Bergman in the background, *The Seventh Seal*, and Kurosawa's *Throne of Blood*.[18] These were part of a common culture at that time which was a lot more interesting than the common culture of *Terminator* and *Mission: Impossible*; they were things we all got incredibly excited about. We all wanted to be serious film-makers. *Monty Python and the Holy Grail* is really no more than a series of sketches, some of which are done more realistically than others – but this is what I liked about it: it was an eclectic jumble and, because the rules kept changing, it has a certain freshness. For me, it was about textures – the mud and

shit – which you certainly hadn't seen in comedy before. And the best jokes came out of this: 'How do you know he's the king?' 'He isn't covered in shit.' You couldn't do that unless you'd set it up properly. My feeling was that the grittier and more realistic it was, the funnier the jokes would be. Anyway, we didn't have time to theorize: we just ploughed into it and learned on the job.

In films, it's when you plan things really carefully that everything goes wrong. On the *Holy Grail*, within two weeks of the first shot, the National Trust took away all the castles we'd chosen. Their line was that they feared we wouldn't respect the dignity of the fabric of the buildings. These were places where the most awful tortures had been practised, where terrible crimes had been committed, and now they were going to collapse because some comedians had come along. So, suddenly we were without castles and we had to make cut-out ones. Besides our principal castle at Doune, the only real castle we could use was privately owned, and we found it at the last moment, so we just had to shoot it on the spot. The whole crew arrived in the morning and we had to wait for the owner's son to fly in on a private plane with the keys to let us in.

We were also supposed to have a sheep to be thrown from the battlements but, because the schedule was all screwed up, we didn't have it. Then one of the crew remembered passing a dead sheep on the road several days earlier, so they went and got this rotting carcass, which had everyone throwing up in the car. We arrived to find the prop master up to his shoulders in gore, gutting this sheep; we were scornful when he warned us not to go near it – until the wind shifted and it hit us. Stuffed with hay, this is what was duly thrown from the battlements. And because we didn't have the costumes for the big battle, the only thing we could shoot was the sequence where a police car comes in blocking the charging army. At that point, I think we had about twelve costumes, as well as banners and pikes, for the army. So the entire crew, with their families and kids, were holding up pikes in the foreground, with a few bits of costume seen in the front row. If things hadn't gone wrong, we would have done it carefully and properly – and learned nothing. What you discover in these situations is that you can get away with murder; also, how inventive you can be if you think on your feet. I love it at the same time as I fear it – and that's how I've gone on ever since. You plan everything carefully – secretly hoping that things will go wrong – and almost always something interesting comes out of it, as long as you have good people around you who can think fast. It happens on every film, and I scream and shout, but in retrospect those are often some of the best moments.

Anyway, we shot the thing, it went out and it was a big success. And the credits said 'directed by Terry Gilliam and Terry Jones', so I was a film director – just like that. Before that, no one would touch me with a barge-pole, but now I had directed a film and the offers started pouring in.

Holy Grail group portrait: *Python* in chain-mail (Gilliam second from right).

NOTES

1 The 'folk rock' musical *Hair* opened, sensationally, on Broadway in 1968 and launched a wave of youth-oriented musicals.

2 Alice wills herself to go *Through the Looking Glass* in Lewis Carroll's second fantasy, entering a world where everything is reversed.

3 Rob Reiner's *This is Spinal Tap* (1983) chronicles the misadventures of an all-too-believable English heavy metal band on tour.

4 A bar in London's Fleet Street much frequented by journalists.

5 British animator Bob Godfrey popularized collage, new graphic styles and 'adult' subjects in his widely distributed shorts *Polygamous Polonius* (1958), *Do It Yourself Cartoon Kit* (1959), *Plain Man's Guide to Advertising* (1962) and *Kama Sutra Rides Again* (1971).

6 Part of the 'new American cinema' movement, Stan Vanderbeek made mixed-media collage and abstract films in the fifties, before turning to expanded cinema, video and computer animation. Unlike many underground colleagues, his work includes a strong vein of political satire and protest, as in *Breathdeath* (1963) and *Skullduggery* (1968).

7 Walerian Borowczyk (b. 1923) was a graphic artist in Poland before collaborating on a series of highly original, macabre animations, mostly with Jan Lenica, including *Once Upon a Time* (1957), *House* (1958) and *Solitude* (1961). Moving to France, he continued as an animator, with shorts such as *Jeux des anges* (Angels' Games, 1964) up to the feature-length *Le Théâtre de M. et Mme. Kabal* (1967), and also made enigmatic live-action shorts. His early live-action features *Goto, l'Ile d'amour* (1969) and *Blanche* (1971) miraculously combined qualities of his previous work within a powerful romantic surrealism, focused on the fragile beauty of his leading actress Ligia Branice. His later, mainly erotic, films have grown coarser and increasingly exploitative.

8 A foldout chart, comparing the pattern of shot composition to Prokofiev's music in *Alexander Nevsky*, appears in Eisenstein's *The Film Sense*.

9 The film historian and critic David Robinson was with Gilliam in Moscow and ensured that he visited the 'Eisenstein museum', a small apartment evocatively furnished with many of Eisenstein's books and mementos from his travels, including a signed cartoon from Disney, whom Eisenstein knew and admired.

10 Marty Feldman (1933–83). Former variety stage comedian who became a prolific television scriptwriter in the fifties, then a regular performer in the sixties before starring in the first of his own series, *Marty*, for BBC in 1968. *Do Not Adjust Your Set* was launched by Rediffusion in 1967, with Eric Idle, Terry Jones and Michael Palin, among others. The second series moved to Thames Television in 1968.

11 Spike Milligan did the first of his *Q* sketch series for BBC2, *Q5*, in 1969, followed by four later series.

12 Peter Cook and Dudley Moore, members of the original *Beyond the Fringe* team in the early sixties, became a national institution with their 'Pete and Dud' duologues in *Not Only – But Also . . .* (BBC2, 1965–6, 1970).

13 Lon Chaney (1883–1930) was the undisputed master of film make-up and bizarre characterization in many of Hollywood's greatest fantasies, including *The Hunchback of Notre Dame* (1923) and *The Phantom of the Opera* (1925). Known as 'the man of a thousand faces', he wrote an article on stage make-up for the *Encyclopedia Britannica*.

14 Barry Levinson, now best known as the writer-director of such films as *Diner* (1982), *Tin Men* (1987) and *Bugsy* (1991), was a stand-up comedy writer and performer in the early seventies, appearing on *The Carol Burnett Show*.

15 *Animations of Mortality*, Gilliam's tongue-in-cheek guide to cut-out animation, was published in 1978.

16 *Cry of the Banshee* was the third of three low-budget horror films directed by Gordon Hessler in Britain for Samuel Arkoff's American International Pictures. One reviewer remarked of *Anne of the Thousand Days*: 'The costumes, beautiful in themselves, have that unconvincing air of having come straight off the rack at Nathan's' (Brenda Davies, *Monthly Film Bulletin*).

17 Filming Terry Southern's anti-capitalist satire *The Magic Christian* in 1969 provided an excuse to add new-style 'bad taste' sketches by Cleese and Chapman.

18 Ingmar Bergman's medieval morality tale *The Seventh Seal* (1956, Sweden) established his international reputation, as well as providing the butt of much subsequent mockery. Akira Kurosawa's *Throne of Blood* (literally *Cobweb Castle*, 1957, Japan) impressively transposes Shakespeare's *Macbeth* to feudal Japan.

Jabberwocky and the joy of real actors; in the footsteps of Zeffirelli for *Life of Brian*

Americans had been playing a big part in British film production right through the sixties, and some of them had become more or less permanent UK residents by the early seventies. Did their success influence you?
Dick Lester was one of the reasons I came to Britain; I'd been so impressed by *The Running, Jumping and Standing Still Film* and then by the Beatles films.[1] I first met Lester when he was doing *The Three Musketeers* and he wanted me to write another project he was working on.[2] At that time, there was no stopping him: he was just roaring through all sorts of things.

Did you recognize a kindred spirit in Lester's historical films? They took an obvious delight in period spectacle and detail, but seemed so desperate to avoid being taken seriously that they kept an ironic modern outlook on their material. Only Robin and Marion *seemed to find as good a balance between the modern and the mythic as, say,* El Cid *or* The War Lord.
In *Robin and Marion* I thought he was doing much better – and with a larger budget – the same things we were trying to do.[3] I really liked the first *Musketeers* film, which is lit so beautifully by David Watkins, with wonderful costumes and the jokes coming out of the period itself – except when Dick can't resist dropping in all those little verbal jokes, and you just want to say, 'Stop it.'

Playing around with history was very much in fashion at the end of the sixties and in the early seventies.
Richard Williams had done animated sequences for *The Charge of the Light Brigade*, which I liked overall, except that I wanted to know exactly what had gone wrong with the charge, and they made it confusing.[4] It was written by Charles Wood – who also wrote *How I Won the War* for Lester – and it had the same acerbic, edgy sense of comedy – taking history seriously but not being solemn. Sandy Lieberson, who was working with David Puttnam at that time, had got me involved in

a project called *World War Three And All That*, which was going to use documentary footage – from the Second World War and elsewhere – with Beatles songs.[5] I was due to direct the whole thing and do the animation sequences. But I just wasn't getting it together, so one day Sandy asked what I really wanted to do. I explained that I had this idea called *Jabberwocky,* and he said, 'Let's do it.' He made one phone call, to John Goldstone, which meant we had the same financing as the *Holy Grail.*

I worked on the script with Chuck Alverson, who had been assistant editor of *Help!* magazine before I took over his job, and who was now living in Wales. There were a lot of things I'd wanted to do in *Holy Grail* but hadn't been able to, and I didn't want to be tied to just doing comedy all the time. I wanted to deal with the whole world – adventure, suspense, romance, textures, smells, atmosphere. And, in my naïveté and arrogance, I thought we could make a medieval film with a lot of comedy, have three Pythons involved – Mike Palin was the star, with Terry Jones briefly and myself – and not be accused of making a *Python* film.

What intrigued me was the idea of a world where the terror created by a monster is good for business. Commerce is a theme that runs through the film. But it's really about a collision of fairytales . . . the tale

Jabberwocky: Dennis (Michael Palin) wants to have a little business and marry the fat girl down the road.

of a reluctant hero who gets the wrong happy-ever-after ending. It's my way of punishing him for having such pathetic dreams. And it's also about craftsmanship: Mike Palin plays Dennis, an early version of the clerk-bureaucrat Sam Lowry in *Brazil*. His father is a craftsman, a barrel-maker, but Dennis is more interested in accounting. He's like a guy somewhere in the Midwest who aspires to own a used-car lot. His aspirations are so low – he wants to have a little business and marry the fat girl down the road – but instead he gets half the kingdom, the beautiful princess, and is doomed. The idea of two fairytales colliding really appealed to me. So off we went and, since it was real fairytale time and there was a bigger budget than we'd had on the *Grail*, I could play with special effects and monsters to my heart's content – until, of course, everything went wrong again.

My first great discovery on *Jabberwocky* was that if you worked with real actors – unlike the Pythons – they would listen to what you had to say and oftentimes actually do it. If you asked a Python to do something, they would usually argue back: 'It's uncomfortable, why should I do that?' Then I would say: 'Listen, you bastards, you wrote this sketch and if you want it to work you've got to do it this way.' It was like babysitting and I just got tired of dealing with them. So now I could say, 'Max, I want you to lie down there and we're going to cover you with Fuller's earth,' and he would happily do it. This, I thought, was fantastic; this is what a director gets to do.

A German television company had just filmed *The Marriage of Figaro* and their sets were still standing. They were the wrong period, wrong everything, but my attitude was: 'Let's have them.' We bought those sets for £5,000 – so they didn't have to pay to have them torn down – and we revamped them into a medieval merchant's house. Then there was the brilliant *Oliver!* open-air set at Shepperton, which we were able to dress as a medieval street. We were some of the last people to use it: now Britain has no standing sets left.[6]

Was Jabberwocky *all shot in the studio?*
No, there were two real castles, Pembroke and Chepstow. What I like doing is mixing something real with something built and – if we do it right – hopefully you can't spot the difference. I also love the business of scavenging around; I was always going out on to the back lot and stealing from the piles of stuff being burned. At that time they were making one of the *Pink Panther* films and Blake Edwards had just built a castle on the back lot.[7] I wanted to use it, but they wouldn't let us, so we started stealing bits from them – things they had already thrown

away. There was a sewer, and I wrote a scene around that – after all, it was meant to be a very scatological film. So we had a scene in which Mike thinks he's found a proper opening into the town, then realizes what he's wading through. But they found out that we were using this stuff and broke it all up before they discarded it. Blake Edwards destroyed it all rather than let us revamp it, even though it would never have been recognized. We were guerrilla film-makers out there, stealing and scavenging whatever we could.

We couldn't afford to build the inside of the castle, so we just hung black drapes. We did have big paving stones, but only for the parts that were lit; otherwise, there was nothing on the studio floor. For the windows we built deep boxes, to give a sense of thick walls, but in fact there were no walls, just black velvet. What fake stone walls we did have only went up to about eight feet; we'd carefully light them to give the sense that there was stone high and low. It was a great way of working. We had a corridor which just consisted of plywood cut-out arches, and I kept changing these so that it became different corridors. It showed how little you need to make things work.

Jabberwocky: conjuring a castle out of drapes and lighting.

In many ways, I look back on those films and wonder why I can't do that now. It's partly because I've become too successful, and you can't do it in this way if you have big names in your films. But, even on a cheap film, the crew don't want to improvise; they want to build real things. There's a scene in *Jabberwocky* where the innkeeper, Bernard Bresslaw, is let out of prison, and they were going to build a cell. I said, 'Hold on, let's use one of our windows, with black velvet and a grille in the foreground, and that's all I need for a cell.' Then there was a scene in a cathedral: again, all we needed was a rose window, an altar and a couple of columns in the foreground. The crew were always complaining, because at that time there was a belief that there were *Python* millions, and they weren't getting a share of them. It wasn't that people wanted the money personally; they wanted it so their part of the film would look as good as possible.

But they didn't understand that there were no *Python* millions. Even when we went to America with *Python*, around this time, the only channel that would show it was PBS, the public television station. So, no big money.

Do you act as a kind of supervising designer on your films? This must make it difficult for your collaborators.

Yes, I do on all of them. I can't not draw stuff and I can't not say it should be this way. But it's always a collaborative thing. I have very specific ideas and either I draw them or I drag in the references and say, 'I want it to look like this.' But, if you get good people, they can interpret this and make it work – take, for instance, Hazel Pethig – the costume designer on *Jabberwocky* – and Max Wall's layers of clothes as King Bruno the Questionable. I drew a cartoon of it and she made it believable, yet it still has the cartoon quality. I like working with good people because if I come up with an idea, they come up with a better idea, then I come up with an even better one, and so on: it's a leapfrog process, and the work becomes much better than it would be if I only did exactly what I want.

That's where I don't agree with the kind of directors I grew up admiring, like Antonioni and Visconti, who seemed to know precisely what they wanted: not one inch more one way or the other. You know from your own experience that it can't be like that, and yet they gave the impression of always knowing everything. But the world wanted to believe in the director as *auteur*. No doubt this was a reaction against the studio system, and I wanted to believe in it as much as anybody, because I wanted to be an *auteur*.

King Bruno the Questionable (Max Wall): a cartoon made believable in *Jabberwocky*.

It's strange how an idea about rescuing directors who seemed to have no room for personal expression, buried within the old studio system and working only on genre movies, has turned into an idea about directors as tyrants and geniuses. I mean, people once needed convincing that Edgar G. Ulmer or Joseph Lewis or Sam Fuller were auteurs, *against superficial appearances. But it seems fairly apparent that, for instance, Antonioni and Visconti, or Scorsese and yourself, apart from all the obvious differences, have at least stamped signatures all over their films.*

Well, I may be an *auteur* according to how the word's used now, but I'm more collaborative than anyone could ever imagine. If you have all this talent available, whether it's actors or designers, then you want to use it to go beyond your own finite vision. I know that everyone who works on my films says they're the hardest they've ever worked on, because they're always more ambitious than the money or time will really allow; yet I think my collaborators feel pretty satisfied in the end because their work is up on the screen, and presented as it should be. So I push everybody and they work hard, because they know I appreciate what they're doing.

The *Jabberwocky* puppeteer: from page . . .

On *Jabberwocky*, I would be on my own in a corner, focused on try-ing to solve some problem, and the props guy would come over and say, 'Have you thought about doing this, Terry?' My first reaction was to tell him to get lost, then I realized he was right and that he'd just told me how to get out of the corner I'd painted myself into. When I went to do *Fisher King* in the States, my problem was trying to get the people working on the film to open up and realize they're part of the process. The Americans are so fascistic in their approach to film-making – the director snaps his fingers and people run because they're terrified – that it took weeks for them to understand I wasn't God, that I wanted their input and wanted them to question me. The more successful I get, the more the onus of having to get it right wants to settle on my shoulders alone, but I just hate that, I freeze up. I want everyone to share the responsibility, the guilt, and I'll shoulder the blame, because that's my job in the end.

. . . to practice, under the director's eye.

Why do you think Jabberwocky *wasn't a great commercial or critical success?*

I think it was mainly because it was sold as a *Python* film and it didn't deliver as such. In Germany, Poland and places like that – where they didn't know *Python* – it was really well received and the reviews were great. But in places where *Python* was known, that was all they saw in it. It's funny, but it's only half as funny; they couldn't see what else I was trying to do.

I had the temerity to write to the New York critics, saying that this was not a *Monty Python* film and, if it was going to be judged on anything, I'd rather they thought of it as a homage to Breughel and Bosch. Of course, they went berserk. You don't write to New York critics and tell them how to look at a film, and their reviews just spewed venom all over it. Even *Newsweek* joined in – 'Gilliam the Questionable' – the whole thing was about me rather than the film. How could I mention in the same breath great artists like Breughel and Bosch and this scatological crap? But hadn't they ever *looked* at those paintings, where people are shitting and peeing; hadn't they seen the humour as well as the humanity in Breughel and Bosch? They're great sprawling worlds: the crucifixion is in the distance, while a carnival is taking place all around it. Of course, it's a transitional film, because I was still very much caught up in *Python*, but I know it works on a very different level as well.

I think children loved it, but they wouldn't allow children to see it because of all the filth – which seems crazy when you consider what drivel children *are* allowed to see. Anyway, it did very mediocre business and took years to break even, although it has now done so, and everybody has been paid and even made a dollar or two profit. Personally, I think there are moments which are just wonderful and other moments that are not quite right, but on lots of levels it's a pretty good film. It was my first chance to break away from *Python* and try different things: there's romance and adventure in it, yet there are still Pythonesque jokes.

But weren't these impulses already apparent in the Python *features?*
Yes, there's a lot of humanity in the *Holy Grail*, but I think there's a different kind of humanity present in *Jabberwocky*. One of my favourite characters is Wat Dabney, the cooper with the severed foot. To me, he's really the epitome of the human spirit: no matter how bad it gets, somehow he goes on and doesn't complain. He's pragmatic: 'All right, so I lost my job. I chop a foot off, take up begging and business is great. Why don't you join me?' When Dennis refuses, he shouts after him, 'You're missing a golden opportunity.' Then, later on, obviously business has deteriorated and he's chopped off his other foot, but he's still perky: 'Morning, morning.' I love that character; he comes quite specifically from a figure in one of Bosch's paintings, who's sitting there, dressed quite differently from the others, with a piece of linen resting in front of him and a severed foot lying on it.[8]

Might the problem with Jabberwocky *also have been due to the title, leading audiences to expect a version of Lewis Carroll's poem?*[9]
The film has nothing to do with the poem – except that it does, because

a monster comes burbling through the woods. Some people got it, and said, well, *Jabberwocky* is just nonsense and this is a film that's nonsense. Maybe it sets people up for Lewis Carroll and then lets them down. I just respond to what inspires me. People still ask, 'Why *Brazil*?' I remember Dick Lester saying he was worried that the title would screw up the film, and that was after he'd made a film called *Cuba*. But I want to push the envelope. It's like that time back in college, when everyone is in the seminar arguing why certain things can't be and I'm outside the window being those things. And there are really oblique titles that work – like *Casablanca* and *Morocco* – and there are others that don't; the whole thing is so tenuous.

In the case of *Jabberwocky*, what inspired me, what got me going, was the Lewis Carroll poem. Right from the first lines

> Twas brillig, and the slithy toves
> > Did gyre and gimble in the wabe;
> All mimsy were the borogroves,
> > And the mome raths outgrabe.

I could see a world already – with characters, textures, shapes and colours. It's all there in those words and it came out as a medieval world, even though it didn't have to take that form. It's only tenuously Tenniel,[10] and much more to do with Magritte, who juxtaposes the paintings with those enigmatic titles just for the fun of it; there's a side of me that can't stop myself doing that – the old surrealist game of putting a name with a thing and the brain has to come up with an association.[11] But I suppose my problem is that I'm using things which already have a lot of associations. For instance, when we said that *Twelve Monkeys* was inspired by *La Jetée*, all the reviews went on about the relationship, despite the fact that I'd not seen *La Jetée* when I made it.[12]

That was an honest statement of what had inspired the script, just as *Jabberwocky* was an honest admission of where that film began, before it went on to something else. It's that vital spark of inspiration. My wife Maggie says that I keep making the same film, except the costumes are different, and I'm beginning to think they *are* the same. Even with the later films – which involve other people's scripts – I'm still back doing the same things, making the same film: there's society and there's the individual within it; there's the guy with the dream; there's the little man achieving something, and not ever quite getting what he wanted: he gets something – sometimes worse, sometimes better – but he seldom gets what he wanted; there's always a quest; there's this sense, as in *Brazil*, of paranoia; there's always greed, like the merchants in *Jabberwocky*;

The Princess who's as mad as a hatter (Deborah Fallender).

there's the love of craftsmanship; and there's always romance, though they're usually misdirected or unlikely romances.

I love the princess in the tower, mad as a hatter, who's living in a dream world of stories, and this guy turns up and falls into her dream world, becomes a victim of her stories – 'my hero' – but she's wacko. I love the idea of people having to do heroic deeds – taking on monsters – even though they're not normally heroic. I think there's a side of me that's trying to compete with Lucas and Spielberg – I don't usually admit this publicly – because I tend to think that they only go so far, and their view of the world is rather simplistic. What I want to do is take whatever cinema is considered normal or successful at a particular time and play around with it – to use it as a way of luring audiences in.

I spent some time talking with George Lucas up at Skywalker Ranch after *Brazil*, and I realized that he really believes Darth Vader is evil. I argued that he's not evil, he's just the bad guy in the black hat, who you see coming a million miles away. Evil, on the other hand, is Mike Palin in *Brazil*: your best friend, the nice-guy family man who, for reasons of his career or whatever, will torture and do awful things. You just don't know where evil is coming from. That for me is truly worrying, whereas what George and Steven are doing are cartoons – good ones, certainly, but they have pretensions to something deeper which I feel is never delivered. Their bad guys are like Disney's ones, who were always the best fun. But I'm trying to turn these things on their head.

In fact, George was making *Star Wars* at Elstree at the same time as I was making *Jabberwocky* at Shepperton. We had our T-shirts and they had theirs, and a lot of the crew worked on both pictures. I remember they'd come over to me and say, 'That guy doesn't know what the hell he's doing; it's a real mess up there. We build these huge sets and he's pointing the camera in the corner.' On the other hand, they loved working on *Jabberwocky*. Then the films came out and all the *Jabberwocky* T-shirts disappeared and the *Star Wars* ones reappeared – 'Ah, George was wonderful, what a great guy.' Crews can be very fickle. This happens on a lot of my films: the crew are excited working on them and we know we're doing good and interesting work, and then they're surprised that the public doesn't see them the same way.

Partly this is because I'm not making it easy for the public, but it's also because the films haven't been sold as vigorously as they should. In the early days, we were with a small distributor, Cinema 5, headed by Don Rugoff, a great man in many ways but also a nightmare. He had his own cinemas in New York and was throwing money at the *New York Times*, but he went round and round on *Jabberwocky*, not knowing how to sell it, before he eventually gave in and started calling it *Monty Python's Jabberwocky* – the one thing I said he couldn't do. We stopped them doing that, because *Python* was always very vigilant about the use of the name for non-*Python* things, both as a group and as individuals. But the audience still didn't know what to make of it.

I think you're right about the problem of titles, about how you lead the public in and what you put outside the side-show, but my obsession is not to tell them anything, so they come in with a completely open mind, even though I know the world doesn't really work that way. That's why I believe in T-shirts, books, magazines, images – anything to creep it out there into the world. Basically, you're planting little seeds in as many different ways as possible.[13]

The terrible thing for a guy who wants to make popular films is that I keep ending up being coursework in film schools. I don't want to encourage film students, I want to encourage the public. But you end up being the darling of film schools. I remember George Perry[14] organized a big seminar that took me to Minneapolis with *Jabberwocky* – the first time I'd been back to my home town since we left in the fifties – and there were a lot of serious people there who loved audiovisual things.

The audience was confused, as usual, when they saw *Jabberwocky*; they didn't know what to make of these beautiful images alongside the crass humour. Then I got up and charmed them, and they all started liking the movie because they liked me. This always makes me crazy because I want the movies to be judged in their own right. But once they get a sense of my personality, then they can make sense of the movie.

I'm surprised that you're still surprised audiences have problems with the tone of your films, especially when they come to them with Python-esque expectations. But, since this was your first real solo experience as a director, I wonder what other lessons you learned?
Right at the end, we had to show the film to some Dutch distributors at the Technicolor lab, and for some reason the soundtrack wasn't with it, so we just showed the images. And it was then that I realized how stunningly beautiful it was, and I wondered why I needed the dialogue at all, with all those cheap jokes. At least on that side we'd achieved exactly what I wanted and I'm very proud of it.

Before that, I'd had a difficult relationship with the editor, Mike Bradsell. He'd been working with Ken Russell and others, and he'd never before worked with a director who was in the editing room every minute – he was a nice man and very good, but he had problems with the fact that I wanted to get my hands on this stuff. This was the first time that I realized how editing is supposed to work. The director shoots the movie and the editor assembles and cuts it together; they look at it and comments are made; then the editor goes back and does the next cut, and the director is brought in again. I was shocked: I always thought directors were real hands-on people, but apparently not. I just wanted to be part of every frame. And, because of my animation background, I was aware of every frame – which is sometimes very useful, especially in the special-effects area. But at other times, I'd be sitting there working on a cut, taking a frame off here and there, and the assistant editors would go mad because there'd be all these envelopes full of single frames, the result of me sitting there at three in the morning wondering about one frame more or less on each cut. Over the years, I've got better and, with the last few films, I haven't edited them in this manner, except for a few scenes. But I still find that I have to restrain myself.

Then there was the monster. I always used to hate how all the monsters in films were obviously guys in rubber suits, with their knees bending the wrong way for animals. So when we came to doing the Jabberwocky – which was roughly based on Tenniel's drawing – and we couldn't afford any other way except a man in a rubber suit, I decided we'd turn the guy round so that he's standing backwards and the knees would bend the right way. What you also gain with a man standing backwards is that his arms become wings. We ran the head of the monster off a crane – like a puppet on wires – and then had a dancer stepping backwards while flapping his arm-wings. The result is quite extraordinary, because you can't quite figure out how this monster works. It was hard for him, acting backwards in sweltering heat; and at one point he tripped and fell, bringing the whole thing down. I decided to keep that – because the shot was wonderful – and rewrote the story to accommodate it. My only regret is not having made a reverse optical of the shot when the feet hit the ground, because when you look at that shot backwards, the feet have real weight and look great.

Post-Tenniel: the Jabberwocky as a man in a rubber suit, backwards.

Jabberwocky: cartoon effects become special effects.

This was a chance to translate cartoon effects into special effects, and to learn something about perception. There's one shot when the Black Knight comes off his horse and falls, and the best take was a hand-held shot that swings around and you see the prop truck. I played with that shot, blew it up and did everything I could to get rid of the truck. But this just made it worse, so in the end I left it in and, somehow, nobody sees the truck, even though it fills half of the frame. It's as if your brain won't accept that big a mistake in the middle of this medieval world, so you blot it out.

And there's another shot where the flagellants come through and we pan up on to a whole stack of camera boxes with tarpaulins over them and, again, you don't see it. Then we get on to situations like the whole armoury collapsing. We had run out of money and somehow had to shoot that scene in a day. You can only plan these things up to a certain point. After that, it's just, 'Roll that across there, Paul, push that, dump this here' – and, amazingly, it works. It's a sequence I like because it's about an assembly line coming apart – my revenge on Chevrolet. But, by doing it in a day, you learn that you can get away with murder. Everyone's saying, you can't do this or that, or we're out of time, and you just stand there, applying animation techniques. If I were to do a sequence like that now, I'd set aside a week for it and it would cost a fortune.

The flagellants' procession in *Jabberwocky* led by the Head Fanatic (Graham Crowden).

Would it be any better because you spent more time and money?
No, in reality I don't think so. The other thing I did was to ask the crew to assemble a kit of bits and pieces that we could carry around with us everywhere, so that we could always get a shot: things like a piece of foreground, the edge of a building, a little Lego kit of parts. I've done that ever since, and it can be invaluable. On *Fisher King*, I always had the edge of a building so that, if we were seeing more than we wanted on the street in New York, we could pull in the foreground edge and block it out. Smart designers understand this, but others used to take great offence because they would want to control and design everything.

We did it in *Time Bandits* too, when we couldn't afford the big mob in the scene with Sean Connery in the square in Greece. We were shooting in Morocco and we only had 120 people, but if you look at that shot you'd swear we had thousands. What we did was push ninety-five of them way down to the end of the square, then took the remaining twenty-five and built them into the foreground, so that they're covering three-quarters of the frame, with the rest far away and Sean and his men standing up on top of the building. In *Jabberwocky*, there's a scene where they're queuing to enter the town and Mike joins the queue. We had only fifty people, so I got a long lens and we positioned each one so that they were slightly overlapping the one in front. They're all standing about fifteen feet apart, but it looks like a huge queue going all the way to the town wall.

I think all of this came out of my graphic-animation side and also because we didn't have a choice. I'm still happiest doing these things, trying to get back to guerrilla film-making. But, unfortunately, where I am now, you can't do it. On *Twelve Monkeys*, with Bruce Willis and Brad Pitt, you have to bring the circus along. And because they're in it, nobody else wants to work for little money – even though Bruce and Brad were working for their version of no money, certainly a lot less than they'd normally get. So the problem is: how do you create a sense of fairness about the whole thing? As soon as I get these big guys in, it makes the films more expensive, but they reach more people and make more money, and so it's only fair that everybody gets a share.

But on the early films, working with independent distributors, we could give all the heads of department a cut, even if it was only a little one.[15] *Time Bandits* actually made a lot of money, so people got cheques and they still get them every year. It may only be £12, but at least they're part of the thing. Since I've moved on to these bigger films, it's been impossible to do that, the system doesn't allow it, and yet I need these big budgets to do the things I'm trying to do now. So it's a delicate balance. If people feel they're part of it and that they're not being taken advantage of, you get twice the amount of work from them for a fraction of the money. But unless you're making very small films, it's hard to recreate that situation and it's impossible to calculate its value in cash terms.

All my films look more expensive than they actually were. *Jabberwocky* cost about £500,000 and it looks a lot more expensive. *Time Bandits* went for $5 million and everyone thought it must have cost $15 million. Even *Munchausen* probably only cost $40 million, but it's still good value. The truth is that nobody knows the real cost of *Munchausen*, because once the finance people took it over, they were loading their other problems on to it – once you've got one in the toilet, throw everything into the toilet with it. You can work out the cost of small films, but big films rarely. For instance, I know what *Fisher King* cost, because I got real cost statements for the making of the film, but then it's the other charges added on afterwards that are impossible to control. The importance of this for me now is that the negative cost does determine certain other things, like whether I have the final cut and whether I get a bonus for staying on budget. Well, I got the bonus for *Twelve Monkeys*.

Gilliam the Resigner on location with Terry Jones, *Life of Brian.*

How did you come to be only the production designer on Monty Python's Life of Brian?

Terry Jones wanted me to co-direct with him, as we had on *Holy Grail,* but I was really spoiled by the experience of *Jabberwocky* and the idea of being a dogsbody for the rest of the group didn't appeal, so I said I would design it. I'd been keeping an eye on the look of things on *Holy Grail,* and here I was running the art department, but it wasn't the same at all because the director wasn't me and sometimes Terry had ideas that drove me crazy, since I have a better eye. So, after a while, I became the 'Resigner' – I just added little lines to the 'D' – when I was getting really pissed off. We'd planned shots with expansive coffered ceilings, then they'd shoot horizontally, completely missing the ceiling. Because I'm always worried about cost, that kind of thing drives me crazy. But there were a few scenes where I managed to get back behind the camera, when Terry was playing Mandy, and so we'd get some of the big shots right. Finally, I went down and shot the Bethlehem exterior sequence at the beginning and we had that looking beautiful. I found it difficult, because I really wanted to make things look great, but the group wasn't particularly interested in that, and Terry had his own ideas about where to put the camera, so it wasn't the best of times.

Meanwhile, back in the manger.

Where did the idea for Life of Brian *come from?*
That was the group. We were in Amsterdam promoting the *Holy Grail* and getting drunk. Eric came up with a great title – *Jesus Christ: Lust for Glory* – and we all fell about. We liked it because it was great subject matter to deal with and everyone did their research seriously. We worked very hard not to blaspheme – because it's really about the guy next door – but the Bishop of Southwark didn't understand this, Malcolm Muggeridge didn't understand it and the people of America didn't understand it either. But my mother, who's an avid churchgoer, had no problem with it: yes, Jesus is up there giving the Sermon on the Mount, and it's the guys at the back who are getting it wrong. I thought we were really clever about this, but we still got lambasted.

The group was running really well in terms of ideas, but directing it was no fun at all, because everyone wanted their own way. One example: the 'Romans go home' scene was a day-for-night shot, which had to be filmed in one direction so that you didn't get the bright sky.[16] So we built a wall in the right place and it was all set up. Then John turned up and said that he'd rehearsed it the other way, left to right, and he wouldn't budge. So we end up with a day-for-night sequence where you can't see people's faces, because they are against a light sky, and the shot has to be printed down until they're almost black. It's still a wonderfully funny scene, but I think it would have been better with a bit more control over those things. It's frustrating when you can't get the group to understand that it's helping the show, and not some artistic airy-fairy visual nonsense – which is what they usually felt I was going on about. For me, the point was always to try to make that world believable, because a lot of the jokes depend on it looking like a biblical epic. The form that we're sending up already exists, so you've got to do it right.

There were some wonderful visual jokes that never quite came off. For instance, I love the Pilate scene – 'thwow him on the floor' – with Bigus Dickus. We were using the set that Zeffirelli had built for *Jesus of Nazareth*; in fact, that's why we'd gone to Tunisia, to follow in the footsteps of Robert Powell and Franco.[17] We were able to grab abandoned bits of their gear, so that their Temple of Solomon became Pilate's palace. Now, there was an architectural joke planned for this: Pilate's palace was previously a weird Jewish tenement, a rabbit warren on three floors, and the Romans were in the middle of building a neat rectangular atrium in the middle of it, cutting right through making three floors into two. You could argue that this was a distraction, but I know it's possible to set up a scene where you can show that at the beginning and then go into the action, so that you get both. You would get a sense that the Romans were caught up in this awful chaotic place, trying to impose their own rational architecture on a place that didn't fit, but doing it ruthlessly and getting caught out by the workers, while at the same time trying to run a court. That was the intention, and the ceiling was beautifully coffered, but you don't see any of it. Basically, Terry shot it like a TV show, with the camera head on, clunk, clunk, clunk. That bothers me, because I think it sets the scene better if you can establish the majesty *and* the madness of the place; you can understand Pilate's irritation because he's got things to do.

But, arguably, this is trying to impose a dramatic depth and complexity which the material doesn't really have, or only has occasionally.
Maybe Terry was right and I'm wrong, and certainly the humour plays brilliantly in the scene. But a lot of it was just practical, too. The art director, Roger Christian, and I found the perfect place for Golgotha, where the sun would be in the right position, the background was right, and there would be a great pit in front of the crosses, a quarry with holes that looked like a necropolis. Perfect. But by then we knew that, whatever we said to him, Terry would go in the opposite direction. So the problem was, how to tell him we'd found the place without him

Hanging around on crosses in *Life of Brian*.

being pissed off that we'd found it instead of him – things can get testy on a film. Anyway, we had split into two groups to look for locations, and Terry had gone in a direction that made no sense geographically, so he came back saying he'd found nothing. I said that we'd not had much luck either, but there was one place that just might work: he'd have to decide. So we took him there and he agreed to use this perfect place – but in the wrong direction! Then we sat Terry down to plan who was going to be on which cross, and have them custom-made – because they were incredibly uncomfortable – but then he changed everything on the day so that everyone was up there, dying painfully on the wrong cross.

Shades of Pasolini's skit on biblical epics, La Ricotta, *where they forget about the extra on the cross during lunch break and he dies for real.*[18]

NOTES

1 American-born Dick Lester (b. 1932) settled in Britain in the mid-fifties and got to know Peter Sellers when directing him in a Goonish TV comedy series, *A Show Called Fred* (Rediffusion, 1956). He then directed a surrealistic comedy short *The Running, Jumping and Standing Still Film* (1960), produced by and starring Sellers. Pop music experience came from directing *It's Trad Dad* (1962), after which Lester was an obvious choice to direct the first Beatles films, *A Hard Day's Night* (1964) and *Help!* (1965).

2 Panama-based producer Alexander Salkind shot Dumas's arch-swashbuckler as two films released separately, *The Three Musketeers: The Queen's Diamonds* (1974) and *The Four Musketeers: The Revenge of Milady* (1975), aiming at a tone of opulent comedy-adventure which Lester achieved with style.

3 Lester's *Robin and Marion* (1976), starring Sean Connery and Audrey Hepburn as ageing lovers, sharply divided critics with its unusual mixture of surface realism, whimsy and anachronism.

4 Tony Richardson's *The Charge of the Light Brigade* (1968), although based on new research into the Crimean War and the disastrous cavalry action at Balaclava, was widely criticized for not making the course of events clear, despite the fact that conveying confusion was also an aim.

5 Sandy Lieberson and David Puttnam's VPS company produced several compilation films in the early seventies, including two on Hitler and Nazi Germany: *The Double Headed Eagle* (Lutz Becker) and *Swastika* (Philippe Mora, both 1973).

6 The period street set built for *Oliver!* (Carol Reed, 1968) was used for many subsequent films before being demolished. Gilliam contemplated building a new standing set for his projected *Tale of Two Cities*.

7 *The Pink Panther Strikes Again* (Blake Edwards, 1976), the fifth in the series, involved blowing up a realistic Bavarian castle set.

8 Hieronymus Bosch, *Temptation of St Anthony* triptych.

9 'Jabberwocky' is a nonsense poem which appears in the first chapter of Lewis Carroll's *Through the Looking Glass*, supposedly in a book that Alice discovers is 'all in some language I don't know'. When she holds it up to a mirror, it reverses into a readable, but nonsensical text that 'seems to fill my head with ideas – only I don't know what they are'. Carroll had written the first verse when only twenty-three to amuse his siblings, calling it a 'Stanza of Anglo-Saxon Poetry' and offering glosses of all its invented words. Apart from many spoof interpretations and parodies, there is a suggestion that it may be a distant parody of a German ballad (see Martin Gardiner, *The Annotated Alice*, Penguin 1965, pp. 191–7).

10 For the book's original edition Sir John Tenniel provided an illustration of a child-like knight with a broadsword facing a gigantic winged dragon.

11 The titles of René Magritte's paintings usually have no obvious connection with the visual image, but invite the viewer to speculate on possible links. More generally, the Surrealists' interest in chance and automatism produced an art of random and unconscious associations between words and images.

12 Although the script of *Twelve Monkeys* was inspired by Chris Marker's short *La Jetée*, Gilliam had not seen the earlier film when he made it (see Chapter 9).

13 The *Twelve Monkeys* marketing campaign featured sprayed-on stencils rather than photographic imagery.

14 George Perry is a film critic and journalist, and author of a book on *Monty Python*.

15 The 'heads of departments' in film production are the director of photography, production designer, costume designer, editor etc, who oversee their assistants and on low-budget independent productions may receive a percentage share of a film's profits in lieu of a high salary.

16 Shooting 'day for night' means that an exterior scene is lit and photographed in daylight to be printed dark as if it were night.

17 Franco Zeffirelli's *Jesus of Nazareth* (1978), starring Robert Powell, was made as a TV miniseries and also released as a feature.

18 In Pier Paolo Pasolini's *La Ricotta* (1962), made as an episode of the portmanteau film *Rogopag*, an extra in a biblical film (directed by Orson Welles) who is playing one of the thieves crucified with Jesus is forgotten during the lunch break, and dies after gorging himself on ricotta.

5

Handmade *Time Bandits* and unlikely heroes; *The Crimson Permanent Assurance* comes aboard

You clearly weren't planning to collaborate again with the Pythons en masse, but you were already working on what would become Brazil *around the time of* Life of Brian. *How did* Time Bandits *emerge from this and how did something as bizarre get financed after the relative failure of* Jabberwocky?

Life of Brian was literally the start of Handmade Films. Things happened at the eleventh hour. On the Thursday before the crew were due to leave on the Saturday, Lord Delfont pulled the plug, so George Harrison put up the money and Handmade Films was formed, consisting of Denis O'Brien, George and the Pythons. I think it was because I was talking to Denis about *Brazil* and getting a blank, while he was pushing to get another film made, that the idea of *Time Bandits* came up. I said I wanted to make a film for everybody and, literally, in one weekend I wrote the outline of *Time Bandits*. I swear I'd never read C.S. Lewis, but I knew the opening would be a knight on horseback bursting out of the wardrobe, and I knew I wanted to shoot it from a kid's level.[1] Because I doubted that any kid could sustain the movie, I surrounded him with people his size; and so it developed in an organic fashion. Knowing that there are holes in time and space, what could be better than to commit a robbery and then escape to a time before the robbery was committed?

So I went back to Denis and he loved it, and said he'd get George to write the music for it. Then I went to Mike Palin and asked him to write it with me, which we did pretty quickly. Unlike now – when I wait for years to get something going – this all happened very fast after Dennis said yes. That's important for me, because I lose confidence and energy when I doubt the likelihood of getting a film off the ground.

But when Denis went out to try to raise the money, everybody turned us down. This was before *ET*, and family entertainment was not what any studio did then. Only Disney did that kind of movie, and they were going through the *Herbie Goes Bananas* phase. We just didn't fit any of the acceptable genres. So, in his arrogance, Denis decided we'd do it ourselves. He and George mortgaged the building they had in Cadogan Square to finance the film, which was budgeted at $5 million. The first actor we brought in was John Cleese, although when Mike wrote Robin Hood he wanted to play that part himself; but Denis was pressuring us to get more Pythons in, and Mike and I agreed that John would be a great Robin Hood.

John Cleese as Robin Hood with the *Time Bandits*.

Sean Connery seems more unlikely casting. How did you bring him in?
The great irony is that the original script introduced Agamemnon like this: 'The Greek warrior pulls his helmet off, revealing himself to be none other than Sean Connery or an actor of equal, but cheaper, stature.' That was before we had any contact with Sean, which happened because Denis was playing golf with him and mentioned the film. I couldn't believe it. Then I went down to meet him at the Grosvenor Hotel and we got on. I think it was a time when his career was going through a bad patch; also I think he was feeling guilty about not having been as good a father to his kids as he would have liked, so it was a chance to be a surrogate father. Shelley Duval was a friend of Eric's – we meet everybody through Eric – and Katherine Helmond was my first choice to play the ogre's wife, but Denis's Hollywood advisers thought

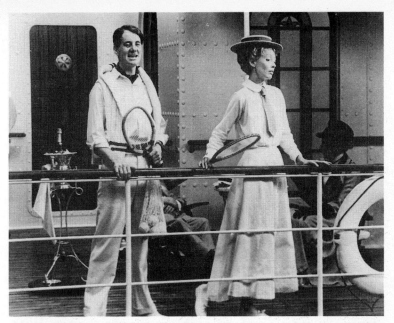

Anyone for tennis? Michael Palin and Shelley Duval on board for *Time Bandits*.

David Warner as Evil Genius in *Time Bandits*.

she was just a television actress. *Soap* was a huge success all over the world at that time, but it didn't count in the movies.[2] So we went for Ruth Gordon, but then she managed to break her leg on Clint Eastwood's *Every Which Way But Loose*, so I was able to get Katherine by default. I originally asked Jonathan Pryce to play the Evil Genius, but he did a heist film instead – for the money – which I think he's regretted ever since. So David Warner got the part.

And the dwarfs?
Well, I've always liked the circus. But I also liked the idea of little guys being as heroic as Alan Ladd, who was only about five foot five. I love watching Ladd's movies; when he's with the girl their heads are on the same level, but when you look at their belts, his is at the level of her chest, and it's very silly. I knew his stunt double in LA, who was six foot two: they would swing Alan in and this six-foot-two guy would jump off the balcony, then Alan would get up. Anyway, I thought, 'If Alan Ladd can be a big hero, then why can't these guys at four foot one?' I think what was most pleasing was that they had never had the chance just to play people and be called upon to do dangerous and heroic things. They all rose to the occasion and were just brilliant. Dave Rappaport had been with Ken Campbell's show for a long time, and was a very smart guy.

Time Bandits: little guys as heroes.

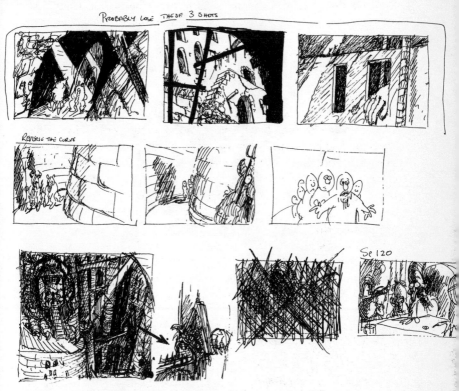

Storyboard sequences for *Time Bandits*.

Kenny Baker is R2D2 in *Star Wars*. And Tiny Ross was the little guy in the Harmonica Gang. They've all had to do extraordinary things to make a living, and here they were as the real heroes of the film.

A ridiculous thing about *Time Bandits* was that the first day's shooting was in Morocco. We had to get all the Greek stuff done quickly, with Sean Connery and the boy, Craig Warnock, who'd never done a film before; and I hadn't directed a film since *Jabberwocky*, four years earlier, and was still trying to learn the craft. First, we had to backpack all the gear up mountain passes to where we were going to do the fight with the Minotaur. The temperature was 120 degrees and I had pages of storyboard to be shot in two days. As soon as I started, it became clear this was a disaster – me with my ridiculous storyboard and a kid who had frozen completely.

The hero as father-figure: Sean Connery and Craig Warnock.

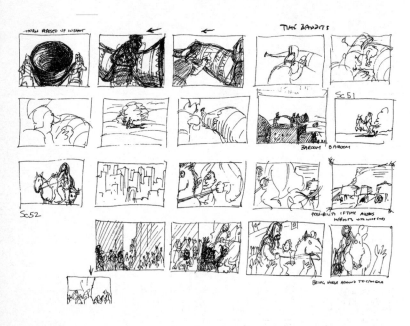

Storyboard for the horn-blowing sequence in *Time Bandits* which summons Kevin.

Taking the bull by the horns: Sean Connery as King Agamemnon.

Storyboard for the bull's head sequence in *Time Bandits*.

Sean was great. He pulled me over and said, 'You just shoot my stuff quickly and keep it simple. Then you can spend time with the kid. And you're not going to get through that storyboard.' So we kept the whole thing pretty much as separate shots; there are only a couple where you see them together. Sean was an old pro, cutting through all the crap, and I wouldn't have got through it without his encouragement. Interestingly, he wouldn't let me shoot him mounting his horse, because he said he wouldn't look good. Obviously, he'd been in situations where he'd trusted the director and they'd used the wrong shots. So all he'd do was stand high in the stirrups and then settle down, and it was up to me to work out how he got on the horse. I didn't mind that at all, because it gave me parameters to work with.

Then we had a crazy horse that wouldn't stand still, and one of the local guys told me that the best way to deal with it was to nail the horse down – right through its shoes – to a piece of four-by-eight plywood. In the end, we found a less painful solution. Next, we had to fake a massive crowd for the arrival scene with only 120 extras, done as I described earlier, and actually easier to control than having 1,000 extras, as I discovered later. Then there was the scene where a great horn is blown from a rooftop. We had found a building for this two months earlier and got permission to use it – until we discovered that the guy who claimed to own it didn't really, and his sister – who did own part of it with her husband – was in Marrakech. This elaborate family feud was preventing us from getting a vital shot. So, until we got the shot, I just sat down in front of the door and said that I wasn't going to move, and somehow it worked.

You did the studio work back in England at Pinewood?
We only used Pinewood for the tank; the rest was at Lee International, the old Rediffusion studio, which I used for *Brazil* as well.[3] It was extraordinary that we managed to do everything there, because the scenes at the end – which involve the big battle – were shot on a stage which is only eighty by a hundred feet. All the sets had been put on wheels, so I'd put the camera against one wall and shoot everything one way, then we'd move everything around and do the reverse angles. For the exteriors, we shot the Napoleonic sequence at Raglan Castle and Ian Holm was brilliant as Napoleon. Holm normally plays straight roles and is never cast as a comic, but I had seen him in *The Misanthrope* and found him very funny. His was the kind of performance that you can only mess up in the editing. He would do these perfect long takes, which you couldn't improve; if you tried to shorten them, you'd damage them.

Ian Holm as Napoleon in *Time Bandits*.

Actors seem to like me, because I'm a good audience, but during the banquet scene – where Ian's drunk – I just couldn't stop laughing. Eventually the assistant director said, 'We're going to have to ask the director to leave the set so we can get the shot.' So I did, and they got a great take.

We used Epping Forest for Robin Hood's encampment, which occasioned another interesting bit of actor business. Derek O'Connor, who was in everything from *Jabberwocky* to *Brazil*, is a great actor, but each time I bring him in he gets rid of his lines. In the Robin Hood scene, Robin would ask him something but he didn't want to reply, so he developed a big gruff grunting sound, which meant that another actor got the line because he had to translate. Derek has managed to avoid saying lines on all three films by talking rubbish. It's one of the things I like about working with good actors: they have these weird ideas – some of which are ridiculous, but others are great – and you incorporate them into what you're doing. It's happened to me on every film so far. It excites me, because by the time you're shooting you're so familiar with the material there's a danger of it becoming mechanical. Then somebody comes up with a silly idea that brings it alive and the adrenalin starts flowing again.

'The shortest, widest person I could find.' Ian Muir as the Giant in *Time Bandits*.

I often try to incorporate things from other films I admire – in this case it was the giant genie from *The Thief of Bagdad*.[4] I started casting tall people but, when you make them giant – using really wide-angle lenses – they just look like beanstalks. I realized I was getting it all wrong and I needed the shortest, widest person I could find. So I got a wrestler, Ian Muir, who's five foot one, we stuck on the wide-angle lens, and suddenly he's gigantic because he doesn't go beanstalky on us. We were shooting at ninety-six frames per second and he's practically running, but slowed down, all those muscles are swinging and his weight seems monumental.

You really prefer these low-tech 'artisanal' special effects to elaborate opticals and computer graphics, presumably because animation is effectively a kind of continuous manual special-effects process?
Always. I prefer them not only because I'm learning all the time, but because also I can discover things along the way which wouldn't happen if it was farmed out to somebody else. I think that's why so many films look the same, when they move into 'effects world': it's brilliant, but it's all the same. In *Holy Grail*, for instance, when they're throwing the animals over the castle wall, all I had to do was make sure that our guys were keeping their heads below the parapet in the foreground. Later we went into Julian Doyle's back garden and threw plastic cows from a farm set into the air; then we matted the two together and what appear to be full-size cows were coming over the wall. It's the most basic film-making technique.

Back to Méliès, with his matte effects and multiple exposures.
Speaking of Méliès, in *Life of Brian* there's the spaceship sequence, which I wanted to do because it was a chance to dabble in special effects.[5] Julian Doyle and I used to have our offices in Neal's Yard in Covent Garden; they consisted of two old banana warehouses, with a studio space of about twenty by twenty-five feet and twelve feet high, and we did the whole spaceship sequence in this tiny space. We'd built a really nice little spaceship, but didn't have any pyrotechnics experts, so we sent a guy down to a joke shop to buy all the exploding cigars he could find. Then we used the filament of a lightbulb as our sparking device, and the asteroid was made of foam polystyrene which we'd carved and painted; we slung them together, blew the powder from the exploding cigars with the bulb, and that was our explosion.

I decided the only way to do the meteor shower was in-camera, so we set up a track, I did a grid and then worked out the tracking for what must have been twelve or thirteen exposures. For each one, we'd track

Low-tech high-tech: the handmade spaceship in *Life of Brian*.

in on an asteroid that was stuck on a stick against black velvet. A dozen of these, and we had an asteroid shower. For the star fields, I just took a brush and splattered paint on shiny black paper, then I airbrushed in a few galaxies and we did several overlays. We moved the full-size spaceship interior by bouncing it around on inner tubes. For the sound I used a motorcycle, so it becomes very funny as they change gear and roar off.

One of my proudest moments came after we'd done *Life of Brian*. I was waiting for my bags at San Francisco airport when I saw George Lucas. I introduced myself and he congratulated me on the spaceship sequence: he loved it – imagine, after all the special effects in *Star Wars*! Since Lucas, Spielberg and I are all roughly contemporaries, I was determined to do special effects as a cottage industry in Merrie Englande, just to show them that you could do it for a couple of fivers instead of millions. After *Holy Grail*, Kent Housten set up the Peerless Camera Company, using my tax write-offs to buy our first rostrum camera and optical printer. Kent had shot my animations as a rostrum camera operator at Bob Godfrey's, and wanted to set up an operation of his own. Now we've got everything, but originally we were trying to compete with Industrial Light and Magic with only a fraction of the resources.

The cage scene is a sequence I'm really proud of because it's so simple. There were three cages – one full size, another half size and the other, one-third, set in false perspective so they're only a few feet apart – on a very small stage, maybe only fifty feet long, hung with black velvet; we did that scene just in the blackness. The escape was only a quarter of a page of script and due to be shot in a couple of days, but it took a week. I knew we had a good sequence there and it was really fun to build up all that tension. I used little models again, but when you shoot with models you just don't know what you're going to get. There's one shot which I think is breathtaking, where Strutter does the last bit of swinging and grabs the edge of the maze. It was just this six-inch figure, shot in reverse, with the camera down low; the little figure was held in place by the fingertips of a guy behind the the wall of the model. We pulled on the other end of the cord around the figure's waist, the guy holding by fingertips lets go, and Strutter swings down and out of shot. You do a lot of these shots and, if you're lucky, one does the trick. In this case, when the shot was printed backwards one take looked as if the figure actually stretches out and grabs the edge of the maze, and that's the one we used.

A lot of this stuff was shot at Lee's, but we have a tendency to end up shooting in small rooms and patching things together. The scene where they're approaching the burning city on their little raft was done at Neal's Yard. We didn't have any decent close-ups of the gang, so we hung black drapes in this very small space, put them on inner tubes and wiggled them, and had some trays of water with pieces of mirror which you bounce the light off to get reflections.

The battle sequence in *Time Bandits* was a complete nightmare, because we were behind schedule and the mechanical special effects weren't ready, so I had to shoot it completely out of sequence, relying on my storyboard. There were some very experienced people on the crew – the focus puller, Bobby Stillwell, had done *Lawrence of Arabia* – and they all thought I was out of my mind. After the première, Bobby said he didn't believe I could do it, but all the bits did fit perfectly.

I love being able to get on the optical printer and fiddle around until I get something the way I want it, so that I can feel my fingerprints are on the stuff and that it's more handmade than other films.

There are quite elaborate rules to keep everyone in film production doing their own job and not someone else's. So you need collaborators who share this attitude of improvisation and love of bricolage?

It's a constant problem, and the bigger the film the more difficult it is. Someone who has been very important for me in all this is Julian Doyle. He first started working on *Holy Grail* as production manager, then he was the associate producer on *Jabberwocky* and came in at the stage when we were re-editing it. He's been a kind of teacher and we were partners on many of these projects. His approach was always to try to be hands-on and challenge the hierarchy of skills and positions among the technicians; and he paid the price of not being liked by some of the crews because he seems too much of a jack of all trades. There's a fine balance you've got to maintain in not alienating people by giving them the impression that you can do their job better than they can. You have to encourage them, even when you want to get your own hands on things; but Julian would often break that rule and stick a camera in my hands, saying, 'Go and shoot that, Terry.' When it came to *Time Bandits* and *Brazil*, Julian edited and we worked again very closely, with a couple of Steenbecks – he at one and me at the other – throwing scenes back and forth between us. He also ran the second-unit mop-up crew on *Time Bandits*, and both the second and special-effects units on *Brazil*, and always knew exactly what we were after – it's hard to find someone who's on the same wavelength as you for this kind of work.

Ray Cooper was introduced to me by George and Denis to try to control the music on *Time Bandits*. He's perhaps best known as Elton John's percussionist – they have done several two-man shows together – and he's helped to educate me musically. He has a huge store of musicians and music which he thrusts at me, to see if I like it. He introduced me to Mike Moran, who composed the music for *Time Bandits*, and since then it's been a kind of triumvirate of Ray, me and the composer, with Ray saying things like, 'I think Mahler would be interesting here, but let's change it from minor to major,' and so on. In fact, Ray's big solo moment in *Time Bandits* is the cage sequence, which he did live to picture. He had his whole kit there, an extraordinary array, with timpani, gongs, matchboxes full of eyes of newts and things like that to shake. The picture would roll and he would start hitting things – it was wondrous to watch.

There seems to have been a lot of improvisation on Time Bandits. *Was the script changed a lot during production?*
Not really, but circumstances forced us to come up with new scenes and events to solve problems created by lack of money or lack of availability of actors. An example of something in the script which isn't in the film would be the scenes in the Land of Legends, after they get off the

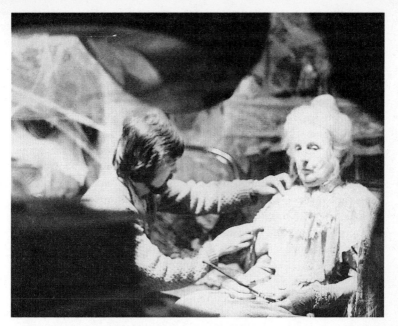

A scene dropped: the Spider Women in *Time Bandits*.

boat on the Giant's head and before we get to the Fortress of Ultimate
Darkness. A scene we had written and actually shot was the Spider
Women. After the gang has escaped the Giant, they're all lost and suddenly Og is snared by some kind of tentacle that drags him into a cave.
What the others find in the cave is that it's not a tentacle but a web that
the Spider Women are knitting to capture young men and blond knights
in shining armour. They're all hung up in the web and there are these
two desiccated and shrivelled Edwardian ladies sitting with their great
wide skirts and six legs, who are desperate for boyfriends. It's a wonderful scene, but we'd run out of money and there was another scene
after it which meant that we would have had to shoot two more scenes
in order to use that one, so we dropped it.

By this point the film was almost finished, except how do we get from
the Giant to the Fortress of Ultimate Darkness? It was one of those
moments that I feel really happy about – we had to make a quantum
leap. How do you get there? The answer is: you're already there, but
you just can't see it; it's an invisible barrier. So we wrote this new scene
very quickly, which gave us a chance to build up the characters. It was
a product of what was happening with the actual guys playing the Time
Bandits. They'd all been on a 'hate Dave Rappaport' campaign, because

Dave didn't want to be a dwarf. He thought he'd got the part because he was a great actor, not because he was four feet one inch. I said, 'Dave, you are a wonderful actor, but you're a wonderful four-foot-one actor and that's why you got the part, so don't forget it.' But he stayed aloof and didn't want to be around the other dwarfs. Knowing that, we wrote the scene in which Randall (Dave) says, 'We're going forward,' and the others say, 'We're going back.' It starts getting ugly and he throws a skull at them, breaking the invisible barrier. The scene encapsulated the reality of their relationship, and for me it was a proud moment of finding a character-based solution to a narrative problem.

The most interesting moment of desperate, but ultimately inspired, improvisation came at the end of the film. In the original script there was a big battle, when the archers arrive with their Frisian helmets: these are Agamemnon's archers. He was supposed to return to save the day; and, although he's killed in the battle, they still win, while Kevin is confronted with the nightmare of his surrogate father dying. We only had fourteen days with Sean for the whole film, and he couldn't come back to England for tax reasons. At our first meeting, he had said the character dying was interesting and very dramatic, but he wished there was a way he could come back at the end. By the time we were to shoot the battle, we had run out of time with Sean, so he couldn't be Agamemnon dying. I didn't know how we were going to end it. Since we couldn't kill him, we killed one of the gang instead, Fidgit, which led to a great emotional scene with Jack Purvis (Wally) raging against Evil. That was all written at the last minute to deal with the problem of not having Agamemnon.

Then I remembered Sean saying it would be great if he could come back at the end, and I had an idea. We'd already shot the boy being dragged out of bed with the fire in his room, so why not make Sean the fireman who rescues Kevin? Sean was back in London for a day to see his accountant, and on his way to lunch I got him to come past the studio and put on a fireman's outfit. Our entire set was just the side of a fire engine. I had him come in, set the boy down and say, 'Are you all right?' and walk out of shot. Then he climbed into the fire-engine cab and winked. At that point I didn't know what the scene was going to be exactly, but two months later we worked out what to do and shot the rest of it, with someone doubling for Sean in the wide shots. In the finished film, when the boy is pulled out of bed, you hear a very bad impersonation by me of Sean saying something like, 'Come on, lad.'

It had all come together in a magical kind of way; and when this happens I feel it's like the film forming itself. I suppose it's really the result of me remembering and half-remembering many things, and they all go into the stew. Then a carrot pops its head up and says, 'Remember what Sean said back then?'

Sean Connery wasn't the only living legend involved in Time Bandits. *What was it like working with Ralph Richardson?*[6]
I had to go over to his house in Regent's Park on a Sunday to be auditioned by Sir Ralph and, although it was the middle of the morning, he started plying me with drink. He was testing me, trying to get me drunk. I'd heard stories about this, about how Jack Gold had wanted him to be in a film and Richardson had sat him on the back of his big motorbike and roared round the park at phenomenal speed, then looked at Jack Gold – still in one piece – and said he'd do. With me, he had this long convoluted argument about what he thought the Supreme Being – having come from a sunny warm place – should be wearing: a pale blue linen suit and perhaps a panama hat. He was describing to me what I knew he'd worn in the play Charles Wood had written about the making of *The Charge of the Light Brigade*, and which he liked wearing.[7] I said no, he'd got to be like a fusty old headmaster, whose clothes aren't quite right. But he couldn't accept that God would be absent-minded or not well dressed, so the argument went round and round. Then he said he'd like to pull out of his pocket a pair of dividers and bend down to

Ralph Richardson surrounded by dwarfs, acting backwards: sublime.

measure Og the Pig, and did I know the William Blake painting of that image? I replied that the image originally came from a much earlier medieval manuscript, which I actually had – it was all a game: I had to keep drinking large amounts of whisky, and yet stay sober enough to keep up with everything he was throwing at me. Apparently, I passed the test, because by the end of the morning he was doing Little Titch song-and-dance impersonations for me.[8]

We had several meetings at his house where we'd go through every line – it was all marked up with his lines retyped in red – and he'd say, with absolute assurance, 'God wouldn't say that.' Then he wanted a red pillar box to put the pieces of Evil in, and I liked that because it was the kind of thing you might find in a kid's playroom. But the suit argument went on and on, and we were getting nowhere, until one day in the middle of shooting, just before he was needed, he turned up for lunch wearing exactly what he wears in the film. During lunch, we talked about everything except the suit. It was a game to see who would mention it first, and I won. He didn't want any grey areas. The worst thing that can happen for an actor, he told me, is to arrive on set and find the director has some hare-brained idea that hasn't been discussed in advance.

So he walks on to the set on his first day and everybody is bowing and scraping, Sir Ralph this and that – and he sees this charcoal statue of Evil. Before he says anything, I can see he's getting twitchy and slapping the script against his thigh; he begins to walk away. It's clear he's angry. I know exactly what's going on – he's claiming his territory and showing who's in charge – so I run after him, tugging my forelock, to find out what the problem is. The problem is, he says, 'What's that statue doing here?' I explain that when he, the Supreme Being, comes down, Evil is blasted and turns into charcoal. 'Yes, yes, but why is it *intact*? It has to be in pieces. The reason I turn Og back from being a pig is that he has a piece of Evil in his mouth – pigs eat human flesh, you see, and he can't eat Evil.'

None of this had ever been talked about before; it was just that he had to take control of the situation. So I told him not to worry and during the lunch break we broke up the statue. We never saw Og the Pig with a piece of Evil in his mouth, but I broke up the statue and then I had to work out how it was going to explode. But after that he was extraordinary. Once he had established that he was the boss, he did everything I asked. And on his very last day, there was Ralph Richardson, surrounded by six dwarfs, while the camera is running backwards and everyone is acting backwards, with dry ice being dumped on his head. He was sublime.

Releasing the film was presumably less fun, since you must have had a replay of the genre problems of Jabberwocky?

The first problem we had was with Denis O'Brien, who insisted that you can't blow up parents at the end of a children's film. I said that this was the whole point: no one had done it before. So we did a special screening for children, and I asked the first kid who came out what was the best part – no doubt about it, the ending, where the parents are blown up. But that was a little boy, and the next kid I asked was a little girl, who said it was awful that the parents had been blown up, because who was going to look after the little boy? But all the little boys knew they could look after themselves, and luckily Denis didn't hear the girl's answer.

Denis was very arrogant in those days; he took the film to the States and asked for $5 million, plus $5 million in prints and ads, and nobody would do the deal. I don't know whether they liked the film or not, but the impression we got was that they didn't know what to make of it, so in the end it went for no money upfront to Avco-Embassy, which was the miniest of the majors, or the majorest of the minis. Their last hit had been *The Graduate*, ten years earlier. But Denis's arrogance paid off: although there was no advance and he and George had to guarantee the $5 million for prints and advertising, we got hands-on distribution. So I did the poster and suggested we did three different kinds of television ads: one for the *Monty Python* fans, one for the kids and one for the family audience.

I remember the first preview we did, in Sherman Oaks, California. *Raiders of the Lost Ark* had just opened and we came on afterwards, and played very well. But the second preview was up in Bakersville, during the fight over the ending, and this is where the silliness of the system came to my rescue. The film is in Dolby stereo, but the projectionist got it wrong and the sound was incredibly muffled for three or four reels, until they realized the mistake and threw the switch. But by this time, people were streaming out. It had been a disastrous screening. Then we got the reaction cards, which I took back to my room to peruse. The next day when we got the numbers it appeared that the ending was one of the things the preview audience had liked most. So I won the argument over the ending. Denis and the other executives had only looked at the statistical breakdown of the numbers. What they hadn't seen were the cards, scrawled with hatred, which showed that people liked the ending because the film was over . . . they had hated it! The other extraordinary marketing decision was that the trailers for television weren't allowed to show dwarfs, because 'people don't like dwarfs'.

What had preceded us was a movie with Chevy Chase called *Under the Rainbow*, about the making of *The Wizard of Oz*.[9] It had bombed, and who got the blame? The dwarfs of course.

Then the film opens and did the best money in America that I've ever done: we were number one for something like three weeks and took $46 or $47 million, which is over $100 million in today's terms. In fact, *Time Bandits* was the most successful independent film ever made until *A Fish Called Wanda* – that bastard Cleese![10] However, it had opened first in England, where Denis tried to sell it like a *Python* film, not as a kids' film or a family film, and it did very mediocre business.

A familiar story, except in some cases success in America it has led to a relaunch in the UK, as with The Crying Game. *Did it get any awards?*
I don't think so. It might have got a BAFTA nomination. I keep getting technical awards from BAFTA, but, in this case, I think not. In Britain, we were still caught up in the slipstream of *Python*, whereas in the States the film was sold in its own right – whatever that was. But the première in New York was a bit of a disaster. It was held at a twin cinema up on the East Side. Now, the whole point of a première is that the famous come to be seen and the less famous come to see. So we were all marched in – my friends and the famous people – and my friends and the less famous are hived off to the left, while the famous people go to the right. This made no sense, since the famous people wanted to have people craning round and looking at them. Anyhow, Mike Palin and I went for dinner – we didn't want to watch the film again – and halfway through Shelley Duvall appeared in tears, saying it was a disaster. She told us that in the *hoi polloi* screen, the third reel had appeared upside down and backwards – it was on a cakestand projector and the projectionist had put it tail out – and for the first five minutes the audience loved it. They were laughing and cheering, thinking it's those whacky Pythons again. Then the lights came up and the manager came on to say we have a problem which will take an hour to put right, so it's best if you all go home. But instead of going home, the *hoi polloi* rushed next door to the other screen and were standing in the aisles. Shelley had been upset by this, but I thought it was great. Any time I'm involved in anything with an attempt at dignity, it falls flat on its face. But the best thing about that night was that I met Robin Williams for the first time.

How did your contribution to the fourth (if we exclude Live at the Hollywood Bowl) *Python film,* The Meaning of Life, *come to extend beyond animation to a special prologue,* The Crimson Permanent Assurance?

We were all working on writing *The Meaning of Life*, and basically my job was to do the animations. But I was tired of doing animation, and so when I had this idea, which would normally have been done as a cartoon, I thought about doing it as live action. The group could never quite pin me down and they didn't know how I worked, so I got to do it. Originally, it was going to come two-thirds of the way through the film. I had my own crew, with Roger Pratt as my DP for the first time, and our own stage.

It followed on from *Time Bandits*, in the sense of taking unlikely people to be heroes. I got these octogenarians who had once been good actors, dancers, sword fighters, and who wanted to do it all again. We built everything and did more experimentation with model shooting and effects to create a heightened, cartoony style that would also be totally believable. The details have to work, so that grappling with a coatstand and the firing of filing cabinets like cannon seem logical. It's also the *Brazil* theme of massive paperwork being used as a weapon and the sense of these great monolithic corporations. There's the romantic aspect of these old Edwardian ways somehow fighting back against the smart young technocrats.

Palin, Gilliam and Idle in search of *The Meaning of Life*.

I think this was the first time – pre-*Munchausen* – that I went over budget simply because there wasn't a budget on it. It wasn't taken very seriously since it was only Terry G. and a sound stage, and Terry G. just went on until it was finished. In fact, it was really frustrating not knowing what we could or couldn't do, and I didn't like my first experience of working with no parameters. Then we found in the previews that it didn't work in the middle of the film, because it had a completely different rhythm and style from the *Python* material: the laughs aren't immediate. So I was under pressure to cut it shorter and shorter, until eventually it got to be too short. At this point I said let's just remove it from the film and – another of those quantum leaps – make it the accompanying short, which gave us the chance of allowing it to come back and 'attack' the main film; so we got a double benefit. As soon as we did this, it worked a treat. It was an instructive process, discovering where things sit and how they do or don't work. On a big screen the *Crimson Permanent* looks extraordinary, while the rest of *Meaning of Life* looks almost like television. But on video, which is where most people are going to see it, *Crimson Permanent* doesn't make such an impact, while the rest of the film looks great. At Cannes in 1983, the audience went crazy over *Crimson Permanent* and, although it's on a different technical level, *The Meaning of Life* worked on the strength of its material, a lot of which is some of our best.

NOTES

1 C.S. Lewis's sequence of Narnia novels begins with children entering an allegorical world through a wardrobe in *The Lion, The Witch and the Wardrobe* (1950)

2 The increasingly satirical and reflexive comedy series *Soap*, in which Katherine Helmond starred, ran between 1977–81.

3 What became Lee International Film Studios at Wembley, North London, in the late seventies was originally the Fox-British Studio, established to make 'quota' films in the thirties, later used by first London ITV company Rediffusion between 1955–67.

4 The giant Djinn in Alexander Korda's *Thief of Bagdad* (1940) was played by the American black actor Rex Ingram.

5 Space flight in various contraptions features in a number of Georges Méliès's fantasy films, including *A Trip to the Moon* (1901) and *An Impossible Journey* (1904).

6 Sir Ralph Richardson (1902–83) was a leading stage actor from the 1930s until his death, noted for such larger-than-life roles as Peer Gynt, Falstaff and Cyrano de Bergerac. His equally long and varied film career included-leading roles for Korda in the thirties, wartime propaganda for Powell and Pressburger; a tyrannical Dr Sloper in Wyler's Henry James adaptation *The Heiress* (1949); and an eclectic range of voice-over and visible roles in the seventies and eighties, ranging from *Alice's Adventures in Wonderland* (1972) to *Wagner* (1983) and, released posthumously, *Greystoke: The Legend of Tarzan of the Apes* (1984).

7 Charles Wood, who wrote the screenplay for Tony Richardson's *The Charge of the Light Brigade*, provided a behind-the-scenes view of the film's production in *Veterans*, first staged at the Royal Court in 1972.

8 'Little Titch' (Harry Relph, 1867–1926) was a tiny English music-hall performer, as popular in Paris as in London, and famed for his energetic 'big boots' dance.

9 *Under the Rainbow*, directed by Steve Rash, was a notable box-office flop in 1981.

10 John Cleese starred in and co-wrote the highly successful *A Fish Called Wanda* (1988) with its director, the Ealing veteran Charles Crichton.

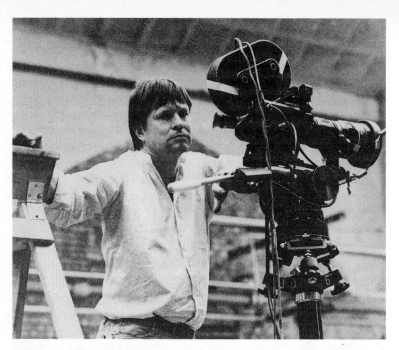

The agony and the ecstasy: at work on *Brazil*.

6

1984½ becomes *Brazil*, with the aid of ducts and De Niro; and what happened next

Brazil was the watershed in your career. Before, you could always be regarded as more or less an escaped Python; after, you were clearly a film-maker of high ambition – maybe too high for some tastes – when you took on Universal in a quixotic battle over the director's rights. But Brazil had been brewing for a long time, hadn't it?

I had this pile of ideas, a general story I was trying to tell, which was a loose collection of scenes running to about a hundred pages. First, I started working on it with Chuck Alverson, who had written *Jabberwocky*, but within a couple of weeks it was clear that we were going in slightly different directions. This led to a break in our relationship and a messy situation. In the end, a deal was done – the scene in the restaurant is the only one that's still close to what he'd written. After that I put it aside for a while, because it had been a painful business. Then one day I was walking down the street and somebody mentioned Tom Stoppard's name.[1] Suddenly, I thought it would be great – his visual skills and my wordsmithing! Anyway, we met and he began to pull it together. For instance, the mistaken arrest already existed as an event, but Tom introduced the name and the single-letter mistake – Buttle/Tuttle – that connects them. This is the kind of thing he was so good at.

Meanwhile, there was the problem of getting the film going, which was harder than getting it written. Even after the success of *Time Bandits* – when I went round all the studio heads in Hollywood, just to meet them face to face – everyone I talked to about *Brazil* said it was a crazy idea. Then I met Arnon Milchan in Paris and really liked him, even though many people had warned me against him.[2] Certainly, he's a pirate; but he's funny, smart and ruthless. He was also a big gambler and at that time he was working with Scorsese on *King of Comedy*. We got on well and he said, 'Let's do it.' When I said I wanted Stoppard to work on the script, he liked that, and so Tom was hired to write three drafts. This was a lot of money for Arnon, but he did it. What he found outrageous was that I laid down the law right at the start. I told him that, even though he was the producer, his opinion didn't mean any more to me than my secretary's or anybody I'd meet in the street. I think he was convinced that I was the guy to work with because nobody had ever spoken to him like that, and he could hardly believe it – 'I'm giving you all this money and you're telling me my opinion doesn't count?'

Tom was doing great things with the structure, but I felt he wasn't getting some of the characters right; he was losing their humanity. In particular, he was making Mike Palin's character, Jack Lint, a real bastard. I explained that he's got to be the nicest man in the world, a lovely family man; he just happens to have this particular kind of job and an anxiety about his career.[3] I knew exactly what the characters were supposed to be, but I'm just not good at dialogue, which is why I always work on scripts with someone else. I can rewrite it well – on *Time Bandits* I could shift Mike's dialogue around really fast and push it where I thought it should be going – but Tom was difficult to rewrite, because if you pulled out one line, the whole structure would come apart.

So I brought in Charles McKeown, whom I'd met on *The Life of Brian*, and we started reworking it. By the end, there was a script that had a bit of everybody in it. But even though Arnon was out there flogging it, the script was still being rejected on all fronts. What really started turning the tables was a film that Fox wanted to do called *Enemy Mine*.[4] This was to be their 'A' film, but Spielberg and Lucas and all the top guys had turned it down, and eventually they reached T. Gilliam – way down on the list. The logic of the situation was that, because this was the top project, the director being offered it must be of top quality too. So when I said no, because I wanted to do this other film called *Brazil*, it meant that my other project must be good – maybe even better than their 'A' film – even though they had already read it and turned it down.

First of all Joe Wizan at Fox – who now saw it in this new light – said yes; then Arnon managed to start a bidding war at the Cannes Film Festival. Cannes can be useful, because of the sun and the wine and everybody being away from their offices, and so becoming human and vulnerable. There had been earlier stages in Hollywood, meeting Jeffrey Katzenberg and Michael Eisner at Paramount, where I'd broken all the protocol by not talking about art but just asking if they were going to give us the money. The system didn't really like Arnon, but I felt that my enemy's enemy is my friend. He and I were being very silly, running up and down the corridors of the Carlton Hotel, feeling like pirates, out there to slash and burn. I remember sitting in the Universal suite with Bob Rehme and the president Sean Daniel. I'm telling the story to Sean and I look over at Rehme, who's nodding off, and behind him Arnon is fast asleep, because it had been a long night. But they're getting a lot of energy and excitement from me: maybe they can't understand what I'm saying, because it's so incoherent and crazed, but they sense the energy. It's like when I first met Quentin Tarantino – it's this furnace that's blazing away – and I think that's why those of us who have managed to succeed in this system are like that, that's why it's recognized us.

We also had a budget problem at this point. The film was budgeted at $12 million, and we weren't getting much respect. So, just as a fluke, Arnon decided that we'd raise it to $15 million, based on nothing more than getting into the higher price category up with the big spenders. So we ended up with a bidding war in Cannes for this now-$15 million-dollar movie, and Fox and Universal agreed to split it. Then they all returned to LA. That was a crucial moment when Arnon had to work fast to get it all on paper before anyone could renege on what had occurred in Cannes, as often happens. He managed to do it, so now we had Fox for the world and Universal for North America.

You had the script and the money: what was the next stage?
Casting. I was looking for young guys – because I saw Sam as twenty-one or twenty-two – and so we went hunting in LA. I had my High-8 camera and was doing videos of everybody I met to take back to London. I really trust the videos, because when I'm sitting in a room with somebody it's quite different from what the camera sees, and what the camera sees is what films are about. Even on location, I always take photographs, because what matters is how the camera perceives things. I remember there was one young actor I saw then, called Tom Cruise, in a rough cut of a film that hadn't been released; but he wouldn't let himself be videoed, because he'd become worried that the tapes would turn up years later – when he'd become the big star he was expected to be – and embarrass him. He was practically in tears on the phone, wanting to be involved, but I couldn't consider him without a video test, even though I could see he had whatever it is that makes a star. Interestingly, the next thing he did was *Legend* with Ridley Scott, so I don't know if Arnon kept that connection going.[5] There were a lot of bright young actors, and at that time I was obsessed with the idea of having unknowns. Because they come with no baggage, the audience discovers the characters as the film unfolds.

Would the film have had a very different feel if you'd cast an American in the lead?

I think so, but then I was always going to make it here, so most of the rest of the cast was going to be English. We spent a long time talking to Rupert Everett, who was hot at that time: I hadn't realized I was considered that desirable as a director by so many actors and actresses. Everyone you could imagine – Madonna, Rosanna Arquette, Michelle Pfeiffer, Kathleen Turner, Jamie Lee Curtis, Rebecca de Mornay – were all people I put on tape. In fact, I chose Kim Griest partly because she wasn't known at all, while all the others were partly known – or maybe they were just too stunning for me. I always get nervous about this business of the leading lady – especially with a character who is supposed to be your dream girl – when you've got a wife and kids. But, in retrospect, it was an extraordinary time: in LA there was Jamie Lee Curtis, who'd just done *Trading Places*, sitting on the pavement on Melrose because Rebecca de Mornay was taking extra time on her screen test. And in New York, the girls would come in and find this guy lying on the floor with a neck brace on – I had somehow pulled my neck muscles – and some of them, especially Kathleen Turner, knew how to do the interview with their legs. I love watching actors deal with situations; how the really smart ones understand that the director becomes the camera, and thus know how to play to the camera.

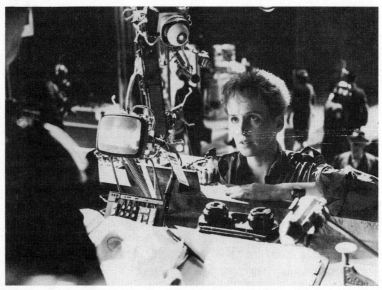

Not quite dream girl: Kim Griest as Jill in *Brazil*.

I remember Madonna came in; she was still working in small New York clubs at that point and hadn't yet become Madonna, so she was just this scruffy, angry, rather unimpressive figure. The casting director Margie Simkin and I ended up going to the Waverley cinema one night to see a John Sayles film with Rosanna Arquette, and who do we bump into but Madonna and her boyfriend. So, the four of us go in with our popcorn to watch Rosanna. Then there were Kelly McGillis, Andie MacDowell and Ellen Barkin. I thought Ellen was going to get the part – she was the best actress of them all – and I actually told her she'd practically got it, until at the last moment I switched to Kim and didn't have the guts to call Ellen directly to apologize. I wrote a note instead. I think that was the most cowardly and shameful thing I've done. I always cite the movie as the justification for such things – it's a convenient excuse. So in the end it was Kim Griest who got the part on the strength of a fantastic screen test, which everybody thought was terrific. Kim had this feral quality: for the screen test she had called on some kind of survival instinct and dredged it up from somewhere; but when it came to actually working on the film – the day-to-day business of just coming to work – this feral quality wasn't there. That was an interesting discovery.

For the part of Sam, there was this guy, Jonathan Pryce, who was a friend and who kept bugging me to give him a screen test. He was too old, but eventually I agreed, just to shut him up. He had just finished making *Martin Luther*, for the BBC I think, and he had put on weight and had a tonsure. He looked dreadful. Maggie got one of Eric Idle's blond wigs for him and he did the screen test with Susanna Hamilton, who ended up as the girl in *1984*. But, despite his weight and the silly wig, Jon was brilliant – no one else had come close to having the character and with such skill – so I had to go to Arnon and say this was our guy. That was the only real fight Arnon and I had: he said I was out of my mind. Then we had to send the test to the studios and they also thought we were crazy; but I bullied my way through and said there'd be no film without this guy.

I've no doubt I was right, because Jonathan is terrific. He is guiltier, he deserves the final punishment far more than if he'd been a twenty-one-year-old kid; he's somebody who has avoided responsibility, who has failed to make the most of himself in life. These things actually add to the character, even though I'd started with a very clear idea about a young guy who's at the turning point of his life where he has to make a decision. Because someone different came along, I was happy to throw out all these ideas, and so the film shifts. This is what intrigues me about the whole process. It's not as if I have this perfect image of the film which I'm

Jonathan Pryce: a guiltier hero than planned for *Brazil*.

going to make at all costs: it grows and it changes. In the end, Kim wasn't able to do the character as written – originally the female role was much bigger. So the film shifts again, since what we had originally were two incomplete characters – a guy who lived in this fantasy and a girl who was so frightened of relationships and the whole paranoia of the system that, instead of being a secretary or having a proper job, she was a truck driver, because there was some freedom within that cab. The price she paid was being isolated and having no real human contact – neither of them did – and so they came together to make a full human being. But because of Kim's inability to handle things, her part kept getting chopped down, so she became more and more a fantasy of his. Even in the real world, she's a kind of fantasy of Jonathan's, and some of her scenes are played on his face, because it wasn't working the other way.

So this is a case of changing partly because you found something better than the original conception, and partly to cover a failure. Do you think this might have saved it from becoming an overly whimsical or schematic allegory, like Legend?

I don't know if it's better or worse. I liked what I was originally trying to do, but we didn't get it. It was so clear when we were writing it that there were two parallel worlds, the real world and the dream world, and the story in the dream world was a complete tale in itself, with the day itself being stolen so that Sam's got to find it. After the tenth or twelfth week of the shoot, it was obvious that if I carried on we would have a five-hour picture and be $10 million over budget. So I told Arnon that we had to stop for a week or two, and I would tear pages out of the script. What had happened was the real world was proving so bizarre that there was no need for the dreams. For example, when I pulled out all the guts of the flat, they were hanging like entrails; but there was a dream sequence where Sam tries to cut through a forest of these entrails with his mighty sword. But there was no need for the dream once we'd done it in Sam's 'real' world.

The great thing was to have the freedom to make these changes while making the film. All I can compare it to is making a big painting, or rather a sculpture: you make the wrong cut and a bit falls off that was going to be a beautiful arm. Whether you go ahead with what you've got or start again with a new block of marble, you've shifted your sculpture, and that's what I do. I've been lucky in most cases to be able to make those adjustments, and Arnon said he trusted me. Someone else who was very important in this respect is Patrick Cassavetti, who had been the location manager on *Time Bandits*, and when my original line producer for *Brazil*, Neville Thompson, couldn't get on with Arnon, Patrick rose to the occasion. He and I were very pragmatic about what was going on. There would be a problem, say, with the cooling tower and the abseiling terrorists: should we do it with models or not? We would argue back and forth, about how much it would cost, and in the end we decided to do it for real. But there was always a price to pay, since I knew something else now wouldn't get done. We worked very well in that way.

I've been in arguments with other directors who don't accept this as a way of working: they talk in terms of art, with the producers on that side and we, the artists, on the other. But, for me, it's more about being able to work the thing: if you want the larger freedom, then you've got to restrict yourself in other ways. You don't get total freedom. At every stage, I'm always thinking about the final battle. What's going to happen then and who's going to be on my side? What troops do I have and who's in the trenches with me? My main concern is to protect the film, and sometimes even I can get in the way of the film. If I'm causing a problem for the ultimate film, then I've got to be stopped, and I tell this to everybody who works with me. They find it hard to believe, but they finally do say, 'Terry, you can't do it.'

'Tie me to the mast' – this is you as Ulysses telling the crew to pay no attention when the sirens beckon.
That's it: I know I've got to get the ship into port. Why I like making films is that, for a period of time, you have a higher cause you're serving, and this may go back, in some way, to my religious background. Everything is for the cause, but it gets complex when that cause is actually the product of my imagination: where's the film and where's Terry in all this? However, it's possible to make that distinction most of the time.

Sam as Superhero in the dreamworld of *Brazil*.

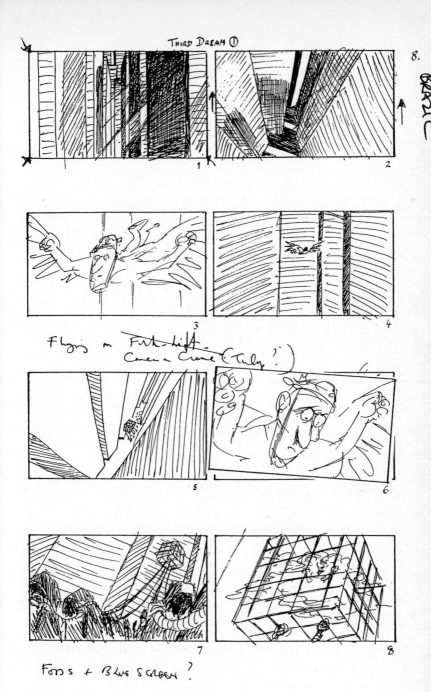

Storyboards for the third dream in *Brazil*.

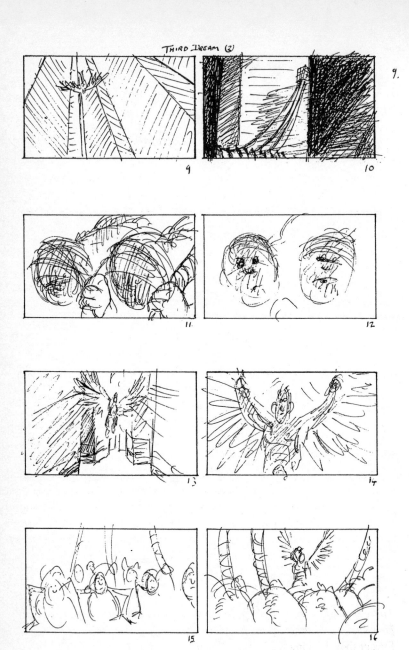

9.

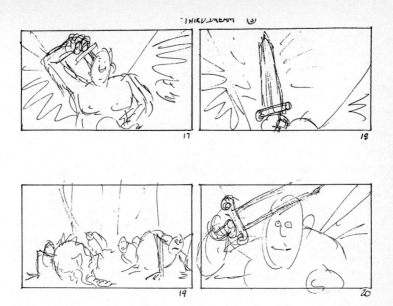

Identifying so completely with the film and making it an extension of your own dreams and fantasies inevitably recalls Fellini. Was he a big influence on you?

Oh, definitely. I always cite him as my great inspiration. Ingmar Bergman too, with *Wild Strawberries*; and Kurosawa's *Rashomon*, which is another way of looking at different realities.[6] But Fellini, most of all, freed that up with *8½* and *Giulietta of the Spirits*.[7] The only American equivalent would be Walter Mitty. We used to talk about *Brazil* being like Frank Capra meets Franz Kafka. The point about *Brazil* is that we're starting at a level that's already fantastic, but we're trying to root that fantastical world in a kind of truth or hyperreality that everybody can understand. The dreams in *Brazil* are more juvenile, they're escape dreams, and they were originally very literal before many of them became redundant.

There is a story that's often told about how Brazil *started with you in Port Talbot, thinking about the incongruity of the song 'Brazil' . . .*

Except that the song was 'Maria Elena', Ry Cooder's version of it, and it used to be there at the beginning of the early drafts.[8] Then it shifted to 'Brazil' via a recording by Geoff Muldaur, from an album called *Cottage Pie*. And it's this version of 'Brazil' that we use when Jonathan is driving to Buttle's flat – it's a really silly version which I loved and used to play all the time when we were going to work. So I went from this sublime version of 'Maria Elena' to a jokey version of 'Brazil' and then somehow swung it back. The choices I make often depend on something that's specific to the moment, even though I don't understand the underlying connections and reasons. I'm eclectic. I feel everything around me is involved in the thing, and in the process of making it I always feel the film is somehow making itself. I think if I ever switched off and didn't listen to the things around me, the films would be very different. They might be easier to follow, but I don't think they'd be as good.

Did you do any other restructuring during the pause in production?
Basically, the restructuring was just cutting things out, because there was so much stuff in it. This is always a problem for me; since there's such an interval between films and I take so long developing them, I try to put everything in the known universe into them, and this is always a mistake. I also find that I've said something with one shot and don't need a whole sequence. In a strange way, I often don't trust the strength of my visuals. I don't appreciate how much information they're conveying until they're done.

Jonathan Pryce was playing your first proper grown-up hero. How did you direct him?
It was very simple. I just told him to keep his voice high. Jonathan's voice can get very low, and become portentous; but if he kept it lighter then he wasn't this heavy, menacing guy. A year or two before, he'd been involved in a projected musical about Laurel and Hardy, and he was going to play Stan Laurel; if you watch his movements, he can be very Laurelesque. He was able to bring out the comedy in the dark scenes. For instance, there's the scene where Jill is in the Ministry and she's having a fight with the guy at the desk, and suddenly the alarm goes off and there are soldiers with guns pointing at her. Jonathan comes up and he whips out his badge, which was his idea and it's just brilliant, and even the idea of having the 'finger gun' in his pocket was his. He was full of ideas which were silly and funny and often great.

How did Robert De Niro come to join what was otherwise very much your stock company of actors?
I think this was the first cameo role that De Niro did, and it was basically because Arnon was working with him on *Once Upon a Time in America*.[9] He came over and I invited him to pick a part, anything he wanted to do, and of course he chose Mike Palin's part, because Jack is

The sinister machinery of surveillance in *Brazil*.

The legendary Harry Tuttle, played by the legendary Robert De Niro.

a complex character and Bobby had always played complex characters. The part he ended up playing, Tuttle, was really hard for him to get his head round because it's such a simple, direct character. I said to him, 'Bobby, you are that man, you're a hero to all of us, and you don't have to complicate it – just be.'

What happened then was that he approached this small part as if he was doing the main part. He kept flying to London and spent months arguing over every piece of costume and every prop. He was going to brain surgeons he knew in New York and watching operations because I'd said that the character, although a plumber, was like a surgeon. The glasses were his idea. We actually built a mock-up of the set just so that he could practise. It was as if we weren't making the main film; the special effects, props and costume people were going crazy because they had so much other work to do, but every time Bobby came in, everything would stop and we had to deal with him preparing for his role. He's just not aware of anything else in the world and he makes the most of whatever it is he has to do. He's very serious, very earnest and very hard-working, but it drove everybody else crazy.

When it came to shooting, it was just the same. I had him on the set for a week in advance so that he could get used to the crew, because it's a terrible thing to come in after a film's started. But apparently he was up all night before his first day's shooting, wearing his costume, and he arrived on the set really nervous. He knew they were all expecting 'Robert De Niro' – whatever that means – and of course he knows he's just this guy Bobby De Niro. The whole day was spent trying to make him feel at ease – to the point where, after I realized that he froze when I said, 'Action,' I would say, 'OK, let's go through the lines again,' and quietly get the camera rolling. The nice thing was that he thanked me at the end of that day, but it was scary. Jonathan was usually at his best in two or three takes, but suddenly with Bobby it was twenty-one, twenty-five or thirty, so in the scenes where they were together, Jonathan would be dozing in the background by the time Bobby had got it. This wasn't an actor being difficult for the sake of it, it was just that he was trying so hard. Of course, we were all in awe of De Niro, then we shifted round 180 degrees and wanted to kill him.

We were supposed to do a week with him, which became two weeks, and by the end he was bubbly, saying this was the most fun he'd ever had, while the rest of the crew were like zombies as we weakly waved goodbye and Bobby floated happily out of it all.

So, after the usual pattern of English actors playing Hollywood villains, you have De Niro playing the hero-cum-villain in an essentially British movie.

I'm sure there was a lot of that going on in my head without thinking about it. Bobby's screen presence is very strong but when we were shooting, I couldn't see it. Then, looking at the rushes next day, there it was: he has a direct relationship with the camera and with the piece of celluloid that others don't. It's almost as if there's a kind of selfishness at work there; it's like he's sucking all the energy out of everything else on the set, focusing it through himself and into the film. That's why guys like this are the big stars they are; they have this weird chemistry, this electromagnetic reaction to the celluloid itself.

But isn't he also trying to lose himself in the part and eliminate everything intellectualized or invented, so that the performance has a massive simplicity that does communicate directly? This is surely why the physical things, props and costumes, become so important in the preparation; and perhaps the multiple takes are the result of, literally, trying not to think.

After spending months choosing the tools, on the day he couldn't deal with them and, finally, I had to choose three and hand them to him under the camera. In the film, when you see his hands at work picking up things, those are my hands, because he was gone by then. I had to put on the costume and I found it was the most uncomfortable, hot, miserable thing to wear. So I think he does all these things that become such a burden in order to take away the thinking, so that what he's doing becomes instinctive, like an animal trying to survive.

His entrance, when he comes in with the balaclava helmet on, was a nightmare to shoot. There's a long preamble: Jonathan is asleep with his head in the fridge, the phone rings, he wakes up, bangs his head, slips on the stool, recovers and reaches for the phone, puts his hand down the garbage-disposal unit, retrieves it in time, gets to the phone, which pulls down, and he crashes to the floor, spends ages trying to plug in the connecters, lifts it up and then, 'Hello, hello, Mr Lowry,' and the camera's now tracking round, we see a pair of feet in the background which are coming forward and we eventually rise up to see a man in silhouette with a balaclava pointing a gun at him. So, after the first take, it was, 'Terry, can I do that again?' 'Oh sure, Bob. Jon, do you mind?' Jon gets back to position one, head in the fridge, and off we go – bang, crash, bump, brilliant fall, etc., then 'Hello, hello, Mr . . . is it Lowry?' I told him not to worry, but he wanted to start again, and again, and again.

By take seven, Jonathan was desperate, and we're getting, 'Hello, hello, Mr Lowry. Put the phone up and your hands down – sorry, Terry, I don't know why I got that backwards.' We must have done eight or nine takes of this, and he didn't even seem to be aware that we were only on his feet. He felt he had fallen out of his character, and by the time we got round to his face he wanted to be in character, no matter what.

Unfortunately, this set a very bad example for Kim Griest, whose first major film it was. She wanted to have thirty takes too, but I told her that when she was as good as De Niro she could have thirty; until then she could have four like everyone else. You have to be careful about something like that spreading, and we didn't have the time or money to make that kind of film. Then Jonathan began to feel pissed off, because De Niro was one of his heroes, but he'd started hating his hero because the hero's taking up all the time and affecting his performance. It was rough, but the end result justified it all. Not only was De Niro great, but he gave the film a certain cachet and, ultimately, he accompanied me on to the major American chat shows for the final battle over *Brazil*. We had the right guy in the foxhole with us.

Were the other cameo actors easier to work with?
Definitely. Katherine Helmond is great. She'd already been in *Time Bandits*; any time I want her in anything, she'll be there. She's a wonderful serious actress and also a brilliant comedienne. She has this rare combination and no vanity; she'll cope with awful make-up or whatever's needed. She's a Texan, and Texan women can be tough, smart and sexy. Katherine also liked the idea of developing a strange kind of half-British, half-American accent. When people are that good, it's hard to say enough about them.

Ian Holm was interesting, because he'd also worked on *Time Bandits*, but on *Brazil* he surprised us. A very controlled and experienced actor, he seemed to be all over the place when we began. Both the continuity girl, Peggy Eyles – who'd worked with him many times – and Jonathan were surprised. Jonathan was surprised to find that another hero of his wasn't the confident, slick actor that he thought he was going to be. My theory was that Ian had liked what we did on *Time Bandits* and now he trusted me, so he wasn't afraid to take chances. His takes were very uneven because he was trying new things all the time. As a result, his performance was fantastic, quite unlike anything else I've seen him do. This was the great payback of having gained someone's confidence, just the opposite of Sean Connery not trusting me over mounting the horse in *Time Bandits*. I think it's a really essential part of film-making, to develop these relationships of trust – like Marty

Michael Palin as Jack Lint, the embodiment of 'true evil' in *Brazil*.

Scorsese and De Niro – so that actors will allow themselves to look like fools sometimes, because the more vulnerable they are, the better they are, and you've got to give them the confidence to be vulnerable.

Jonathan was also surprised by how nervous Mike Palin was. This was the first time that Mike had played a very different kind of character. Normally he can lose himself in outrageous characters, but this was basically a normal guy. I would give him business to concentrate on, like keeping his mouth full of food in the party sequence, so that he didn't have to worry about making the character more complex. I found it helped to give him props, and the only scene that we reshot in *Brazil* was the scene in his office, which was one of the first we'd done. It just didn't work. For a long time I couldn't figure out why, then suddenly it hit me. We were talking about him being a father and husband, an all-round nice guy, but we weren't showing it. So we brought in my three-year-old daughter, Holly, to play his daughter. Same dialogue, but now he's down there playing with bricks and blocks and she's got her little lines, and the scene just goes *whoosh*, because now he's talking about torture while playing with a kid.

Brazil *is, above all, a weird self-contained world and it looks as if it was a huge construction job, quite apart from the found locations. Did you build much?*

Not as much as you'd think. What interests me more is altering a location, because there's so much of reality there to begin with. Our main builds, like the gigantic Ministry foyer, were done at Lee's on a relatively small stage. We built that very cheaply using four-by-eight-foot sheets of hardboard, which were marblized, just as you would marble paper. We built a giant marbling tank, full of water, then swirled oil paint on the top and dipped in the sheets of hardboard and then put gloss on them; the whole place is made out of these. It was built like a stage set, where what you see are basically flats, except they have a return on them, and the square columns are two sides of a cube. So when the camera was looking the other way for reverses, we just pivoted them all. You save a fortune that way, and we reused things, which is also nice. For example, the information-retrieval foyer is the same place as the Ministry of Information: foyer mark one is decked out with statues as the public face, then we stripped it for the other. So there's a sense of having been here before, familiar yet unfamiliar; I like the idea of the same place being two different things, depending on the mood at that moment.

An economical Ministry of Information in *Brazil*.

A feature of the design of the Ministry is that it was supposed to be rectilinear and, the further you get into it, the more squared up and sanitized it becomes. As Sam goes higher, he reaches the floor with all the white tiles, and the torture room was going to be a forty-foot-square cube of white tiles, completely boxing you in. But when we were looking for locations, we visited Croydon Power Station, because we were searching for big façades. I looked inside a cooling tower – something I've wanted to do for most of my life. There was this great circular parabolic space that rose up 200 feet and I immediately knew we had to use this. But for what? Then I realized it was the torture room – almost completely the opposite of what I was planning, but I just knew it was right, because it would be a bigger surprise than finding the white cube which you're more or less expecting. So that leap, and all the other leaps, saved me from my own mediocrity. I think my dreams and fantasies and images are often mediocre, until reality intrudes and transforms them.

Where and when is Brazil *set? What were your visual references?*
It's everywhere in the twentieth century, on the Los Angeles/Belfast border. I wasn't thinking of retro particularly, but there are bits of everything coming from all directions. There's a lot of growing up in America in the forties: progress and the utopian vision were always there, with technology as the answer to all our needs, so you see a lot of that. The posters are very much the kind of thing you would see in *Popular Mechanics*. In fact, we were using all those magazines from the forties and fifties as sources and, because we couldn't afford to build things, we had posters extending the world beyond what you see with images of, for instance, holidays and technology.

Some of the technology was a deliberate mixture of the futuristic and the Victorian, like the typist who has this weird thing on her hand. I think it's a Victorian invention that was supposed to be for exercising the fingers or for giving them electric shocks; I thought it would be interesting to use it as a kind of typing machine that was recording her movements. There's also a sense of German Expressionism, but because the Expressionist films were always in black and white, Roger Pratt used colours from Expressionist paintings, mixing yellows and oranges with blues and greens in the lighting. You see a lot of mixing warm and cold colours today, but people weren't doing that in the mid-eighties; we took our cue from the way German Expressionist painters put contrasting colours together so that they jarred.

We also used a lot of stuff by Ferriss, the American illustrator who drew the Rockefeller Center.[10] Then there were wartime anti-spy posters, which we adapted. A lot of the design of the machinery was done in a totally organic, sculptural way; it wasn't designed by the art department and it wasn't done from drawings – that would have been expensive. You use what you can find, and I got everybody thinking that way. It was like found art. George Gibbs, in special effects, got these old teletype machines for £25. They were still in their original crates and when we opened them they were amazing, but we took off the shell, the carapace, which revealed their guts; then we thought of hooking them up to a television – but the smallest television, which would then require a magnifying screen like televisions needed when I was a kid. Once I got everybody thinking that way, we built all sorts of things and that's what populates the place.

And the famous ducts?
The ducts which everybody talks about came from two sources. One was the Pompidou Centre in Paris, which has its guts on its outside; and the other was me coming to England and noticing these Regency buildings with beautiful cornices and mouldings which have been smashed through to run the pipe from the toilet down the outside. It was the violation of an aesthetic for the sake of the mod cons. You'd see all the piping and wiring that's been applied to these beautiful old buildings to get the gas, the electricity or the telephone in, and you'd wonder why people don't bother to put these behind the exteriors. The answer is, of course, that it costs more and their sense of aesthetics isn't great enough to justify the cost – and that greed to have the goodies at the expense of beauty started me going.

Norman Garwood started bringing in ducts, and I would say, 'No, bigger!' So we ended up with this huge duct collection at the back of Lee's Studios; the biggest were used in the restaurant, those gigantic ones with the reflective tiles around them. The first sketches I had done were of the Buttle house. Originally the Buttles didn't live in the city, they lived out in the country. There was this little house on the prairie – somewhere out in Wales, maybe – with ducting strung on telephone poles coming to it – ducts about four feet in diameter delivering goods to this little house and ruining the landscape in the process. It was about showing how you link to the system. When we were promoting the film in Chicago, people asked about the ducts, and I said, 'Well, don't you realize what's behind the walls and the suspended ceiling and under the floor in this room we're sitting in?' It seemed these kids had no idea of the connections needed for all these things, and of the price to pay. I

Service umbilical

Guy turns up for work wearing several nasty looking bandages - he had been OK the previous day - "What happened?" "Oh, I had to go to the doctor's last night" "Oh, I see" This continues with others "Been to the doctor" "Yes"

Handjim's kibbe ? (not his) Kovalis

Improve Scale

Hausner - Ark of Odysseus

Try Flashy Bruegel's Tower of Babel

INSIDE THE HEALING STOKESHIP

First drawings for the Buttle house: 'Somewhere in Wales, maybe?'

said this was the balance I was dealing with – what is the price? – and they were stunned by that.

The other question that always came up in these discussions was: are the terrorists real? To which I would always say that I don't know if they are, because this huge organization has to survive at all costs, so if there is no real terrorism it has to invent terrorists to maintain itself – that's what organizations do. This always came as a big surprise to them, and they wanted answers: was the explosion in the restaurant a terrorist one? Again, I said I didn't know, it might just be part of the

An alimentary vision: the giant ducts in *Brazil*.

system that went bang, which happens all the time. But if you assume that technology works, then, if it blows up, it must be because someone blew it up: this is what I was trying to get across in *Brazil*. When I left that session and got in the car, I noticed that people were ashen-faced and I asked what was wrong. The *Challenger* had just blown up.[11] Systems go bang, don't they?

In fact, the initial spark for *Brazil* really came from a seventeenth-century document I stumbled across, from a time when witch-hunts were at their height. This was a chart of the costs of different tortures and you had to pay for those inflicted on you; if you were found guilty and sentenced to death, you had to pay for every bundle of faggots that burned you. I started thinking about the guy who was a clerk in the court and had to be present while the tortures were going on, to take down testimonies. It's an awful job, but this man has a wife and kids to support, so how does he deal with it? That's actually where *Brazil* really started, before Port Talbot. There was a theory that the witch-hunts died out because they were a system that got too big for its boots and started going for ever bigger fish. They started nibbling at the lower nobility – at which point the aristocracy just clamped down and that was the end of witch-hunting; there was a pan-European collapse. Before that, it was a self-perpetuating organization that needed to find witches; they found them and, what was really grotesque, you paid to be punished.

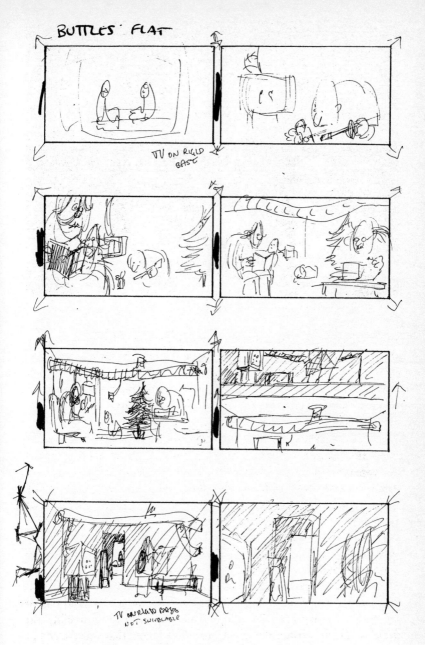

Storyboard for the Buttles' flat sequence, *Brazil*.

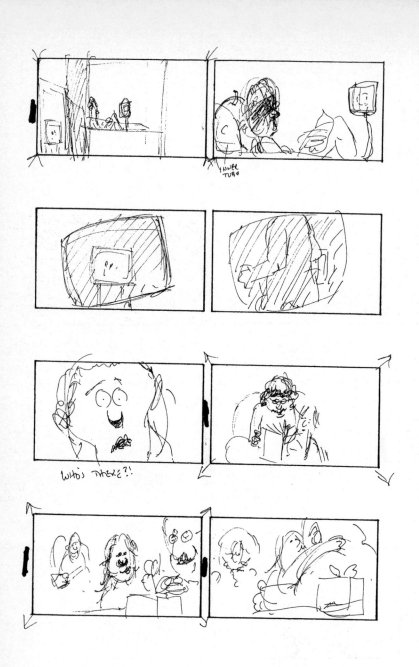

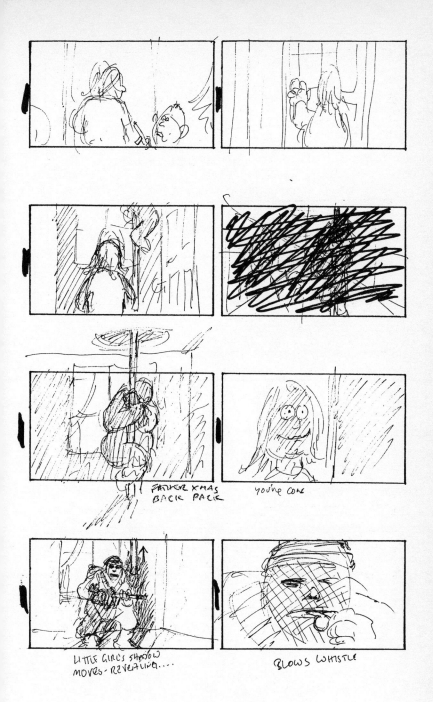

FATHER XMAS
BACK PACK

YOU'RE COOL

LITTLE GIRL'S SHADOW
MOVES - REVEALING.....

BLOWS WHISTLE

135

WIND BLOWING

BROKEN SERVICES

136

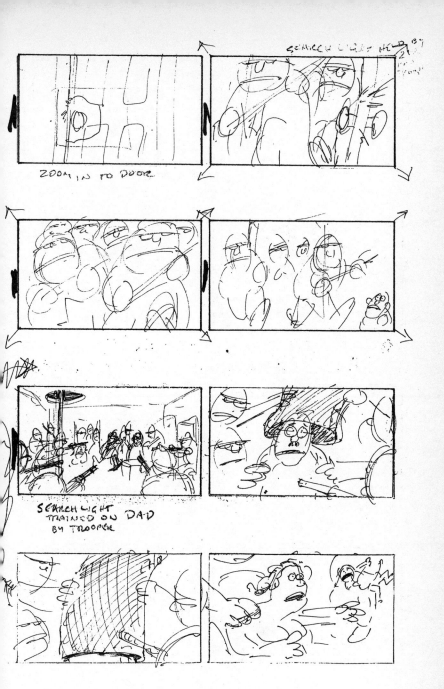

ZOOM IN TO DOOR

SEARCH LIGHT HELD BY
SEARCH LIGHT
TRAINED ON DAD
BY TROOPER

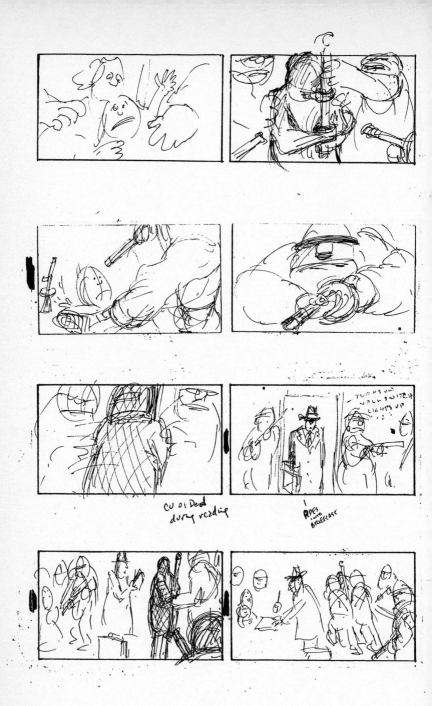

CU of Dead
during reading

PIPES
INTO
BRIEFCASE

138

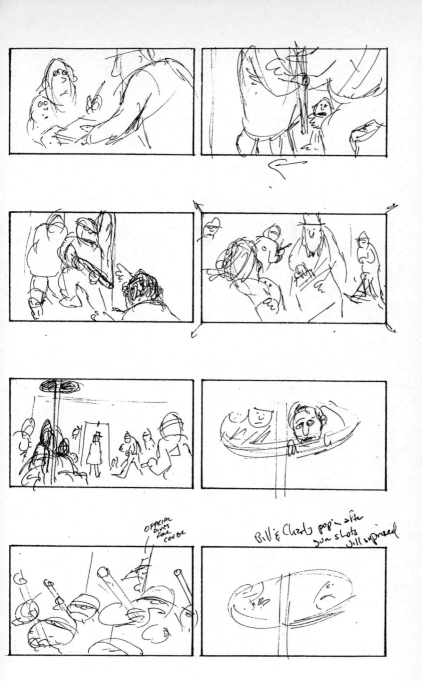

OFFICIAL DIVES FOR COVER

Bill & Chuck pop in after gun shots Bill surprised

WIND

GUARD
COUGHING

BROWN WRAPPING
AROUND DISC — WITH NR'S

THERE MUST BE SOME MISTAKE

OFF SCREEN FROM JILL
MRS BUTTLE? MRS BUTTLE?

CLERK'S POOL

FLOP

This became the idea of the Buttles' cheque, which was one of the earliest scenes I wrote.[12] I knew that Sam thinks he's a good Boy Scout; it's Christmas time, so he's doing his best for everybody by taking his chance. Normally you wouldn't do that in the system, but he thought this was a great humane gesture, without understanding what he was doing. I think this is an important scene.

During the witch-hunts, there was nothing better than to have one come to your town. If you were an innkeeper or a local merchant, this was the big time: the circus comes to town and everybody pours in from the countryside to watch the burnings – great for business. Everyone benefited, except for a few, and it was the little guys, the Buttles, who fuelled this horrendous system.

You wanted to show the logicality as well as the banality of evil? There's no Big Brother.
I didn't want it to be a totalitarian system like in *1984* or *Brave New World*. Even Mr Helpmann isn't the top guy, he's the deputy. There probably *is* no top guy, since everybody abdicates responsibility; the buck doesn't stop here, it always stops at the next person up. Although it's often described as a totalitarian world, I don't think it is, since the sum of the parts isn't quite the total that we're looking at in a totalitarian system. This may be why people around the world, whether in Eastern Europe or in Argentina, all recognized the place; it's not *1984*, it's now. People have often said to me, surely you've been to Brazil, Argentina, Chile, Poland and so on, but I haven't been to any of these places; this is just what's going on, more or less, in every society; we only needed to push it a bit further in the film.

The ducts led us into the morality or the politics of the film . . .
One of our locations was the National Liberal Club, which seemed a perfect setting for this non-liberal society. We used it for Sam's mother's luxurious apartment, and again we ran the ducts through it. If you look carefully, you can see ducts going through antique tapestries, violating everything. On the other hand, Sam has this modern flat, with all the ducts tucked away neatly, so that he can go through life not having to bother about how it works – except that it never does quite work properly: it promises everything but only does half the job.

For me, the architecture in the film is as much a set of characters as those that speak and wear clothes. All the sets have a function within the whole process, they represent specific ideas. I think this probably sets me apart from many other film-makers, who think of background as just that and not as an integral character. For instance, Croydon

Power Station, which we used for the exterior of the Ministry, was built in the thirties, at a time when we believed we knew the answers. There was a collective dream of progress and a centralized belief in the perfectibility of man – either through technology or through fascism, which effectively amounted to the same thing. The plastic-surgery clinic was shot at the house of Lord Leighton, the Victorian painter and collector, in a lush Moorish atmosphere that was just right for it.[13]

What I love about London is the variety of buildings from a great variety of times. You can go from Lord Leighton's to Croydon Power Station, from the National Liberal Club to Victoria Docks, where we found a huge flour mill. In fact, the desks in the clerks' pool are Victorian wooden flour-milling equipment that we converted. I really liked the idea of putting them through the looking glass to make them into something different. When Sam rises to Warrenn's level, we were using the base of the great grain storage silos. You can see the circular holes in the ceiling where the grain was emptied from the bottom of the silos. We only had the money to build one corridor, which ran about fifty feet before it ended with a painted false perspective; then, between the uprights, we put the walls with doors – although only two of them actually opened. When Sam is looking down all the different corridors, we did a whip pan from our single corridor to blackness, then continued the movement with a whip back to the corridor, and repeated this. So there's just one corridor used again and again, which I like – even though we were forced to do it – because the uniformity is really disturbing.

Another thing I really love, which few people notice, is the corridor with the white tiles and the one drop of blood. When we were building that, the tilers put little pieces of cardboard in between the tiles to separate them as the adhesive dried. I walked on to the set and saw these little bits of cardboard sticking up, and decided we'd keep them. So when you see that scene, it looks like normal tiling, apart from these peculiar sticky-out things. I had a memory of Arnon telling me about when he was a kid in Jerusalem, and how the women would put prayers in their section of the Wailing Wall; then at night he would sneak in and steal them to see if the girls were writing about him. I think that was at the back of my mind; these little pieces of card are like the prayers of the people who are marched up and down that floor.

Things like this are really in my own head and probably don't translate to anyone else, but I like the peculiarity – and the possibility that somebody is going to watch the film and wonder what those things are. For me, raising questions, instead of giving answers, is what I want to do in films. You don't cross all the t's and dot all the i's.

What about the film's different beginnings and endings? Why so many versions?

There was a wonderful beginning that Tom wrote, with a beetle in an idyllic rainforest, who is disrupted by a great tree-gobbling machine that reduces the forest to paper pulp, which is then poured into a truck that heads towards the city as the beetle flutters overhead. The truck enters a paper mill that spews out huge rolls of paper which are taken to a printworks, which then churns out reams of printed pages that are bound into a document, which lands on a technician's desk. As the technician picks it up to swat the beetle that's now buzzing around his office, we can see the title page: it is a government paper on saving the rainforests. I thought that just encapsulated everything, but we couldn't afford to do it.[14] Now it begins with a Central Services commercial that was written by Charles McKeown.

Doesn't it begin with clouds?

No, the clouds are in the American version. The English – or European – one just has the time come up, followed by 'somewhere in the twentieth century'; then, from the Central Services ad, there's a pull-back, and you see the window of a shop with TVs and videos, before it blows up.

And the American version starts with the song 'Brazil', an idea apparently suggested by Sidney Sheinberg at Universal, before your feud with him became public?

I'm not sure if it was Sid, but that idea came from somewhere and I thought it was fine – it just shows what an easy-going guy I am – and then we added clouds. We already had these anyway, because when we started work on the film we thought we were going to need cloudscapes, since we were planning to use back-projection blue screen for the flying sequences, and we were able to buy out-takes from *The NeverEnding Story*.[15] In the end, we didn't use these because our own manufactured clouds worked; so you get a beginning with *NeverEnding Story* clouds, but the ending relates to *Blade Runner*, which used out-takes from *The Shining*.[16] There's a weird connection going on there: it's about out-takes from different movies all tying together. The happy ending of *Blade Runner* so appalled me that I was all the more determined I would end *Brazil* as we did.

The American version allows the song to be heard at the beginning. We start with 'Brazil, da, da, da', then from that beautiful soaring, sweeping thing, it comes down to earth. There were two versions of the end in the original script and I could never make up my mind whether to leave the torture room bare, as we did in the European version, or to have it slowly fill with clouds, leaving Sam strapped in the chair while they float around him, which we did for the American version. Deep down I prefer the European version, so after looking at both for the laser disc, I went back to the original, hard, no-compromise European ending.[17]

I remember after a screening in Chicago bumping into someone who had already seen the film in Europe and asking him if he'd noticed that the ending was slightly different. Interestingly, he thought there *were* clouds in the European version; he had experienced the effect of clouds filling the room through the music, which was what we had intended. In a strange way, it was meant to be a hopeful ending, since the film had started from the challenge: can you make a movie where the happy ending is a man going insane? I always thought the ending was chilling, but then it bursts out musically and suddenly it's wonderful – wonderful in the context of all the possibilities open to our boy – at least he's free in his mind. Again, with clouds at the end, the clouds at the beginning made sense: there was a nice book-end feeling to it. Whereas, in the European version, you start hard and dark and you end as you began.

I feel that in films you should let the audience know very early on what they're in for, then you can take them in other directions, but at least you've warned them. I don't like it when endings are out of keeping with what's gone before, like the tacked-on ending of *Blade Runner*. That could have been a brilliant film, except that the compromises at the end betray the intelligence of the audience.

Apart from the Universal executives, were you surprised by the response to the film?
People were stunned by it and the reaction was very polarized; there was no middle ground. They either thought it was fantastic, or terrible, awful, unwatchable.

Many said they found it hard to follow.
That even happened with *Time Bandits*. A lot of people just don't seem to be trained to watch this kind of film, because everything is always handed to them on a plate. I think many were overwhelmed by the visuals and missed the performances. I remember the British reviews were mostly like that: only one mentioned Jonathan's performance. They seemed to think it was all about visual pyrotechnics. But the great revelation was when I went to Paris to promote it. All the reviewers and journalists were thanking me for this wonderful work, and calling it 'poetic' and 'symphonic'. This came as a genuine surprise, because there's a side to me that's trying to be the eternal bad boy, to stir things up and get reactions. It's too dangerous to hope they love me, but at least I can

make them hate me and wake them up. The reaction in France made me stop and think, 'Maybe I *am* an artist?'

Around Europe generally it was a young person's film, which is all right by me. If I ask myself who I was making it for, the answer would be myself at about the age of eighteen, when I was just waking up to the potential of film, to all sorts of books and ideas. Students loved it, but this also worried me because I didn't want to be just an intellectual film-maker. I wanted to be a popular film-maker, yet much of the general public didn't know what to make of it and just walked away.

I would say that about 60 per cent of the US reviews were really good, and the rest were hateful – which is fine. The worst thing is being dismissed: you want to be hated or loved, but not ignored. I remember the screening at Universal for the studio execs, in the Alfred Hitchcock Theatre. I made a little speech, being silly in order to get all these stiff men in stiff suits to relax. Then the film started and I left. Five minutes before the end, I sneaked into the projection box. All I could see were angry red necks, with muscles knotted; their shoulders had risen and nothing was moving. I realized they hated it, but of course they came out lying through their teeth, saying it was 'interesting' and 'we've got to talk' – anything to get out of there. But Arnon was bubbling; he thought they all loved it and it was celebration time. That's what I like about Arnon: he was naïve because he loved the film, but I had to break it to him that this was not where we were.

Before that, we'd done a lot of shifting around in the cutting. We would pull dreams from one place and put them somewhere else, or we would cut them in half and move bits about. *Brazil* was a bit of a jigsaw in that way; after each screening, we'd shift something or put a line in. In the restaurant scene, we had a line about how Sam must believe in something, he must believe in dreams – 'No, I don't believe' – and we cut this because it seemed unnecessary, but in the end we had to put it back in. I was always stunned by how people had difficulty following what is basically a very simple story, but I think the problem is there's so much detail in *Brazil* they get distracted. Hitchcock, for instance, will go into close-up on something that's key, and hold it until he's sure everyone's got it. But I make it harder to spot what information is vital. The result is that you can see the film again and again and discover things; it's a real world there and, as in life, it's not always easy to judge where the real story is. I'm cursed by constantly wanting to bring real life – the reality of life, the experience of life – into the movie house. I may do it in a way that seems totally unreal, but this is only because I'm trying to deal with the unreality and weirdness and confusion of life itself.

After you delivered a version of Brazil *eleven minutes longer than contracted to Universal, this started a struggle between you and the studio, with Milchan initially trying to mediate before he came out fighting on your side, which eventually became almost as famous as the film. Since Jack Mathews's book,* The Battle of Brazil, *covers that in detail,[18] I'm going to suggest we don't go over the same ground again. Except I can't resist quoting your famous whole-page ad in* Variety, *which read in full, 'Dear Sid Sheinberg. When are you going to release my film, BRAZIL? Terry Gilliam.'*

Most of the stuff is in Jack's book, including how Kenneth Turan was first to write about it in the States and described it as 'the masterpiece you'll never get to see'.[19] That was a good start. It let people know that there was an interesting film being suppressed, and soon there was a whole range of troops lining up for the battle. I think one of the nicest articles was Salman Rushdie's piece on the film, in which he said, 'We're all Brazilians, we're all strangers in a strange land.' He was sharing the fact that he and I are both expatriates. I discovered later that Rushdie is a great comic-book fan, and *Brazil* is done very much like a *Marvel* comic. While everyone else is trying to film actual comic books – and I've always wanted to do them too – in the end I think *Brazil* is as close to that as anything. The way it's shot, with a lot of wide-angle lenses to force the perspective and distort things, makes it visually a kind of caricature. It's trying to drag this second- or third-rate art up into the premier league, not as the *Batman* or *Superman* films, but by dealing with what really goes on in comic books.

No superheroes or supervillains.
That's right. And where there is an attempt to create a comic-book superhero in the dreams, we can see how escapist and simplistic it is. However inspirational, comic-book heroes don't solve any of the problems of real life.

1 Tom Stoppard (b. 1937 in Czechoslovakia) is best known for the philosophical ingenuity and verbal pastiche of such plays as *Rosencrantz and
Guildenstern Are Dead* (1966), *Travesties* (1974) and *The Real Thing*
(1982). After an early comedy script, *The Engagement* (1970), he became
associated with complex literary adaptations, including Thomas Wise-
man's *The Romantic Englishwoman* (1975, dir. Joseph Losey), Nabokov's
Despair (1978, dir. Rainer Fassbinder), Graham Greene's *The Human Factor* (1979, dir. Otto Preminger) and J.G. Ballard's *Empire of the Sun*
(1987, dir. Steven Spielberg).

2 Arnon Milchan, an Israeli entrepreneur with international food and technology interests, was drawn into film financing by Elliott Kastner in 1977
and had his first success with *The Medusa Touch* in 1978. Producing
Scorsese's *The King of Comedy* (1982) brought him prestige in Hollywood, and Leone's *Once Upon a Time in America* (1984) further strength-
ened his links with De Niro. He had already worked with Sidney
Sheinberg on the Universal miniseries-cum-feature *Masada* (1982), for
which he produced the Israeli exteriors; and when Gilliam first met him in
Paris, he had a stage production of *Amadeus* running, directed by and starring Roman Polanski.

3 Jack Lint is a contemporary of Sam's, who has risen to Level Five Security,
where he conducts torture, while being a bland 'family man'. In a crucial
scene reshot by Gilliam, he can't distinguish between his own triplets.

4 *Enemy Mine*, a sci-fi version of *Robinson Crusoe* with a pacifist message,
was eventually directed in 1985 by Wolfgang Petersen, whose *NeverEnding
Story* would provide spectacular sky footage for *Brazil* (see n. 15 below).

5 Milchan was the producer of the much-mocked fairytale *Legend* (1985),
directed by Ridley Scott, with Tim Curry and Cruise.

6 *Rashomon* (1951) offers four contradictory accounts of an ambush in
twelfth-century Japan.

7 In *8½* (1963), Fellini's alter ego (Marcello Mastroianni) fantasizes about
solutions to his personal and professional problems, while in *Giulietta of
the Spirits* (1965), his real-life wife (Giulietta Masina) explores an equivalent fantasy life beyond her timid bourgeois experience. An early title for
what became *Brazil* was '1984½'.

8 Early drafts of *Brazil* bore various titles, including, apparently: 'The Ministry' and 'The Ministry of Torture, or Brazil, or How I Learned to Live
with the System – So Far'.

9 De Niro had played only leading parts since his breakthrough in 1973, but
no doubt relished some diversion after the heavy demands of Scorsese's
protracted *The King of Comedy* and Leone's sprawling *Once Upon a Time
in America*.

10 Hugh Ferriss (1889–1962), an American architect, city planner and utopian, noted for his futuristic drawings.

11 On 28 January 1986, the space shuttle *Challenger* exploded shortly after take-off, in full view of television viewers throughout America and the world.

12 When Sam's boss Kurtzmann discovers that a refund is due to Buttle, after he was confused with Tuttle and accidentally 'deleted', Sam volunteers to take the cheque to his widow personally – which leads to him glimpsing his dream girl, Jill.

13 Frederic, Baron Leighton (1830–96), a President of the Royal Academy, was a noted aesthete who specialised in painting classical scenes and decorated his extravagant house accordingly.

14 Trying to develop Gilliam's story into a script, Stoppard worked on creating a chain of accidents which would explain why the protagonist rebels against the tyranny and absurdity of the system. But Gilliam found this script too cerebral, so turned to McKeown as a collaborator more on his own wavelength.

15 'Blue screen' technique enables actors photographed against a bright blue background to be matted on to location or other footage, in this case to create a flying illusion. Wolfgang Petersen's *The NeverEnding Story* (1984), made in Munich, generated much aerial material for its flying dragon sequences.

16 Ridley Scott's *Blade Runner* (1982) used spectacular landscape material originally shot by Kubrick for *The Shining* (1980).

17 The Criterion Collection laser disc edition of *Brazil* includes both Gilliam's 'final final cut', restoring some scenes cut from the European version, and Universal's optimistic cut intended for television, labelled by Gilliam the 'love conquers all' version. It also has documentaries on the film's production and subsequent 'battle'.

18 Jack Mathews, *The Battle of Brazil* (Crown Publishers, 1987), includes an annotated screenplay and drawings, as well as a detailed account of the production and aftermath.

19 Kenneth Turan wrote the first enthusiastic American review, after seeing the film in Europe, for *California* magazine in late 1985. This was in time to influence the LA Critics Awards in December, which gave *Brazil* an unprecedented line-up of Best Director, Best Screenplay and Best Picture (Mathews, pp. 67–8).

7

Bernini, Doré and light filtering through the pines of Cinecittà while *Munchausen* hovers between life and death

After the very public and exhausting battles over Brazil, *you might have turned to something more straightforward. But* The Adventures of Baron Munchausen *became even more of an ordeal, although for different reasons. What first got you interested in the Baron's tall tales?*
I think it was seeing a picture from Karel Zeman's *Munchausen* in a National Film Theatre programme that got me excited. It seemed to be a combination of live action with drawn backgrounds, and somewhere along the line I got to see the film.[1] Then Ray Cooper dragged me out to George Harrison's house to see the German version and they said that we really ought to remake it.[2] I didn't like the German version particularly, but Munchausen was in the air. I read the book and in many ways it was the Doré illustrations that seduced me.[3] This is what happened with *Don Quixote* as well – it seems to be my mission in life to make Doré come alive.[4]

Since the relationship between Arnon Milchan and myself had been so good, I suggested we develop *Munchausen* and off we went. I got Charles McKeown to write it and Arnon went to Fox – because they'd had *Brazil* for the non-US territories – and did a deal with them to develop it. They took an ad in *Variety*, announcing the world's biggest, most outrageous, mostest film, and we started working on it. But Arnon wasn't paying Charles, so I had to pay him, and I thought this was rather odd. It was as if Arnon had had too good a time on *Brazil*: an affair was one thing, but now he was pulling back from a marriage.

At this time we were trying to set up Prominent Features, the Python production company, with Steve Abbott, who had been an accountant at Handmade Films and subsequently became Python's. So we approached Arnon about a joint deal, but he wasn't interested. But before the parting took place, we all went to Lake Como, where Jack Mathews was writing the book on *Brazil* and Arnon was making *Man on Fire*, with Scott Glenn and Jonathan Pryce. It was there that he introduced me

No Roman holiday: Gilliam at Cinecittà during *Munchausen*.

to the guy he had in mind to be line producer on *Munchausen*, Thomas Schühly; and when things with Arnon started falling apart, Thomas came forward and suggested that we could do it on our own.

Thomas is a very interesting character. He's a big bull of a man and likes referring to himself as Rambo because he has energy and is highly intelligent. He's also crazy, but the intelligence and sheer size of him make you think he's solid; not air and smoke, but the real stuff. I liked his energy and ambition, because I knew *Munchausen* was going to mean taking on more than we could imagine. He also convinced me that it could be 30–40 per cent cheaper in Rome, and I had already been thinking of going there anyway, so this was the perfect excuse.

I sat down and started doing my storyboards, and in no time at all I had the film finished – ready to go. That had happened before with *Brazil*, and this time I caught Thomas asleep: he hadn't done any of the things needed to advance the project. So off we went to see Jake Eberts, formerly of Goldcrest, since they had both been executive producers on *The Name of the Rose*.[5] Then came one of those great moments which illustrate how cinema works. We go to Jake's office and it turns out that they had never met, even though they'd been credited with the same job on the same film. In fact, I was giving Thomas credibility in Jake's eyes, and Thomas was more credible to me because he seemed to be good buddies with Jake; everyone is proof to the others that we're all working with good guys. Jake was wonderful on that occasion. He asked how much money we needed to start pre-production and he offered the money right there, with a one-page agreement to be signed – simple, cut out the lawyers. So off we go to Rome, where Thomas further impressed me by securing Dante Ferretti and Peppino (Giuseppe) Rotunno.[6]

As production designer and director of photography, respectively. This was an exciting prospect for you, to work with people who'd been involved with legendary films.
They were gods for me. From the early films like *Jabberwocky* and *Holy Grail*, I was heavily inspired by Pasolini's texture and sense of reality, and it was Dante who had put those together before he'd gone on to work with Fellini. And Peppino was involved with Fellini too; so for me this was like working on Olympus.

Meanwhile, we were budgeting the film – based on my storyboards, and trying to raise the money. Jake, Thomas and I went to LA and the first office we walked into was David Picker's at Columbia, where David Puttnam – who was the new president – had just said they weren't going to make this kind of big-budget film any more. But even before I'd opened my mouth, David Picker announced that he wanted the film. This was too good to be true. We still went round all the other studios – just to cover our backs. The one we weren't going to approach was Fox, since they had done the development deal with Arnon, and then ultimately passed on it. Everyone from that period had gone – the Hollywood parade marching on – and there were new people at Fox, with Scott Ruden, whom I'd known for years, as president. There had been a 'key man' clause in Arnon's contract, so that if the people he'd signed with were no longer there, it was void; so we assumed we were clear from Fox. Then I got a call from Jake to say that Scott claimed they owned it.

We had a meeting and it turned out that Arnon had taken $150,000 from Fox to develop the film. This was the first I'd ever heard of it – in my naïve way, I was just pleased to be making a film – and I'd never seen a penny of the advance; on the contrary, I'd been paying Charles McKeown myself. I confronted Arnon over this and didn't speak to him again for six or seven years until he came up to me at the Golden Globe awards after *Fisher King*. It was very sad, because I liked him – even though he's a pirate. On the other hand, if you're partners you don't do things like that. In the end, we had to pay Fox back the $150,000 *and* give Arnon points in the film! Clearly, in Hollywood crime pays.

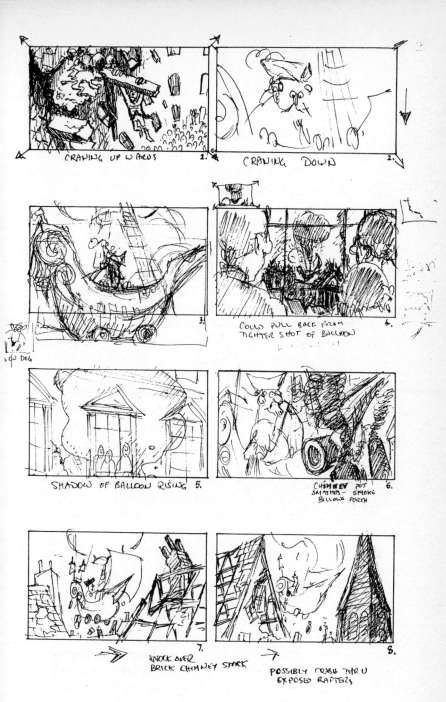

Storyboard for the balloon sequence in *Adventures of Baron Munchausen*.

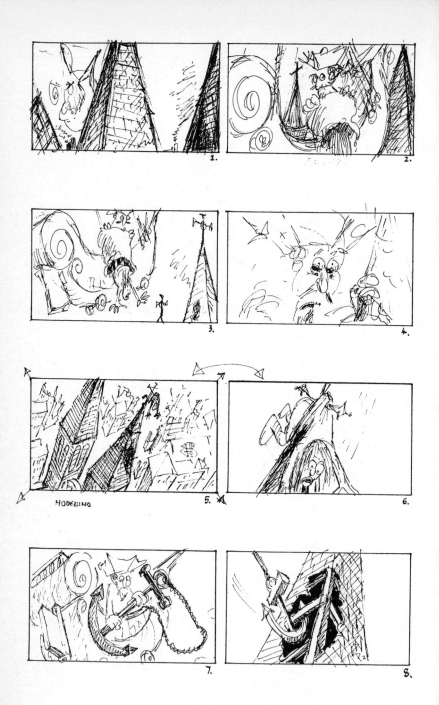

MODELINO

1.

2.

3.

4.

5.

6.

7.

8.

156

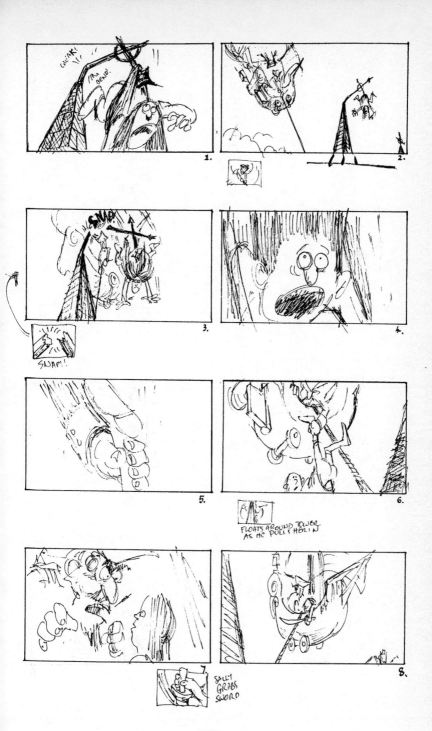

157

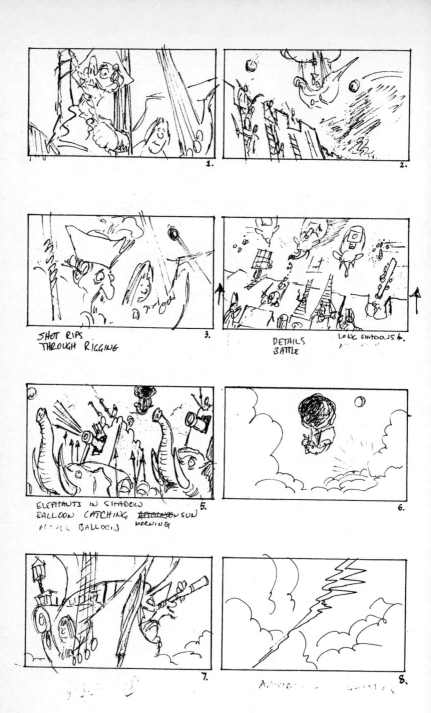

1.

2.

SHOT RIPS
THROUGH RIGGING 3.

DETAILS
BATTLE   LONG SHADOWS 4.

ELEPHANTS IN SHADOW
BALLOON CATCHING AFTERNOON SUN
MORE BALLOON   MORNING   5.

6.

7.

8.

LANTERN'S ALIGHT   1.

SUDDEN
FUEL
ON FIRE

2.

EARD
SLIDES DOWN
ROPE

3.

4.

LIGHTNING

5.

6.

7.

8.

159

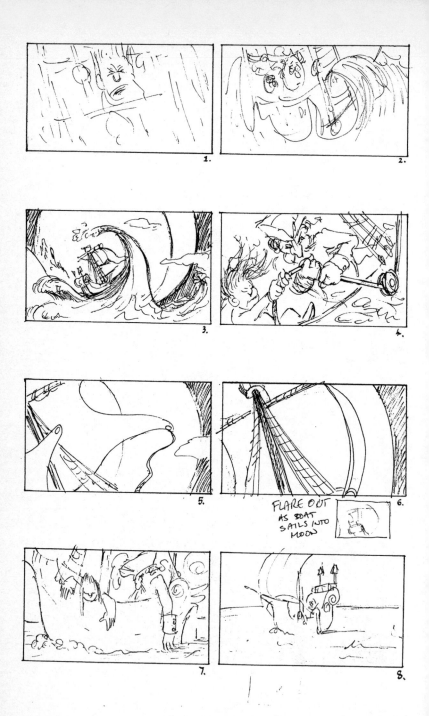

FLARE OUT
AS BOAT
SAILS INTO
MOON

1.

3.

What was going on back in Rome?

We finally pulled together $23.5 million, with some of the money from the Italian company Cecci-Gori, some from Germany and the rest from Columbia and from RCA-Columbia Video, who paid over the odds because there was a guy there who likes what I do. I kept making the 30–40 per cent adjustment: if *Brazil* cost $13.5 million and we have $10 million more – and it's really worth a third more – then we should be able to do the movie. Because I'm not good at figures, I just do these rough sums. Thomas, on the other hand, was getting proper budgets done, and when the first one came in at $60 million, he fired the accountant. He hired another accountant and the budget came in at $40 million, so he fired that one. We finally reached the fourth accountant who somehow managed to make the budget fit the money we had. Later, he was fired.

Ironic, or appropriate, considering the villain of the piece, Horatio Jackson, is an accountant who wants to destroy Munchausen and everything he stands for.

The production was basically a disaster. Dante and I would find locations and be told there was no problem getting permission to use them. We'd spend a month designing around them and then hear we hadn't got permission. We redesigned the film three or four times because of this. The worst case was when we decided to use the Alhambra in Granada for the Sultan's harem. Dante and I went out and did a recce: we measured everything, worked it all out, designed and built the model. Then, just over a month before we were due to start shooting, the entire team – special effects, stunts, camera crew – goes up to the Alhambra on our final technical scout and Bob Edwards, the line producer at that point, explains to me that we have a little problem. The problem is that we can't use any smoke, we can't lay tracks or move the camera and we can't have a horse inside – in short, we can't do the scene. Shouldn't he have told us this before we all got on the plane at vast expense? I just went berserk, but that was how it went on. They couldn't agree a deal with Jim Acheson on the costumes – which was fair enough – and we were lucky enough to get Gabriella Pescucci, who is brilliant, but so much time had been lost that she had only six weeks to prepare the whole show.[7]

I actually set up my office in the middle of the art department, because theirs was the biggest budget and I felt I had to be on top of it. So I had a partitioned-off area with a big table where we held our production meetings. This meant that as everybody came in every day they

162

would have to pass by the sets and see the problems; there is a tendency in films for people to be concerned only with their own department, and I feared it would be even worse in Italy. Thomas, the producer, came only twice to these meetings, and each time there were almost fisticuffs. With only a couple of weeks to go and people angry that they hadn't been paid, he suggested that those who had been paid should share their money with those who hadn't. With such madness going on, I knew before filming began that we were doomed. But we were so far into it there was no alternative but to go forward.

Thomas was spending an inordinate amount of time, at the expense of other, more important problems, trying to get Marlon Brando to play the part of Vulcan – and it nearly happened. One of the great memories I have from *Munchausen* was that I got to spend some time with Brando in LA. *That* was worth the price of admission.

What other problems did the film being based in Rome cause?
I was going out there for something like eight months. Thomas was based in Rome and, because he'd been executive producer on *The Name of the Rose* – which had gone well and was successful – he was credited with being essential to it. Later, it turned out that everyone had been fooled – he was really the frontman for the man making the real decisions. Thomas had power because they all saw him as this big producer who had brought *Munchausen* to Rome, the biggest film there since *Cleopatra*.[8] It was one thing for the creative people to fool themselves, but for the financial people to do so was even more stupid, since they claim to be the adults in this business. It turned out that the creative team was actually clearer about how close to the abyss we were, but we just couldn't stop.

I remember the first day of shooting – or what Jake Eberts thought was the first day. He arrived in Rome to crack open the champagne, but there was no shooting because it had been postponed for a week. Thomas hadn't bothered to tell the executive producer! It was ostrich time, head in the sand. There had been a convenient accident: a crane had fallen over and brought down some of the set, which necessitated the delay – which was fortunate since Gabriella was still trying to finish the costumes. Later, Thomas foolishly bragged in LA that he had organized the accident, and the insurance people refused to pay.

The worst part was going in every day knowing we couldn't possibly finish the film. It brought back the nightmare of when I was drama coach at the summer camp, and had to cancel *Alice in Wonderland*.

When the shooting finally did get under way, difficulties arose due to my Protestant method of film-making, as opposed to the local Catholic method. Peppino Rotunno wanted all information to go through him and he would then dispense it. By contrast, I've always worked in a completely open way where everybody has access to me. This became a real sticking point and I decided that, if I had to be God, then I would be a Protestant God, where priests aren't necessary because everyone can approach Him directly. But Peppino was the Pope and took great offence at this non-hierarchical regime. He could be surprisingly petty about sharing information, not even telling the continuity girl which filters were on the lens. He is a truly brilliant cameraman, and since we were in Rome he was running the show and many of the Italians felt beholden to him.

Thomas was making press announcements every day, crowing about the size of the production, and I told him to stop; everything we did was costing twice as much as it should because everyone wanted a slice of this huge cake. Transport is one of the things that can get out of control on a film, and the Roman transport person on *Munchausen* just happened to be the boyfriend of the production secretary. So, with his company, it cost about $12,000 to ship each of the cannon to Spain, and the same guns came back with a Spanish company for $5,000. Then I wanted exotic birds for the harem – $10,000 was the asking price. I said that was ridiculous and we'd manage with half the number for half the price. But we still got the same number of birds; obviously the price was whatever they thought they could get.

There were secretaries being sent to Munich for attaché cases of money to keep things going. There were two sets of books being run on the production: the white books were for the taxmen and then there were the real accounts, the black ones. Apparently, this happens all the time in Italy. And, with a couple of weeks to go before shooting, the first assistant director, who has been holding the production together for months, quits. So the nightmare begins: we start shooting and by the end of the first week we're two weeks behind schedule. This isn't possible, but we did it.

I notice David Tomblin gets a special credit as 'man of the match', as well as associate producer, and I've heard a lot of other film-makers pay tribute to him.[9]
David really got us through *Munchausen*. He only made one mistake, right at the beginning. Because he didn't want to be the first AD, he became a kind of 'super first', but his second AD – who would normally have stepped in and taken over on the 'floor' – had to return to England for family reasons. The best alternative we had was the Spanish AD, whom

David brought to Italy, but it turned out that the Italians didn't want to take orders from another Latin, especially a young one. It was chaos.

We tried to shoot in the theatre in daytime, putting a big canvas over it, but the heat was so intolerable that we had to switch to night shooting. So what was supposed to be two days' work went on and on. All my worst fears came true. David moved me about like an automaton – ordering me out when things got too bad, then sending me on to the floor when we were ready to shoot. My translator – who had never worked on a film before, although she was the granddaughter of Robert Flaherty – found it astonishing.[10] She'd see this dark, festering heap – me – that just growled its way through the horrors of the day; then she'd watch the rushes and they would be beautiful, charming and funny. She never worked out how one could produce the other.

Then we set off to Spain and that proved to be another kind of nightmare. First, we got on the plane and found it piled high with Italian suitcases. I was worried that we'd never leave the ground, but they said, 'Don't worry, we've lightened the load.' I looked out of the window and saw these big hampers on the tarmac – they're the costumes and we've left them behind to make room for all the Italians' evening wear. 'They're coming on the next flight,' I'm told, but instead they end up in Barcelona, at the start of a customs strike, so they can't be sent on to us in Almeria. We didn't have any of the principal costumes needed for the Sultan's camp sequence, but what we did have was 400 Turkish army costumes. So we staged the battle – which was supposed to be done several weeks later in Saragossa – there, and somehow we managed to fake it. There were also gales blowing, so ships' masts were destroyed and tents blown over. But when we did the scene where Gustavus blows and we needed a hurricane, it was dead calm.

There was one unbelievable day, just before we started sending things to Spain. First, the three horses we'd been training to be the Baron's horse, Bucephalus – we needed several to do different jobs – couldn't enter Spain because there was an outbreak of African horse fever, and all horses were quarantined throughout Spain; then the Baron's dogs got sick; and, finally, David Puttnam got the sack at Columbia – all in one day. The job was like being Job. Every time we thought we could take a few steps forward, things came crashing down all around us. The only thing that made it almost bearable was the beautiful light filtering through the umbrella pines at Cinecittà, casting shadows on the ochre-coloured buildings.[11] At weekends I would wander around Rome, not speaking to anybody, and that would resuscitate me, because Rome is such a wonderful, vivacious place.

The Baron on his trusty steed Bucephalus: 'Flamboyant and fabulously over the top'.

Anyway, we're in Spain and everything is going wrong. Thomas has disappeared and we're having big meetings to try to bring everybody together. This is six weeks into the twenty-week shoot and Film Finances – the financial guarantors – announce they're bringing in their own accountants.[12] They start to work, and after a couple of days we're told that we're going to be $3 million over budget; then, a day later, it's $6 or £7 million over; and by the end of the week the projection was $10 million over budget. They said they were going to close the film down. Meanwhile, I'm going crazy trying to get Peppino to do more set-ups a day, because we were only doing seven; we were running two cameras, which I've never done before, just to get shots. But Peppino wouldn't budge: he felt we were doing something for posterity, and he wasn't going to sell out his art.

This sounds more like you.
The whole thing was about to collapse. Richard Soames of Film Finances had come down to Almeria in his pith helmet and shorts, and decided there were too many documentary crews on the set, slowing down production. Well, there was a BBC crew wandering around, but this certainly wasn't what was slowing us down. The problem was much deeper. They didn't seem to understand how films are made, which made me furious. While all of this was going on, Maggie was pregnant with our son Harry, and Film Finances were threatening to sue me for misrepresentation and seize all my assets. So Maggie is trying to get the house out of my name, they're talking about bringing in another director to replace me, and we're still trying to work.

Eventually, they sent out David Korda, one of the Korda boys, who is actually quite nice, but he's shy and when you first meet him he's very cold.[13] This was the last thing I needed – a cold judgemental man coming into the midst of this nightmare – so I asked David Tomblin to keep him away from me. But while we were getting ready for a night shoot, I bumped into him in the production office. I started raging about how dare he threaten my wife and family, and they had to pull me away before I attacked him. So I'm downstairs where the cars are parked and I catch sight of him up on the first floor: instead of throwing a rock, I started hitting the car nearest to me, until I put my fist right through the windscreen, smashing it to smithereens. It felt very satisfying until I looked at the car and realized it was my own. So I had to drive around the rest of the time with no windscreen. But the adrenalin was flowing and we had a great shoot that night – I was flying.

But they closed the production down. I asked them to give us an extra day in Spain, because we'd built everything and with one more day we'd be finished with the scene completely. Jake Eberts was willing to pay for the extra day and I begged them not to interfere – it would cost them extra money in the end. But all they knew was how to pull the plug, so we went back to Rome.

With the scene shot?
No, half shot. It's when the Baron comes flying off the cannonball on to the battlement. Everything was rigged and ready to go. Anyway, back in Rome, they said we had to cut back, but I urged them to keep construction going, while we closed down for two weeks, just as we did on *Brazil*. It was worth the investment, I pointed out, even if somebody else took over. In fact, we were in a good position, because Columbia were insisting that they had paid for a Terry Gilliam film. I remember a meeting with Film Finances where they all came in suits, looking very stern and headmaster-like, taking the line, 'Gilliam, you've been a very naughty boy.' To which I responded by pointing out that we'd all been made fools of by Thomas. He had cleverly woven a web: he knew that he didn't have enough money to finish the film; and his plan was to get everyone in so deep, especially David Puttnam, that they would have to cough up the money.

Well, David had got the sack and there was nobody to cough up because, under Dawn Steel, the studio was basically taken over by accountants. Again, wonderful for *Munchausen*. There was Victor Kaufman, who would soon be selling the studio to Sony, and Film Finances' Richard Soames: nothing but accountants, factual men, men who claimed to know the truth, just like the character that Jonathan played in *Brazil* – it was my nightmare: everywhere I looked, he was there.

You seem to have this ability to make the making of your films mirror their themes.
It's always this way: the making of the film *is* the film; it's all the same thing. In many ways, the Munchausen in all this was Thomas Schühly; he was the biggest liar. I was a bigger dreamer, but he was a bigger liar and it probably took the pair of us to become Munchausen. If he hadn't done what he did, we probably wouldn't have ever made the film; so, for all my screaming and shouting, we owe a lot of this film to Thomas's madness. He had three heroes whom he modelled himself on: Alexander the Great, Napoleon and Dino de Laurentiis.[14]

When we were in Spain and things were just awful, I remember getting some photo contact sheets and among the photo sheets from the previous week's shooting was one of Thomas, back in Rome in the gym he'd had built for himself, posing as a boxer; he was trying to get an article about himself in *Playboy* as the battling producer!

Once we started talking about cutting the script, I said, 'OK, fire me. I just want out.' I insisted that I'd never lied to anyone about the situation on the film. I'd even advised Richard Soames to check on certain areas during pre-production, which he hadn't done. Now they brought in a guy named Stratton Leopold, who'd worked on one of John Carpenter's low-budget films: they sent a boy to do a man's job. I warned them that this wasn't going to work, not in a place as sophisticated as Rome, but they didn't know what to do except threaten to make life difficult.

I really did want to leave at that point, until Charles McKeown, who is a very mild-mannered person, suddenly said: 'You can't, it would be betraying everything.' He really got on his high horse – it was like Sally berating the Baron for giving up. So there was nothing for me to do but stay and finish the job. The main issue was the moon: they wanted to cut the whole sequence, but I insisted we had to go to the moon. The original moon sequence was gigantic. It had 2,000 extras, with musical numbers, heads changing bodies, palaces; it was all there in the script, storyboarded. It was almost a film in its own right, about what happens during an eclipse of the moon, the time of forgetting: sins, indiscretions, betrayals are all wiped out. Sally's terrified that they'll stay there, get caught in an eclipse, and the Baron will forget his mission.[15]

When they said we couldn't do the moon, my response was that if Munchausen can't go to the moon, then there's no point in continuing. Our first solution was to do it like a *Python* film. Munchausen arrives on the moon: he and Sally open a door and step into my office at Cinecittà, where we're all sitting around in street clothes reading the script, and we end by blaming the insurers before the two of them step out again and continue the film. We laughed about that for a couple of days, then we felt it would be cheating. Eventually, we came up with the idea of just two people on the moon and the mind–body Cartesian duality, which is actually much neater. I think that was another instance of the financial strictures forcing us to find a clever solution, because what we were planning before was really my bid to be Cecil B. DeMille.

All that's left in the film of the original DeMille banquet set is a big semi-spheroid structure that you can just see the ribs of: it was the framework for a huge inverted dome of St Peter's which was going to be a massive amphitheatre. Basically, we adapted what we already had. In the sequence when they arrive on the moon and the buildings are zipping around, these were literally the drawings of the buildings we were going to build full size. We mounted them on plywood and coloured them with felt-tip markers, Dante added a few sequins on pins to give them some glitter, then we put them on tracks and pulled them back and forth fast on ropes – another interesting result of the cuts imposed on us. For me, it was a moment of being free from the responsibility of what we had set out to do; we could throw it all up in the air and see where it landed. Sean Connery was going to be the king in the Cecil B. DeMille version, but after we had rewritten the sequence, he thought it was a completely different character and that he wasn't right for it. I agreed, no problem, but Thomas went crazy . . .

I can understand why. Letting your biggest star go before you'd even found a replacement?
Thomas said I'd offended Sean, but Sean and I were just being pragmatic. I didn't talk Sean out of it; I just didn't try to keep him in because both of us knew he would have been wrong for it. So we lost Sean, but Eric Idle had been taking a break out in LA and he told us that Robin Williams was interested. Robin had actually been on the set during the first week's shooting when he was on holiday in Europe, and he had come to say hello, because he had worked with Peppino on *Popeye*; also, our make-up guy, Fabrizio, had done his arms on *Popeye*.[16]

Robin Williams appears in the credits of Munchausen *as 'Ray D. Tutto', the 'king of everything'. Why is he not named?*
When Robin agreed to do the film, his managers were very much against the idea, because they thought we were going to 'pimp his arse' – in other words, sell the film on his back, even though he only appeared in a small part. So the deal was that he could do the film, but couldn't be credited. The crazy thing is that, once the film came out, Robin was delighted with it and he got great reviews. You would have thought that at this point they would have allowed him to speak openly about it, but that didn't happen. It's 'contractual', as they say.

At any rate, you were back in business.
By this time we'd been through three assistant directors and about the same number of line producers and accountants. Everybody was being sacrificed. Dante and I had a running gag about *i caduti*, 'the fallen': we were always making memorials to the fallen and each day we would check to see who was new on the crew list. When Film Finances took over, there were a lot more sacrificial victims, but we got going again after two weeks. They agreed our cuts were sufficient; also, they couldn't find another director willing to take over. The fact that Columbia were being totally negative became a positive thing in my favour.

But because they hadn't kept building sets, we would still arrive in the morning to find the paint just going on, so we were still losing time. Finally, David Tomblin agreed he had to go on the floor and take charge. That was after the best AD in Italy had come on – soon after having multiple bypass surgery – and quit after three weeks, saying that he didn't intend to die on this film. Then, at the eleventh hour, Vulcan was finally cast: we got Oliver Reed instead of Marlon Brando – who was really never going to do the film – and he proved to be brilliant. The second AD had worked with him on *Castaway* and assured us that he didn't drink at all. Well, everybody lied on this film – Olly, of course, did drink, but he was wonderful and enjoyed working with John Neville – they both admired each other. As for Venus, this was only the second film that Uma Thurman had ever done. She was just seventeen and a half, and the day she was doing her nude scene, her mother was on the phone trying to persuade her to go back to high school to get a diploma. I said, 'It's too late, Uma, you're a fallen woman, there's no way back.'

How did you come to cast John Neville as the Baron? He's not usually considered a film actor, much less a star, although he's famous in theatre circles.
I was trying to find an actor whom people didn't know too well. At one stage I went to meet Peter O'Toole, who would have been perfect, but for a variety of reasons he didn't want to do it. At another point, Fellini himself was suggested as Munchausen, because he's one of the great liars and charmers. In fact, we had thought of John Neville earlier, but were told by his agent that he didn't do films, since he ran the Stratford Ontario Shakespeare Festival.[17] Then a make-up girl asked if we'd thought of him, and said that she knew his daughter well. She called him and it turned out he was a big *Python* fan; so we met and talked and he agreed to do it. The punishing thing for him was that this was the first film he'd done in years, and it turned out to be one of the worst films of all time in terms of its making. Having enjoyed the immediacy of the stage for so long, to be involved in a process where you sit around for hours, then get up and say two words and go back to sitting again, was really painful. I think at times he regretted having got involved. John had a terrible time with his false nose: he was in make-up for four hours every day and some days he wouldn't even be used because the schedule was so screwed up. It was only after months had passed that I discovered the reason he was so grumpy wasn't just the time spent in make-up or even the waiting; it was because his glasses wouldn't sit on the false nose, so he couldn't read. Fortunately, Thomas found him a pince-nez that did the trick. When it was all finished, I think he was pleased with the result, but the process was a nightmare.

Uma Thurman as Venus in only her second film, 'already a fallen woman'.

John Neville, an infrequent film actor, had to undergo four hours of make-up daily to become the Baron.

Films come to be about their making: Jonathan Pryce as the accountant
Jackson, aghast at what he sees of Munchausen.

Valentina Cortese: the great queen of Italian cinema.

Jonathan Pryce had wanted to play Munchausen, but he was the wrong shape – not enough like the Doré image – and I liked the irony of him playing the opposite of his Sam Lowry character in *Brazil*. Bill Paterson was outrageous and he made me laugh more than anybody because he was so into Henry Salt; he believed in that character on and off camera, and was constantly working on the script, changing his part to be at the centre of everything. I feel bad about Alison Steadman, because I got her in and then her part was cut down to almost nothing.

Valentina Cortese was incredible.[18] Here was the great queen of Italian cinema; she was sixty-four when we did the film and looked stunning. She was very worried about playing the queen to Robin's king because he was half her age, yet on film it works fine. Every day she would glue strips of material to the side of her face, pull them back and tie them behind her head. Then she would say, 'Terry, can you do my shots fast, because I can only stand this pain for a few hours.' She comes from the rugby school of film acting, and wherever the camera was pointed she knew exactly where the cross-hairs were, so that in scenes with lots of people she would always be dead centre. The other actors used to complain to me that she was kicking and elbowing them out of the way to get to the centre of the shot. Valentina got her comeuppance on her very last day, when we were shooting the scene where she enters with the headless king. That day there was a Swiss documentary crew doing a piece on her and she was being wonderfully grand, but the girl who was playing the king's headless body was pushing and shoving her mercilessly. Suddenly she sank to the floor, sobbing, 'Terry, make her stop, I can't stand this.' It was an experience she probably deserved and, being a tough nut, she recovered. In a strange way, we all got our just deserts: we were all punished for previous sins in different ways.

Your original inspiration had been Doré's illustrations, but what were the other visual and stylistic sources? After all, despite its Arabian Nights *fantasy, this is also your only full-scale historical film to date.*

Apart from Doré – who is frustrating, because you can't recreate him for real – the other big influence on *Munchausen* is baroque architecture and art. Once I got to Rome I realized I had chosen the right place: it is *the* baroque city and that's what *Munchausen* is about. The Age of Reason had taken over and returned to classical forms, but before that came the baroque and *Munchausen* is very like that – flamboyant and fabulously over the top.[19] All over Rome you can see marble becoming flesh and flying in Bernini's sculpture.[20] So the king and queen of the moon are made out of stone, and yet they float. Those great volutes we used for the king's

Art imitates life: the theatre was built in a sound stage that had been bombed during the war.

bed were pure Baroque. And that's why the theatre setting worked so well: it had all the extravagance, and yet here was a world that was trying to be precise and civilized – like Jackson's office, which is white, spare and very crisp. Of course, I was also cheating and using nineteenth-century stuff, such as the morbid romantic image of death, who is feminine and embraceable. I was trapping the Age of Enlightenment between the baroque and the romantic. We were also looking at a lot of the *pompier* artists, like Gérôme, and that's where Doré comes in.[21]

One of the great things about shooting in Rome was working with Roman craftsmen. There were three sculptors there who did various things, from the little boat to the great equestrian statue and the King of the Moon's bed. That bed is extraordinary: you would never find anyone in England who could build something as complex as that. The Italians are all classically trained, so they've done their volutes and their equestrian statues. They were also prima donnas; they all had to have their own studios and worked as if the others didn't exist. The painters were also phenomenal. And Dante was a great politician, who could get more than anybody else out of Cinecittà – at times I thought he was producing the film.

We built the theatre inside a sound stage that had been bombed during the war and still had no roof, so it was like history continuing in some strange way. The walls supported our set and it was great to be inside a building that had died the way our theatre had died. We got them to rebuild the backing of the tank on the back lot, and most of the boat sequences were done in that tank. And we also got them to build a new blue-screen stage, which they wanted to do as part of the studio's modernization. Unfortunately, someone changed the plans; they thought the stage only needed to be as wide as the screen, but this left no space for the lights, so the stage didn't work properly.

It must have been more difficult than on Brazil *to reconcile cartoon stylization with all the craftsmanship and visual richness available at Cinecittà.*

I was trying to do a Disney cartoon in live action. I mentioned that amazing coincidence of reaching for *Munchausen* in the Eisenstein Museum and knocking over the cartoon that Disney had done for him. The sequence inside the belly of the whale is my *Pinocchio*.[22]

It was interesting working on the costumes with Gabriella, who is great and had worked with Visconti. I wanted to keep things slightly cartoony, so that the Baron's in red, Berthold's in yellow and so on – all very primary. But it was hard for her to deal with primaries; normally her colours are beautifully muted. It was interesting to force these styles together – my cartoony view and her sophisticated feel. It raises the film to a different visual level. Of course, the detail in Disney cartoons like *Pinocchio* is exquisite, which is what we were trying to achieve.

If you look at the great Hollywood films, like those designed by Grot, they were never naturalistic but always stylized and quite fantastic.[23] This is what Coppola – together with Dean Tavoularis – was aiming for in *One From the Heart*: a graphic, slightly abstracted, artificial world.[24] He was trying to mix stylization with naturalism, although I think what lets down that particular experiment is the overuse of ad-libbed dialogue.

One of the things that intrigues me about *Munchausen* is the moment they come out of the whale's mouth and end up on the beach. There's an incredible feeling of relief because we've been in artificial environments – like the moon and the belly of the whale – for so long and suddenly it's real sea, real sky and real sand. I remember the first time I saw it put together, the effect was really powerful: 'Ah, we're back in the real world.' It wasn't planned that way, or maybe it was planned on a subconscious level. When I look at my films, I'm always surprised how well thought-out these things seem in retrospect. But other people are much better than me at putting into words what I'm doing instinctively.

That sounds like a good working definition of the auteur *theory – finding coherence after the event in things that are very much the product of intuitive decisions and chance events. Film directors surely know better than most how many elements in a film lie outside their control.*
You start out thinking that you know what you're doing. Then you get lost in the forest and come out the other end and look at the film, realizing that you somehow made it. But along the way there are many surprises, things you didn't know you were going to do. I keep trying to demystify the whole *auteur* approach to films, although I think I'm probably more of an *auteur* than most. I know that it's the product of a lot of people who all contribute in different ways, yet, somehow, it ends up being something that can be described as 'a Gilliam film'. The best way I can explain it is that I'm the filter that lets certain ideas through and stops others. That's my function; I have an idea of what the film's supposed to be, but half the things that end up in the film I would never have thought of myself. However, many of the Italian crew just wanted a maestro who would say, 'I want this or that; no, don't come up with your own ideas . . . just give me *that* shade of green.'

Isn't that specifically the Italian tradition of the maestro-director?
Perhaps there are directors like that, but Dante told me how Fellini used to work: Dante would design the sets, Gabriella did the costumes, they would all work collaboratively. Then afterwards Fellini would draw cartoons based on what was done, and would take credit for visualizing the whole thing, thus maintaining the mystery of the maestro. I really want to try to break that down.

But doesn't somebody have to have an overview of how it's supposed to add up? You can't expect each person working on a film to know their part of the whole.
The reality is that most directors don't know either. The number of sets I've gone on to and talked to the crew who say they don't know what the director wants. But they read the script and think it should be like this, so they do it and the director gets the credit for it. I remember Dante saying about one of his more recent projects, 'I don't know what he wants: I show him these things and I don't get a yes or a no, so I just build.' What I've discovered is that this is the norm. Directors or producers hire good people who do their stuff and, in a lot of cases, you could make quite a respectable film without a director. So what's the difference? Certain directors do have vision, ideas of what they're trying to

achieve. These are the real directors as far as I'm concerned – and some get called *auteurs* – but they're definitely in a minority.

We need to go back to the production process, which wasn't finished when David Tomblin took to the floor and the last members of the cast dropped into place after your lay-off.

At every point, magical and outrageous things were happening, but Peppino was still going slowly, even though David was managing to move it a bit faster. The offence that Film Finances were trying to nail me for was 'enhancement' – that's the capital crime when they're in charge; they assume that the director is always trying to make it bigger, but the reality on this film was that everything was getting smaller. The Turkish army had gone from 800 to 400; in fact, there were probably only 350 soldiers. The Cyclops were down from eighty or a hundred to about twenty-five. The numbers kept going down, yet they kept trying to hit me for 'enhancement', since time was still running on. In reality, the second unit wasn't working well because it was locked in battle with the special-effects unit, and Peppino had put his son-in-law on camera there, which proved to be a controlling move. In this tense situation, everybody blamed each other: the Italians were calling the English arrogant imperialists; and the English were cursing the incompetent, untrustworthy Italians.

Italians love doing things at the last moment, extemporizing in a very spontaneous way, and when they do they're brilliant. But you need to plan this type of film very carefully and we never got the balance right. The one scene I wanted to do most of all – the one that got me into this project in the first place – never got done, which tends to happen on my films. It's the tale of Munchausen chasing the retreating Turks. His horse is so fast it roars right through the Turkish army into the Turkish town as the portcullis crashes down behind him. He rides to the fountain to water his horse and, as it goes on drinking, he notices that it has no rear half – it was cut off by the portcullis, so the water is running straight through the animal. He goes back and finds the rear half, now free from the front and having a great time in the fields; he sews both halves together with laurel branches, which then grows into a bower. So he rides in the shade of his laurels – a nice pun. For me, that was where the whole project had started – and it was one of the first things to be cut when I realized what a mess the production was in. Something had to go, so I cut my favourite scene. That's why I get so angry when I'm accused of being out of control and irresponsible.

What David did in the last stage was to guide things through to the point where we decided that a lot of the model and special-effects work

– which were supposed to be concurrent with shooting – could be done back in London. This bought us time so that we actually got through on schedule to within a few days. After I left Rome, they shot a few things and everyone worked for nothing. By the end, the crew were completely dedicated to this project – even though it had been so awful and painful – because they knew there was a wonderful film being created. We spent another three months on special effects, shooting at Pinewood, and somehow got through. But the constant pressure was incredible. During the latter part of the shoot, Film Finances' liability ended, and because they were reinsured through Lloyds – this is how mad it got – Lloyds became the film's producer. They brought in Joyce Herlihy, a great line producer who'd worked with me on *Jabberwocky*, and that was a relief: she really knew what she was doing.

So when the insurance adjuster from Lloyds came in and we explained what was wrong and what needed to be done, he would say, 'Yes, that makes sense, do it.' At last, things were sensible, instead of Film Finances constantly panicking and trying to cut back, which cost more money in the long run. Once the train has left the station, you have to try to keep it on the tracks. Lloyds were pragmatic: they would approve spending when they saw what it was for. But, eventually, their liability ended and it was back to Film Finances and Stratton Leopold, a nice enough man but out of his depth. He would call Richard Soames in LA every night asking for guidance, and Richard would be handing out instructions with no idea of the reality of things.

Speaking of reality, where was Thomas, the producer, in all this?
Thomas was amazing. They wouldn't fire him; I think it was because he was blackmailing them over the black books, which they had somehow condoned. Thomas undermined them and countermanded Stratton Leopold's orders, which he was able to do because a lot of the Italians were loyal to him, as the producer, and because they believed he had a big future in Italy. Thomas took to walking around with a gun; he claimed he was afraid that Film Finances were going to assassinate him because he was the only one standing in their way, protecting the film. Then, after we got back to London, there was another great moment with Thomas. They were reneging on what they had agreed to pay him, so he stole the negative from Technicolor in Rome: he had a gun on the negative: 'Pay up or I kill it.' Labs aren't supposed to release negatives like that, but in their eyes Thomas was still the producer of the film and he had said that he needed it, that they should pay no attention to those other jerks. So he had it for a while, until they got it back. Whatever

was mad about *Brazil* was nothing compared with this – and the craziness was exactly right for the tone of the film, except it kept getting in the way of making it.

There was a lot of bad advance publicity even before anyone had seen the film.

That had a lot to do with the studio politics at Columbia. David Puttnam had affronted Ray Stark when he took over and Stark was instrumental in getting him out.[25] I'm convinced that *Munchausen* was being used as an example of Puttnam's folly – even after he'd gone – because the articles that were coming out were outrageous, just factually untrue. We couldn't work out where all this stuff was coming from, until Jack Mathews at the *LA Times* realized he was getting it from the Stark camp; it turned out that Stark's partner had a son who worked for Film Finances. When you read the articles, it looks as if Film Finances are in charge and doing really smart things to handle this nightmare, and that I'm completely out of control. There was always some specific detail that could only have come from someone on the inside.

It was also, post-*Brazil*, Terry getting his comeuppance. It was *Magnificent Ambersons* time: he got away with it once, but now the little bastard is going to be seen for what he is.[26] So everything got blown out of proportion and is still talked about this way today: whenever there's a failure like *Waterworld*, *Munchausen* is still wheeled out as one of the most expensive disasters in the history of cinema, etc. It probably cost about $40 to $41 million and the budget was $23.5 million. That's a big difference, but it's not unusual. I talked to Neil Jordan about *We're No Angels* and he told me that went over budget more than *Munchausen* did, but no one talks about it; and *The Mission* went over budget even more.[27]

It seems to me there are only a few stories in Hollywood and they're just waiting for new people to populate them, like trappers hiding in the bushes ready to pounce: 'You're in my story and that's the story with . . .' I had been the beneficiary of one of those stories on *Brazil* – David versus Goliath – and now everything was turned round as it became 'director out of control'.

It also played into the original cinema disaster story of Cleopatra *running out of control in Rome.*

Ridiculously, that was what Thomas was almost selling it as – 'the biggest disaster since *Cleopatra*'. I always worry that I sound defensive when I talk about *Munchausen*, but my biggest problem is the myth that I was out of control, that I was enhancing all the time when, in fact, we were doing just the opposite. This is the part of the story that never seems to get through: that we were constantly cutting everything down. And the reason I've spent so much time blackening Film Finances' name is that I think they were greedy and lazy and didn't do their job properly. When we got to Spain, we discovered all the money had gone: somehow Thomas had managed to get it out of the bank. Film Finances had nobody countersigning, or they would have known what was going on.

Anyway, the real crunch came when we had the first screenings and people started walking out. Panic hit and I did something I regret more than anything else. I felt I had to get the new regime at Columbia to feel that it was their movie, not a left-over Puttnam project. So when the previews didn't go well, and the pressure was on to cut it down to two hours, I agreed – and I think the film suffers for it.

What are the most important things missing from the final release version for you?
It's not any one thing. It's a question of pacing; I think we ended up rushing some sections, so it becomes a bit of a jumble – like conducting an orchestra too fast. An extra five minutes would make a big difference. In my films there's always a danger of being swamped by the visuals, that's my albatross; and I think the longer version of *Munchausen* wasn't so frenetic, so you had time to absorb the ideas. Our first cut ran three hours and I thought it was just perfect. It was so dreamlike, it floated; you could just wallow in those images or listen to the ideas. Now I find it whizzes past in a rush and Michael Kamen's music is probably too loud and too in your face. By the end there was so much energy pushing to get the film out that it actually hurt it.

I keep being caught out by trying to include a lot of ideas, but in this case it's about fantasy – it's about going on a big adventure – and hopefully the ideas sprinkle down and the audience gets them. For people who like the ideas, this can be a frustrating experience, because the pictures are saying, 'Look at me! Look at me!' So we made some mistakes along the way, and not only by condensing things.

For instance, I let Jonathan play too broadly; he would be a more interesting character if he were more subdued and menacing. Also, I don't think we had enough time to establish the town: it's too abstract and you don't care enough about it as we go through all these adventures to save it. The town was supposed to be personified in the actors' troupe, so that even if it remains an abstract idea at least we'd care about them, but they're not well enough established as individuals. Visually, the film is extraordinary, but I was constantly arguing with the Italians, who have this innate sense of beauty, that it didn't *all* have to be beautiful – we could have crummy bits, visually quiet moments – but I never seemed to achieve that. I believe there are a lot more ideas and attempts at conveying ideas in *Munchausen* than in *Time Bandits*, but they're rather jumbled.

Have you thought about making a restored 'director's cut'?
I don't think I have the energy for it. I had a chance when we did the laser disc, but it would be a hugely expensive process to dig out all the stuff and I would have to recut the film, so it would cost hundreds of thousands of dollars.[28] Nobody's going to give me the money for that, since the film didn't make any money in the first place. What the editing down didn't do was solve the problem of getting the film released properly – which is what I was aiming for. I would have been happy with two hours twenty minutes – which would have been a better film – but we ended up with two hours.

In the end, I felt totally betrayed when Columbia released only 117 prints in America; an art film will often have 400 prints. They opened in fifty-two cinemas, where it played to the best business and reviews they'd had since *The Last Emperor*, but they didn't want to go with it.[29] They were trying to balance the books to get Sony to buy the studio, and they discovered that if they spent no money on either marketing or production, they might just succeed. Other films suffered too, but we were the most obvious casualty. There was even a publicist on our side who was banned from the marketing meetings. So I got on to Larry Estes at RCA-Columbia video, who had paid $7 million for the video rights, and asked him to find out what was going on, since it would affect his investment if it didn't do well in the cinema. He said he'd never seen anything like it; everyone was busy justifying what they were doing and using exit polls to prove it would only work in major cities.

Interestingly, in the places where they went out and sold it seriously – especially France and Spain – it opened number one and stayed there for a couple of weeks. But distributors always get caught up with previous things you've done; because of *Brazil*, they thought this was a sophisticated adult film. I convinced the French distributor that it was a family movie. Why not put on matinées? They did, and they were a huge success. In England, it just died. There had been all this press coverage about it going out of control, a big disaster – everything was about 'big' – and then you notice that there are no ads, so something is clearly wrong and nobody bothers to go. Columbia had this idea that, if it worked in Germany, this would give them some sense of how it would do in the States. So that's where it first came out, and the Germans hated it. I suppose it's as if a German or a Russian came and did *Tom Sawyer*; it would seem presumptuous. The reaction I got in German press conferences was a fear of the extravagance of *Munchausen*. The last time anyone was that outrageous, with that many lies and dreams and big plans, was Hitler; you could see the Germans backing away, not wanting to admit that a lie might be more powerful than the truth – plus, of course, their outrage at me for taking one of their classic films and remaking it in my own image. The only place we got good reviews in Germany was in Munich.

Very appropriate, in the former home of mad King Ludwig, who built all those fairytale castles and backed the original megalomaniac artist, Wagner. Do you think the film could have done better with more sympathetic handling?

No question. I know that every time we had screenings with kids, they came out loving it, dancing. I said at the time that I was writing it for my daughters, and I think it's important that kids get ideas thrown at them, even when they're too young really to understand. People with any sense of art or music always respond to the film. Perhaps others have to be guided towards it. What was fascinating was going to the Academy Awards with Maggie. She had been nominated for the Make-up Award, one of the four awards we were up for. As each film was announced, you could feel and hear the buzz of interest from the audience until they came to *Munchausen* . . . nothing, a void, no reaction. They hadn't seen the film – didn't have a clue what it was. This happened in each category. The lack of distribution had been even more successful than I had imagined.

The nice thing about *Munchausen* now is that it has its own life. I'm always running into people who say it's the best of my films, or that it's their favourite film, or that their kids watch it all the time – and I just say I'm glad they like it.

Actually, it's great to have made a lost classic, like Korda's *I, Claudius* or *The Magnificent Ambersons* – 'one of the greatest films ever made, that nobody will ever see'.[30] And, if they do catch a glimpse, they'll discover the shadow of what it might have been: the great 'if only'. It's important to make at least one of those in your career.

Keeping a child's-eye view: Gilliam with Sarah Polley as Sally.

1 Czech animator Karel Zeman (1910–89) turned from shorts to a series of feature-length fantasy films, of which *Baron Munchhausen* (1962) is one, using a distinctive combination of live action against animated and graphic backgrounds.

2 An earlier version of the story had been made by the Hungarian-born Josef von Baky (1902–66), who worked as a director in German cinema from the thirties until the early sixties. His lavish *Münchhausen* (1943) was commissioned by Goebbels to mark the twenty-fifth anniversary of the UFA production company and made in still-rare colour.

3 Rudolf Erich Raspe (1737–94) was a librarian in Cassel who stole rarities from his employer's collection and took refuge in London, where he published in 1785 (and in English) *Baron Münchhausen: A Narrative of his Marvellous Travels*. The 'real' Baron Münchhausen is said to have been born in 1720 and served in the Russian army against the Turks before embellishing his experiences.

4 Gustave Doré (1832–83) first became famous for his illustrated Bible in 1866, then produced richly detailed engravings and drawings for a wide range of classic and contemporary works, including Dante, Cervantes and Tennyson's *Idylls of the King*.

5 The independent Goldcrest company's collapse, after a spectacular rise to prominence, was exhaustively chronicled by Eberts and Terry Holt in *My Indecision is Final* (1990) Jean-Jacques Annaud's *The Name of the Rose* (1986), as an Italian–French–German co-production, boasted three executive producers and two co-producers.

6 Dante Ferretti (b. 1943) had worked as production designer with Pasolini and Fellini, and most recently on *The Name of the Rose*. Giuseppe Rotunno (b. 1923) had been cinematographer on most of the great Visconti and Fellini films from the sixties onwards, as well as working intermittently in America.

7 Jim Acheson had designed the costumes for *Time Bandits* and *Brazil*. Gabriella Pescucci was responsible for costumes on Fellini's *Orchestra Rehearsal* and *City of Women*, as well as *Once Upon a Time in America* and *The Name of the Rose* before *Munchhausen*.

8 *Cleopatra* (1963), largely written and directed by Joseph Mankiewicz, and starring Elizabeth Taylor and Richard Burton, long held the reputation of being the most expensive and extravagantly mismanaged film of all time. It was made at Cinecittà.

9 David Tomblin started as an assistant director in the sixties and has become one of the most respected profesionals in this field, working on films directed by Kubrick, Spielberg and Lucas.

10 Robert Flaherty (1884–1951) pioneered the feature documentary of exotic

cultures with *Nanook of the North* (1922) and subsequently made films in the South Seas, India, Ireland and finally Louisiana, many in collaboration with his wife Frances.

11 Cinecittà was established under Mussolini's regime in 1937 as Italy's biggest studio complex; and during the fifties and sixties it served as a base for Hollywood's European productions, as well as for countless spaghetti westerns and ancient-world epics.

12 The role of the completion guarantor, such as Film Finances, is to indemnify a studio against a film going over budget, in return for a percentage of that budget. The guarantor is empowered to intervene if an overrun seems likely, to minimize its risk, which is in turn reinsured.

13 The descendants of the Korda brothers – Alexander, Vincent and Zoltan – who dominated British cinema from the thirties to the mid-fifties, have continued to play prominent roles in the media. See Michael Korda's *Charmed Lives: A Family Romance* (1986) for an insider's account of the clan.

14 Italian producer Dino De Laurentiis (b. 1919) produced his first film at twenty and had his first international success with *Bitter Rice* in 1948. Thereafter he produced a mixture of films by the likes of Fellini and Visconti, along with heavyweight spectacles such as *War and Peace* (1956), *Waterloo* (1970) and an ill-advised remake of *King Kong* (1976). His American-based company folded in the late eighties.

15 The Baron has gone to the moon to find his trusty servant Berthold, as part of his promise to return to the besieged city with reinforcements.

16 Robert Altman directed this stylized live-action version of the comic strip, scripted by cartoonist Jules Feiffer, in 1980.

17 Despite his distinguished theatre career and frequent television appearances, John Neville (b. 1925) had appeared in few films before *Munchausen*. Among these were Peter Ustinov's *Billy Budd* (1962) and Jerzy Skolimowski's *The Adventures of Gerard* (1970).

18 Valentina Cortese's credits began in the early forties. She made her American debut in Jules Dassin's *Thieves' Highway* (1949) and starred in Thorold Dickinson's political thriller *Secret People* (1951). Thereafter she appeared internationally as well as in Italy, with notable roles in Fellini's *Giulietta of the Spirits* and Truffaut's *Day for Night* (1973).

19 The baroque period in art and architecture ran from the mid-seventeenth century to the early eighteenth, which is the 'true' setting of Munchausen.

20 Gian Lorenzo Bernini (1858-1660), Roman sculptor and architect, was the key figure of the Italian Baroque, noted especially for his sensational fountains and elaborate decoration of St Peter's.

21 The *pompiers* of nineteenth-century France were highly regarded specialists in large historical and religious paintings – Leon Gérôme (1824–1904) is famous for his *Death of Caesar* – supported by traditionalists against the Impressionist avant-garde, but now largely forgotten. Their derogatory

nickname (literally 'firemen') is thought to be a joke at the expense of the helmets worn by their classical figures.

22 The Baron and his companions are swallowed by a whale during a storm at sea, as in Disney's *Pinocchio*.

23 Anton Grot (1884–1974) studied design and illustration in Poland and Germany before entering the American film industry in the 1910s. He worked on the spectacular 1924 *Thief of Bagdad* and designed DeMille's late twenties films, before going to Warners, where he designed and over-saw their leading productions from 1930-48, including gangster movies, swashbucklers and *films noirs*.

24 Francis Coppola's romantic musical *One From the Heart* (1982), set in Las Vegas, was entirely shot in his shortlived Zoetrope studio (which it helped to bankrupt) and designed with notable anti-realism by Dean Tavoularis.

25 Former agent turned independent producer Ray Stark had a longstanding deal with Columbia, which David Puttnam questioned when he took over, ensuring Stark's opposition to his regime.

26 After having *carte blanche* on *Citizen Kane*, Orson Welles faced studio interference on *The Magnificent Ambersons* (1942), culminating in the film being shortened and the ending re-edited in his absence.

27 *The Mission* (1986, produced by David Puttnam) and *We're No Angels* (1989, produced by Art Linson) both feature De Niro expensively in priest's costume; the former a Cannes prize-winner and the latter a notable box-office non-performer.

28 The Criterion Collection laser disc from Voyager features a commentary by Gilliam, but unlike *Brazil* has no supplementary material.

29 Bernardo Bertolucci's Chinese epic *The Last Emperor* (1987) was respect-fully reviewed and widely shown, despite its exotic subject.

30 Unlike *The Ambersons*, which was released, even if truncated, Alexander Korda's *I, Claudius*, begun by Josef Von Sternberg in 1937, was halted after a month's shooting, and the results not seen until Bill Duncalf's BBC documentary, *The Epic That Never Was* (1965).

Knights errant and distressed damsels
in Manhattan: *The Fisher King*

What did you do after the disappointing release of Munchausen *in 1988? There was talk of various comic-book adaptations.*
I don't have any idea of a 'career', so all that mattered to me was the fact that I was depressed by the whole experience. I didn't want to make films any more, so in interviews I would say that I wanted to make a really small film; a film about a schizophrenic, but about only half of his personality. Then George Ayoub, who sold Handmade Films around the world, approached me about doing a Raymond Briggs adaptation. He originally wanted to do *The Snowman*, but I pushed for *Fungus the Bogeyman*.[1] Ray Cooper, George and I went down and talked to Raymond, and there seemed to be a chance of getting together a group with Terry Jones, Neil Innes, David Leland and Charles McKeown. But it didn't work, because we'd all gotten too old and set in our ways to be a gang any more, in the way that *Python* had been a gang. I think after *Munchausen* I had a real wish to have the support of a group and to be part of something again.

Fungus was going to be live-action?
Yes, the idea was to make something very British that could be done here. After *Fisher King*, we made a little pilot with Val Charlton, who had made the three-headed Griffin for *Munchausen*. She built a creature suit with a big head that could be worn, so that there could be a person inside as well as levers to make things move. But it now looks as if it's going to be done in Canada, with none of the original people involved.

Then Joel Silver approached me to do *Watchmen*, which is a project that keeps coming up.[2] *Watchmen* is the *War and Peace* of comic books, and Joel told me he was sitting on $40 million and a green light. There was a script by Sam Hamm that had some nice things but didn't quite do the job, so I brought in Charles McKeown and we rewrote it. The

Working with an American crew on *Fisher King*: 'The biggest shock was discovering I had a reputation.'

difficulty was trying to condense this vast comic book into two hours and I wasn't really happy with what we'd done. Then it turned out that Joel couldn't get the money anyway. It was such wonderful arrogance on his part: he had just done *Die Hard 2*, which had gone way over budget, and I was fresh from *Munchausen*, also famously over budget. We were running round Hollywood together trying to make this very dark film that was going to cost a fortune and, of course, nobody wanted to do it. Joel was very upset. He'd made billions of dollars for Hollywood and he thought that at some point he'd get a chance to do what he really wanted. But it doesn't work that way: even someone like Joel doesn't get what he wants.

The other thing that happened at this time was that I joined CAA.[3] Up to then I'd stayed away from Hollywood, but it was Joel who convinced me, I was so disillusioned by the way things had been handled on *Munchausen*. At the end of the film, the completion guarantors had asked us to hand it over and trust them, and the *Python* office had said that they seemed to be honourable men. Once they had it, they announced that they weren't going to pay me – the film world can be very brutal. So we said we'd sue and they said they'd counter-sue, and it all became a bad dream. I felt I wasn't up to going to court and reliving the whole nightmare, and I just walked away, still owed a lot of money. So I got one of the biggest agents of all, Jack Rapke of CAA, and that was the beginning of the end of my virginity.

Do you regret taking that step?
I don't know if it's been a good or a bad thing. But I do know that, once you dip your toe in that water and have access to that kind of money, it's very hard to go back. You know you can get it and do the things you really want to do that are expensive. I may have spent too much time waiting to get my hands on their money, rather than just working in a smaller way and using European money. But the thinking has been that I can always get the European money, while you have to grab Hollywood finance when it's available to you. The truth is that all money for films comes and goes: there are certain moments when new companies are being formed, money has been gathered and that's the time to strike. Some people have struck brilliantly, like Bertolucci and Jeremy Thomas with CiBy 2000, when they got *Little Buddha* off the ground.[4] But I've always been bad at taking advantage of those situations. There's a side of me that's perverse enough not to want to go the obvious route, and then I always regret it.

Anyway, I explained to Jack Rapke that I only wanted to do my own scripts, except I wasn't actually producing anything. Then Scott Ruden, whom I'd known for ages, said he had a script he wanted to send me, but it wasn't quite right so he kept postponing. Finally this 'just right' script arrived and it turned out to be *The Addams Family*.[5] I couldn't see what we'd been waiting for – it was just a lot of gags with complicated special effects – and I certainly didn't want to do something like that after all the effects of *Munchausen*. But in the same package there was another script, *The Fisher King*, which Jack thought had some very interesting writing. I read *The Addams Family* at the kitchen table and decided it was crap, and was heading up to bed around 1 a.m. when I opened the other script and sat down and read it right through. The writing was absolutely wonderful; it was funny, with great characters, and seemed to come from the same mental state that I was in. I knew these people, but they were written more wittily than I could have done. So I told Jack I was interested and he arranged for the producers, Debra Hill and Lynda Obst, to fly over with Steve Randall, who was an executive at TriStar. We had dinner, I said I wanted to do it and off we went.

This was the *Enemy Mine* situation again. They wanted Robin Williams, so they had gone through the list of directors who had worked with him and eventually reached Gilliam. I was the bait to get Robin. I think Lynda and Debra also liked the idea of taming the wild beast: my reputation for being troublesome sends some running in the opposite direction, but others want to prove they can handle me. But the first thing I had to do was convince Robin to do it. I thought he was signed and sealed, but no, my job was to convince him and then start looking for the other actors.

It seemed a nice idea to do *Fisher King* because it broke all my rules: it wasn't my script, it was set in America, it was a studio film – everything I'd said I wouldn't do. But I'd tried doing things my way and got into a mess, so why not break my rules and see what happens? In a sense, everything I'd done had been reacting against America or trying to show America that there was another way of doing things. That's why I was doing optical effects down at Peerless, to demonstrate that you don't need Industrial Light and Magic. And I remember how angry I was after reading William Goldman's book *Adventures in the Screen Trade*, because he implied that there was no other way of making movies than in the Hollywood system – it was as if what the rest of us were doing didn't exist.[6] So this time I decided to do everything differently. This was the first time I didn't have final cut. It was head-in-the-lion's-mouth-let's-show-'em time. The point was to make sure I came in on budget and did all the right things: it was like putting together a new business card.

Did you do much work on the script, considering that this was what had hooked you in the first place?
When I read the script my fear was that someone like Rob Reiner would make it, and it would be very lightweight and flat, the way that New York films tend to be shot, like a Woody Allen film. But this is a fairytale, dealing with the mythology of the Fisher King and the Grail, and it should be done like a proper fairytale. So where Jack's apartment was just a loft somewhere in Lower Manhatten, I decided to turn it into a hi-tech tower. The one I liked was the Metropolitan Tower, which is like a

'If there's no magic, what's that?': the Grail legend's Red Knight errupts in New York.

Jack (Jeff Bridges) comforts Parry (Robin Williams): 'I was constantly afraid of making it sentimental.'

great razor-blade slicing the sky: there's a point where the edge cants backwards that I decided would be where Jack lives. Amazingly, that turned out to be Mike Ovitz's apartment and, since I'd just joined CAA, we got to recce it.[7] I wanted a very photogenic place, the kind you see in design magazines – beautiful and stylish, but with no soul, just hard-edged steel.

I started altering the script to make it more fairytale-like, giving each scene or setting a resonance that in some cases wasn't already there. So Perry has to live in a basement, below ground, because Jack has to die to be reborn. It's basic mythic stuff. I liked the idea of the city being a kingdom with a moat around it, in the form of the Hudson and East rivers. Then the video shop became the little peasants' hut in the forest, nestling at the base of these skyscraper towers, that looked to me like the trunks of giant trees. When the king leaves his castle and gets lost in the forest, he ends up there: it's all earthy and messy compared with the world he's left, full of life instead of design. Lydia is the princess imprisoned in the tower, so we had her working in a stone tower-like insurance building. In general, I tried to heighten this sense of the underlying myth.

I also pushed things harder and made Perry's nightmare more disturbing. The scene where he meets Jack – in front of what turns out to be a castle – and first sees the Red Knight, was very simple in the original script. Jack says, 'There's no magic, Perry,' and Perry replies, 'Well, if there's no magic, what's that?'– it's the Red Knight at the end of the road and he chases him. That's not what we have in the film, because for me the Red Knight had to represent all of Perry's nightmare, his great torment. So when Jack says, 'There's no magic, I know who you are,' he was trying to break through the illusion that Perry had created around himself. Perry starts to get really violent and ends up frothing at the mouth in the gutter, because his little shell has been pierced. Then the knight appears and Jack holds him to try to shake him out of his terrified fit; this is the first real human touch he's had since his slide into madness. So two things are happening simultaneously: Perry is being embraced for the first time, and Jack is making the first breakthrough in his own life by holding this smelly, awful creature that he's been trying to escape from. At this moment the Red Knight begins to recede, as Perry regains his confidence and chases him. That's how I changed the script: it was all there, but it needed those little pushes and shoves to bring it out.

The biggest change was the Grand Central Station scene. Jack is talking to the Tom Waits character – the Vietnam vet who's begging – and suddenly a black woman starts singing. People on their way to the trains hesitate for a moment and listen. That's what was written: 'They stopped in their rush' – Jack has a momentary epiphany – 'then they went on their way.' Other people do scenes like that better than me, but there it was in the script. So I went to Grand Central to hang out and get a feeling for the place again; I wanted to feel the rhythm of it as rush hour was developing and, as it got faster, I said, 'Wouldn't it be great if everybody, just as they passed each other, glanced over, fell in love and started waltzing?' I remember walking down the street afterwards, and the producers, Lynda and Debra, thought it was a fantastic idea and told me I had to do it.

My response was that I would do it in one of *my* films, but this was the writer Richard LaGravenese's film, which I was merely working on as a hired director, bringing his vision to the screen. I actually worked hard on that film trying to get the Gilliam out of it – and this is where the film and its making begin to merge, because the film is about becoming selfless and breaking down the ego. That's what I was trying to do, to take a good script that nobody else wanted and make it as a selfless act, without 'Terry Gilliam' intruding. Of course, I failed miserably, since my fingerprints are all over it, but it was an interesting approach. Before, it was always my ideas and therefore my ego; it's me trying to get me up there and say this is who I am, this is how I see the world; so there's a lot more defensiveness and tension. With this, I could say, 'It's all Richard's stuff, I'm just the hand that's writing.'

How did the explosive Mercedes Ruehl character, Anne, develop?
Well, Richard writes great women and Howard Feuer, the casting director, started gathering a few actresses, but as soon as Mercedes came in, that was the end of it. We began talking and she clearly knew all there was to know about the Fisher King myth; amongst everything else she is a very intelligent woman, and we had an instant rapport. The same happened with Amanda Plummer, who plays Lydia. Whoever played Anne had to be brassy and smart and down to earth. Mercedes's performance is very big and at times she's almost theatrical – yet she's supposed to be the earthiest, the most real, the most solid character, and it works.

I don't quite understand it, but I think my films allow people to play much bigger than they do in other films, yet still be believable. Maybe it's because the settings are so big that you can play it big and the balance works out. Within the context of *Fisher King*, she *is* the real thing, the earthy one, but if you put her in another film with that performance, she would just go bang – there wouldn't be room for anyone else in the film.

'Whoever played Anne had to be brassy and smart and down to earth':
Mercedes Ruehl in award-winning form.

Amanda Plummer as Lydia, a cuckoo settling into Anne's nest.

She does seem to represent a new kind of character in your films.
The problem is that I couldn't write that character, but once it's written
I understand it totally. They're the kind of people I would like to have
written, but I don't have the ability to get that on to paper.

*The other thing that's new is the sense of closeness between the charac-
ters – they touch, hug, kiss – which reminded me how little touching,
certainly of an affectionate kind, there is in your earlier films.*
That's part of what I was trying to do. I've often been accused of considering the sets more important than the actors – to put it bluntly, of
not being interested in the individual characters and actors – when in
fact I've always felt that the characters are what hold the films together.
It's true that most of my films have dealt with some kind of alienation,
or with a sense of not being able quite to come together, but this was
different – it was basically a nice, romantic comedy. In fact, it was such
a huggy, kissy, feel-good kind of film that I was constantly afraid of
making it sentimental – after all, it's very easy to slide over from world
domination to mawkish sentimentality: just look at Hitler.

*There did seem to be a danger of this in the scene where Jeff Bridges and
Robin Williams lie naked in Central Park watching the night sky.*
I know. It was a scene that I didn't think we would get away with. All
through the making of the film I was on edge, because I didn't want to
be sentimental and yet we were dealing with very sentimental material.

*There are film-makers who've spent their entire careers working with
material that walks the line between sentimentality and sentiment, or
emotion. I'm thinking of Sirk and Ophuls, for instance. Is it just that
this was unfamiliar territory for you as a director?*
One of the films I admire most, which I only discovered about three
years ago, is Ophuls's *Madame de . . .* [8] Someone told me it's one of
Kubrick's favourite films; and I swear that the beginning of *Schindler's
List*, when Liam Neeson's preparing to go out to the restaurant, is really
Madame de . . . I think it's just stunning at every level, even from the
dodgy old tape that a friend loaned me.

*So how did you set about countering the potential sentimentality of
Fisher King?*
One of the key things was to get someone as solid as Jeff Bridges,
because Robin can be mawkish and so over-the-top and silly that I was
quite likely to lose it with him, because I'm vulnerable to these things
too. I was meeting all sorts of actors – like Ron Silver – hunting for a
character; I wanted to meet Kevin Kline, but never did at that time. I

really wanted a young Jack Nicholson. In the end, I was travelling on a plane from LA to New York which was showing *The Fabulous Baker Boys*, and there was Jeff Bridges.[9] I couldn't wait to get off the plane and tell everyone that I'd found our man. We went back to the original list of actors we'd made, and all the names were in capital letters except one in lower case – right from the beginning the finger had been pointing at Jeff. So we got him, and what Jeff did was make sure that Robin and I didn't take off on flights of silliness.

'One of the key things was to get someone as solid as Jeff Bridges.'

Robin Williams as the traumatized Parry, who is anchored by Bridges' performance.

JACK WALKS INTO SHOT

Storyboards for the first film Gilliam didn't completely previsualize.

He always pulled it back and anchored Robin, which worked a treat. Jeff is a very slow, meticulous actor, and during the two weeks of rehearsals I thought we'd made a big mistake, because nothing was coming out. Then, on the penultimate day of rehearsal, there was a scene where he kisses Mercedes and takes her upstairs to her apartment. We were just going through it and suddenly, as the two of them embraced, I realized that was it – this is what we pay money for, to see people like that kissing each other on the screen; we don't want them looking like us, we want them to be gods and goddesses. Jeff was suddenly the character and everything fell into place.

Your previous experience of stars had mostly been with cameo appearances and always in Europe. Did you feel nervous working with Hollywood stars on their home ground?
Actors have always liked working with me and I know I can work well with them, yet I never seem to be credited with being an actors' director. So here was a chance to throw away all the special effects and just concentrate on four performances, which was easy compared with what I'd been doing in the past. In fact, it was the easiest thing I've ever done; I just floated through it. Maybe I'm stupid and I ought to keep making those kinds of films; certainly my life would be more enjoyable, but I'm

drawn to more difficult, complex things. At least I should try to alter-nate between the weird ones and the sweet ones.

The other thing about *Fisher King* was that, for the first time, I didn't use storyboards. In the past I'd always worked out everything in advance; this time I wanted the actors to lead, to be pushing the film forward, so I decided not to storyboard. We'd done rehearsals and got ideas from them, then we went on set and worked things out. Take the scene where Jeff and Mercedes have their big break-up after Robin has been stabbed. I knew where I was going to start this shot, but when we went through it on the set I changed everything I'd planned because I was taking my cue from what the actors were doing. So I placed the camera on a dolly and danced around them. It's one of the scenes that I'm most happy with from a directorial point of view, because I did the right thing: I put the camera in the right place and gave the actors the space to do what they needed to do without me getting in the way with the camera. We all did a perfect dance and the shot runs four and a half minutes before the first cut. I shot some coverage on it, just for insur-ance, and when we first cut it, using the coverage in the normal way, it didn't have the power.[10] But by holding on that shot for four and a half minutes, with the camera moving and the characters moving, you're just there, suspended, and the first cut really kicks.

I was watching *Strangelove* the other night, and Kubrick does these really long takes in wide shot, where you just hang in the air because what the actors are doing needs no punctuation.[11] Cutting has its own uses, but it can so easily break the tension. I hadn't worked like that before, trying only to be sensitive to these characters rather than fol-lowing some preconceived idea in my own head.

How had you originally planned to do the scene?
I was going to begin with Mercedes coming out and finding Jeff. But, instead, I started on Jeff sitting with his feet up, and that shot worked perfectly because I knew it was coming right after Robin being attacked. What better than to see a guy laughing on the phone immediately after someone else's brutal beating? The first time we cut it together, it really hurt: you think this guy's a total asshole. Yet Jeff's a likeable character, so no matter how much of an asshole he is we never lose the audience, which is important. You never quite know how far you can go before you alienate them, but I knew my chances were pretty good with Jeff.

The exteriors look like New York, but where was the film shot?
It was shot half in New York and half in LA. We did five weeks in New York, then moved to LA for financial reasons. The worst thing for me

was having two different crews. New York crews are spiky and tough, but the biggest shock was discovering that I had a reputation. They all approached me with far too much respect. As I've said, I only know how to work in a reactive, collaborative way, so it took three weeks before the New York crew was relaxed enough for a dialogue – you get the impression that American directors must all be fascist dictators.

Did they not see you as a foreign director?
Yes, at first, until I spoke and they knew they were stuck with an American. But they'd seen the films, *Time Bandits*, *Brazil* and *Munchausen*, with each one getting bigger and more elaborate, and they assumed that here was a true *auteur* who worked out every detail in advance. English crews are much bolshier and don't treat directors with the same respect as Americans do. They always question whether or why you want to do something, which would often make me come up with a decent justification. In the end, we had a great time shooting *Fisher King*, except for having to break in a new crew in LA. Most of the interiors were done in LA, apart from Grand Central Station and the Chinese restaurant. We had one night to do each of those.

How tight was the budget?
It was $24 million, but shooting in New York with big stars isn't cheap, so it felt as if we were making a low-budget movie. We also had some major challenges, like turning Madison Avenue traffic round so it travelled north–south. We had to close down about four blocks for the scene in front of the castle. The castle was supposed to be opposite Central Park on Fifth Avenue, where the traffic flows north–south. So we had this potential tidal wave of traffic just two blocks away, beeping furiously while we were doing our shot. What also happens in New York when people are pissed off with you is that they call the Fire Department. You've set up an elaborate tracking shot and are ready to shoot, when suddenly there's a siren and the fire trucks have to go just where you've laid the tracks. That's a little New York joke.

The interior we had to shoot at the last minute was the Chinese restaurant, which was planned for LA and so was the one scene we had never rehearsed. It was the single bit of weather cover for the entire New York shoot – a ridiculous gamble the studio was willing to take, but which I would get the blame for if things had gone wrong. We were shooting in the park when it started raining. I decided we'd better head for the Chinese restaurant, but there was no set, apart from the elaborate back wall. So we had to go in and dress the whole thing, fit banquettes, and by 1 a.m. we were ready to think about starting to shoot.

We had none of the proper gear with us, apart from a camera dolly, so I decided that we would track in to start, then lock off the camera and do take after take until we had enough material. Basically, it was all ad-libbed and there was no real coverage, apart from a tighter shot of Mercedes and Jeff. Then Roger Pratt noticed the reflection on the tables and, since I didn't know how we were going to get out of the scene, I decided we'd pull the camera back across them. We didn't have a crane, so we had to build a structure on the dolly out of two-by-four beams and then hang the camera from it, just like in the early days of cinema. This was all nailed together and, as we pulled back, the whole crew worked at sliding the tables back in. The reflections made a great shot and it was a wonderful evening, because everything was faked or improvised. Later, in editing, we did those wipes which are totally stylized but work terrifically. It was a test of our skills, and we came out with a scene which is many people's favourite. For me, this was exciting film-making.

How difficult was it filming in Grand Central Station for just one night after you'd adopted the waltz idea?
We started to bring our stuff in at around 9 p.m. and at 11 we had the run of the place after the last train. We had 1,000 extras who were supposed to come from dance schools, on a special dispensation from the Extras Guild. So, by 11 p.m., we had six or seven choreographers on hand and a sound system all set up. Then we made two discoveries. The first was that most people couldn't dance the waltz, so we had to turn Grand Central into a gigantic dance school. And the second was that the acoustics were so bad that nobody could hear the beat of the Strauss waltzes we were playing, so the head choreographer had to get on a ladder with a bull horn and shout, 'One two three, one two three.'

I needed a top shot, but 1,000 people in Grand Central Station looks like nothing, so the AD was going crazy trying to organize all these extras to cover enough of the floor. By now it was about 3 a.m., we still hadn't shot anything major and we had to be out by 5. Joe Napolitano, the AD, was going crazier and crazier. First assistants tend to love handling big scenes because this is their moment, but then they become obsessed when things aren't quite right and it looks as if we're never going to turn over. This is when the director has to say, 'That's it, Joe, time's up, we shoot no matter how awful it is.' So we did, but nothing quite worked properly. We got a top shot that was vaguely acceptable and then we got on the floor with only an hour and a half to shoot all the walking through and waltzing.[12]

I had five cameras and we slammed them in all over the place and things went quickly. Then 5.30 came, the trains started to arrive and we were supposed to be out, although we just retreated from the main floor to the edge. In the last shot of Robin – when he's looking for Lydia – those are real commuters plus the crew, and trains were arriving non-stop. It was now 7 a.m. and the PR people at Grand Central were trying to get us out, but I told Robin to stay in there and look lost as we kept pushing the crew through the shot, and so we got it. Sometimes those shots are best when they're done in a panic, so the actor doesn't have a chance to start acting. It's just, 'Go in, look left, look right, keep going, bump, knock him over, keep going.' In actual fact, we had to go back a couple of nights later and pick up a little piece at the very end of the waltz.

I heard that Barbra Streisand was there for several days to do basically one walk-through shot for *Prince of Tides*, which was nothing on the screen. But we'd done this huge sequence, with a great Musco light, which is rather like stadium lighting, and which had to be moved in the course of the night from one side of the station to the other. Quite often in my films there's a huge idea that really needs longer to do it properly, but we do it anyway and, even though it isn't perfect, it ends up having great life and vitality. It never becomes the great classic 'clunk' where everything is perfect; instead, it relies on a lot of things to make it happen, and I love those moments, with their sheer panic. The crew hate me because they're not given enough time to do everything right, but afterwards they're proud to have done it and for the next week they're strutting around feeling like kings. Also, they're not blamed for the bits that didn't work, which is important, since so much of film crew's time is spent worrying about getting blamed and covering their asses accordingly. That's why films cost so much money, but if you can somehow convey that they're not going to be blamed if something doesn't work – that you know how impossible and unfair it is – then they feel much better about it.

What happened when you moved to LA?
We kept some key people: the camera operator and heads of departments. Our prop master quit while we were in New York because he hadn't been allowed to come with us to New York – instead he was forced to stay in LA, setting things up there. So we had to start with new prop guys, who were desperately trying to hold things together, and they managed to do it. We built some interiors in LA. Others, like the mental hospital, which was in an old walnut storage place – a nut house! – were locations. One of the interesting problems in LA was getting the extras

to impersonate New Yorkers' behaviour. LA people are polite when they come out of a lift and their body rhythms are totally different, so we had to badger them to push and shove. Fortunately, my AD was a New Yorker and could spot the difference immediately.

In fact, the assistant directors had a hard time, and this has happened so often that I realize the common denominator of these problems is the director – me! They're all guys who are loyal to me but feel the production is fatally compromised, and they become so determined to save the film that they end up sacrificing themselves. Joe Napolitano did that on *Fisher King*: he was so enraged by the production not giving us what we wanted and needed, and not enough time in New York, that by the time we started shooting he was a madman and he lost control of the crew, which the first AD can't afford to do, because he was taking his frustrations out on them. So he quit in New York, and Tony Scott recommended a new AD, David McGifford, who proved excellent. He found himself in an odd position: he had responsibility for the schedule but he hadn't actually put it together – so he didn't have to prove he was right. This meant responsibility began to float a little, which can sometimes be useful. At any rate, we did eventually manage to get back on schedule and on budget, which is what it was about for me on this film, but it still ended with a silly episode when the studio came in.

In reality, the producers had been holding back certain information from the studio, because we were actually over schedule and were projected to be over budget. This came out with just two weeks to go. It's an old Hollywood trick and a rather dangerous one. We had a meeting with the production people from the studio and they all looked at me, but I had to tell them it wasn't my fault on this one. I hadn't concealed any information. What we needed were five more days, but the studio said we had to find a compromise, so they gave us four days. I thought this was stupid: we just couldn't do it all in four, but we did – although ultimately it cost them six days, because we just kept shooting through the final day and night to get everything done.

We were doing a foreground miniature, looking down the stairway in the castle, and Roger Pratt and I were up in the lighting grid of the studio, which we'd had to alter structurally. The wrap party was going on downstairs, with executives from the studio and everybody coming in for drinks. But it wasn't over, folks! I think we quit at dawn on Friday morning – I know the sun was up when we finally came out at 6 or 7 a.m. The studio were able to claim that we finished on Thursday, but with the overtime it would have cost them less if they'd given us five days. The dangerous side of these games is that you're driven to lie: you say you need seven days, knowing they'll give you five. I've never done that, but they still think it's a bargaining thing. We actually went over two or three days on the shoot, which was nothing, then we managed to claw back the overages in post-production. So we came out on budget in the end.

To give some idea of how stupid and unfair Hollywood can be, everybody hides behind the word 'precedent', and this affected what they wanted to pay Roger Pratt to shoot *Fisher King*. The previous film he'd done was *Batman* and you'd have thought that would have given him some standing. But at that point he didn't have an agent, and if you look at the posters for *Batman* you won't see any mention of the director of photography, because it wasn't in his contract. Roger got a ridiculously low rate on *Batman*, about a third of the going rate for someone as good as him, and I wanted to pay him the amount we actually had in the budget for DP. But Gary Martin, the production chief, objected because this would have doubled Roger's last rate – a dangerous precedent. We had a huge fight and in the end I won by stamping and screaming and shouting: if Roger doesn't do it, I won't do it. The key to being a good director is knowing when to flounce out. So we got Roger paid properly, and Gary Martin – whom I disliked at the beginning though eventually I grew to like – thought I was terrific. I was desperate to show Hollywood that I was a responsible film-maker and that I'd always stuck to budgets, despite what they'd heard.

Did they finally believe you?
Everyone in Hollywood talks to everyone else and, when I came to do *Twelve Monkeys*, the people at Universal checked with Gary Martin, who gave me top marks. But I was still on the black books of the completion guarantors, not only Film Finances but also Lloyds of London. We had a film guarantor on *Twelve Monkeys*, and during negotiations they said that *Fisher King* didn't count, because it was a studio film and had no completion guarantor. I had to do *Twelve Monkeys* on budget to get that black mark finally off the books – it's taken me that long to clear my name. Mind you, their attitude towards studio films is justifiable because the budgets are fudged all the time. They have these 'adjusted' budgets, so that even if the film ends up on budget, it's nowhere near the figure they started with. Whereas if you're doing an independent film, it's a fixed thing: you go to the bank, get the money, and that's all you have.

This was your first film set in what's more or less the contemporary urban world. How did you go about the design of it?

The funny thing is that I didn't want it 'designed'. I was trying very hard not to let the design dominate the film. I got Mel Bourne, a New York designer who's worked with Woody Allen and is a wonderful, cranky old guy.[13] But the problem is that designers like designing and my job here was to hold back from too much design so that it didn't overpower the film. I think that the design is really down to the medieval fairytale approach that I had in my head; everything we chose supported that.

But the castle was something you had to create?
We were looking for a regular town house – which is what it was in the script – and were in fact on our way to one where Woody Allen was shooting, when I got out of the van and suddenly saw this castle on Madison Avenue. It was an old armoury, one of a whole series built around the turn of the century. Now it's just a façade with a school behind it. Roger said, 'Look, we've got the castle.' But my immediate response was that we couldn't use it, because it's what people would expect me to do. It took a month for me to be convinced, with Roger lobbying heavily for it. He would say, 'Come on Terry, it's what you want to do'; but I didn't want to do what I wanted to do – how perverse, trying to run away from all the things you really like. The castle seemed so much on the nose, unlike more abstract representations like the sterile castle Jack lives in: the idea that we get there and it really *is* a castle seemed almost too obvious a leap, yet I'm really glad we used it because it does the job.

We didn't invent things for this film; we just chose from what was already there and made a patchwork out of that. The most satisfying moment was when I saw the film in New York with New Yorkers. It was as if the scales had been lifted from their eyes. They came out enthusing about what a wonderful city they lived in, how magical it was, with all these details and places they hadn't noticed before. For me, that's exactly the point of making the film – to lift the scales. I still meet New Yorkers who ask me if there really is a castle in the city.

The location we chose for the homeless bums was an actual cardboard city under the Manhattan Bridge. It already looked fantastic, like Piranesi.[14] I loved the idea of cardboard boxes beneath this vast stone and steel structure, vermin clustered around the foundations of the empire, and we got to know a lot of the guys who lived there. Most of them were Vietnam vets, who couldn't reassimilate into society after the war. They had TV sets hooked up to the streetlights; there was a latrine – which was foul – and a barbecue, and they were protected from the elements to a degree by the bridge. Most of the guys were black, but

Cardboard city under the Manhattan Bridge: 'It looked fantastic, like Piranesi.'

there was one, known as Crocodile Dundee, who was white and gap-toothed; and there was Larry, the leader, who, if he'd chosen to, could have been running a major corporation. He was really organized and sharp, and his line was, 'We're homeless but we're not helpless. This is a drug-free zone. Whatever you guys want, we're here to co-operate.'

So we set them to work to sort the place out and look after things. They were also to guard against the Auto Gobbler, a guy from New Jersey who came over and took cars to cannibalize from where the police dumped them under the FDR Highway. We wanted to keep enough cars there for the scene where the punks start to beat up Jeff, so we sent Crocodile and those guys down to make sure the Auto Gobbler didn't take them away. Then, a week before we were due to shoot under the bridge, we arrived to discover that everything had been razed. The guys had got fed up with Larry trying to organize them, they had a big fight with him, and he came back later and torched the whole place. So we had to provide new cardboard and plywood and help them rebuild their hovels.

There's an obvious irony in this. Did you feel bad about trading on the picturesqueness of their misery?
It was madness. Being dutiful, socially conscious people, we hired a lot of homeless people as extras, but this didn't work out either. You would

have thought being part of a film was exciting, but they just fell asleep on us, or they would wander off and not be there when we needed them. In the end, we had to hire extras to be homeless people. There are no simple stories about the homeless and you can't just give them money and responsibility and expect them to cope. It's more complex, but at least we tried and in the process I learned a lot.

What about the overall shooting style of the film? Although you were working with Roger Pratt again, after the Rotunno interlude, Fisher King *looks totally different from* Brazil.
I don't know how much this shows in the end, but I decided on the first day of filming that we'd shoot it like a Sergio Leone western. I don't know why – it just came to me. I think all directors get bored and we do something like one of our heroes would have done, to persuade ourselves that we're making serious films. Sometimes it works, but other times it doesn't and you get a pointless shot like that one in *GoodFellas* where Scorsese does a track-zoom on Bobby De Niro and Ray Liotta in the diner.[15] I don't know what he thought he was doing in that shot, but the camera wasn't making that moment stronger; it was a total mannerism.

I don't agree. I think every scene in that film has its own distinctive camera pattern, and that they're related either to the narrator's memory of an event, or to revealing what's going on beneath the surface, taking us into the characters' minds.
Well, he may have a justification for it, but that one didn't work for me at all. What's interesting about these choices we deliberately make is that they provide an excuse for doing what we do. We can say we did it for intellectual or academic reasons, but whether or not it *works* is something totally different. You walk into some scenes not knowing how to deal with them, and you take a pattern off the wall that works somewhere in your memory of films; you use it, and sometimes it's correct and other times it's not. I like it especially when we're really wrong and yet it works – those are the moments when you learn something. In fact, it's often difficult to remember why you were doing something in the way that you did it at the time, even though you usually have a reason for it. There's another shot in *GoodFellas* I remember talking to Marty about, which is when Ray Liotta comes to see his girlfriend and there are drugs in the room. He does it all in one shot and basically he's doing that to keep it interesting. He obviously had very little time and couldn't do coverage, so you wiggle the camera about. He wiggled it very nicely, and it kept the scene alive.

By this time you're so close up to the film, it's hard to keep the whole design in your mind.

Apparently, David Lean would talk through and tape his thoughts on the whole script before he started shooting, because when you're shooting you often forget the point of scenes. So he would click on the tape and be able to check what the scene was meant to be about. Time and again, you're in the middle of shooting and you realize it's all wrong. There was one scene I actually reshot in *Fisher King* – it's where Jeff is being beaten up by the punks and Robin rescues him – which I'd got wrong because I was shooting it from two points of view. Normally, there's the main character and I identify with that character, but this had two main characters and, as I got into the scene, I was shooting from both viewpoints. But it has to be from Jeff's point of view, so I went back and got some shots to accentuate that. In reality, it was an evening lost: I kept shooting and, from the outside, it looked as if I knew what I was doing, but I didn't because I was caught in the dilemma of trying to be both characters at once.

This is one of the main issues in directing, isn't it, getting the emotional geometry right?

It's really the key to it, and in *Fisher King* there were just four characters that I had to deal with, each in the right way. There's one scene I really enjoy, which is when Amanda comes into Mercedes's apartment for the first time. Both of them are stage actors, so it was really interesting to see how they worked at the first walk-through. Amanda comes in and starts wandering round the room, invading, touching, taking up a lot of space. Mercedes just stood still by the door, with her back to it: rigid, wary, trying to judge this cuckoo that seems to be settling into her nest. It was absolutely right for the characters. So that's how I filmed it, in just one wide shot, watching the two perform. As I said before, this was me learning to direct in a different way, where I watch the actors and, when I see them do all the right things, try not to interfere. You see so many films now where the camera is doing all the work, because the characters don't exist.

Where did you edit?

We edited here in Britain, which was part of my deal, and it was edited by Lesley Walker. Lesley is the Thelma Schoonmaker of England; I particularly wanted a woman editor, because I wanted a more emotional touch to the film. This was partly to control me, to keep me from going down paths that I'd been down in the past. But I also needed her to support the sides of me that I wanted to reveal in this film. And that's what

Lesley did. She's got a wonderful sense of character, and she developed an incredibly strong emotional side to the telling of the tale, so I was able to avoid the need to be 'clever'. I don't know if other directors are like this, but I have a lot of facets and I choose people who will support, or help bring out, those facets that I want to show in a given project. I'm very aware of this when I'm setting something up.

With Fisher King *was there the usual problem with your work when it came to marketing, of it not fitting into a well-defined genre? I suppose it could be described as a 'therapeutic myth', but that's not very catchy.* Maybe it's right, though. I didn't do any study of mental illness, but Robin's character awaking from his catatonia after Jeff brings him the 'Grail' was something I wanted to believe in. I felt it was right, although I had no basis for this other than my instinct. Then I heard that Dave Crosby, of Crosby, Stills and Nash, contacted Richard LaGravenese after the film came out and said that he'd been through the same experience as Robin's character. His wife had been in a fatal car accident and he never got to say goodbye: for ten years he lived in a state of booze and drugs, unable to come to terms with her death and his sense of guilt. When he saw the film, he broke down sobbing and it just flushed him out; it worked as a total catharsis and he says he's clean now. Another person working on the film had a similar experience. I remember some reviews accusing us of sentimentality and lightweight Hollywood crap, but these were two real cases, which suggested we'd been truthful on some level.

The other thing that was intriguing was the endings. The studio would have been happy to end when they're doing a little singalong in the mental hospital, where Jeff's hair is down and he's the most beautiful-looking guy on the planet. Fair enough, but I'd promised Mercedes that he would come back, that they would have that moment, although I added her hitting him and the two of them embracing in a cascade of porno videos. Then there was the ending of the two guys in the park, and this seemed to be just too much. I was convinced we would never end the film with the two of them naked on the grass in Central Park. We were giggling as we shot that, thinking it was ridiculous and pathetic. It would never be used. When I saw the first assembly, I was completely won over and I'm happy to be proved wrong. Just for fun, we added a fourth ending, with fireworks and a big Hollywood musical finale. There are those who criticize us for this, these multiple endings, but I know they work for me. End of conversation.

The critics took us to task for dealing with 'serious social issues' in a not serious-issue kind of way, as if you're only supposed to deal with homelessness and mental illness solemnly and earnestly. But this was never the intention of the film. We were making a modern fairytale, with contemporary warts.

And how did Fisher King *fare at the box office?*
Exceedingly well. It was the second most profitable film of that year for Tristar, after *Hook*. We made them more money than *Bugsy*, which took slightly more at the box office, but cost twice as much to make. We also got nominated for a lot of awards. When Mercedes won the Academy Award, I sent her a fax, rather than the usual flowers, saying, 'It's all downhill from now on, your career is finished,' and that's been rather prophetic. I hate awards, because they're not about excellence; all they can do is draw attention to your film. But I'm glad Robin got a Golden Globe, and I think Richard won the LA critics' award, so he became a hot writer. But what was frustrating was that the film should have taken more money. We were number one for almost five weeks and we were running away from the competition – but nobody was going to the movies because of two things: the World Series and the Judge Thomas Supreme Court hearings.[16] That's show business.

NOTES

1 Children's illustrator and writer Raymond Briggs's *The Snowman* had already been a huge success as an animated film for Channel 4 in 1982. His *Fungus the Bogeyman*, a kind of underground comic book for kids about a loveably disgusting monster, appeared in 1990.

2 Independent producer Joel Silver (b. 1952) is best known for the *Lethal Weapon* and *Die Hard* series of action movies, but has also produced such comic-strip subjects as *Tales from the Crypt* (TV series, 1989) and *Hudson Hawk* (1991).

3 Creative Artists Agency, reputedly the most powerful agency representing actors and directors in Hollywood, was founded in 1975.

4 CiBy 2000 (intended to sound like 'C. B. DeMille' in French) was launched in 1992 and enjoyed a string of critical, and occasionally commercial, successes with films such as *The Piano* and *Secrets and Lies*.

5 *The Addams Family* was directed by Barry Sonenfeld in 1991.

6 Goldman's *Adventures in the Screen Trade* (1983) offers a cynical but widely accepted view of Hollywood screenwriting.

7 Ovitz had co-founded and was head of CAA at this time.

8 *Madame de . . .* (*The Earrings of Madame de . . .* , 1953) was the penultimate film, and one of the most profoundly elegant, directed by Max Ophuls.

9 *The Fabulous Baker Boys* (1989), written and directed by Steve Kloves, starred Jeff Bridges and his brother Beau Bridges, with Michele Pfeiffer.

10 'Coverage' means shooting a scene from different angles, so that it can be edited in a variety of ways.

11 *Dr Strangelove: or, How I Learned to Stop Worrying and Love the Bomb* (1963), directed by Stanley Kubrick.

12 The overhead shot was later optically doubled to increase the number of waltzers.

13 Mel Bourne worked for Allen from *Annie Hall* (1977) to *Broadway Danny Rose* (1984), and was production designer on Michael Mann's early features *Thief* (1981) and *Manhunter* (1986); and immediately before *Fisher King* had designed *Fatal Attraction* (1987) and *Reversal of Fortune* (1990).

14 Giovanni Battista Piranesi's etchings of 'Imaginary Prisons' (1745) create a gloomy, labyrinthine underworld.

15 De Niro and Liotta are in profile sitting on opposite sides of a diner table and the camera zooms at the same time as it tracks, so that the depth of the image 'flattens' as we watch.

16 In October 1991, public attention was focused on Senate hearings in connection with charges of sexual harassment brought against the Supreme Court nominee Judge Clarence Thomas.

9

The Defective Detective *in development hell;*
A Tale of Two Cities *untold;* Twelve Monkeys *unleashed;*
early cinema as *The Last Machine*
and the art of *Spellbound*

You had hoped that bringing The Fisher King *in on budget would open the doors of Hollywood. What happened next?*
You would have thought that when Richard LaGravenese and I went with our next project to Tristar they'd say, 'Come on, boys, what do you want to do?' We brought them a Philip K. Dick story – not to make, just to develop and write – and they wouldn't do it.[1] We came up with the idea for *The Defective Detective*, which was turned down, and I started going crazy. What are the rules of this town? I keep thinking it's about money, box-office and critical success and all of those things, but even when we achieved them we still weren't given *carte blanche*. We weren't even looking for a major *carte blanche* – just let's go and develop the next project. I couldn't deal with the fact that Hollywood is so irrational, so unpragmatic – which is what they perceive me to be by their standards. I had shown I wasn't out of control; we made a successful film; *now* can we do another thing that interests us? *No*, that didn't seem to be possible. They didn't quite understand the new projects.

There are these Hollywood axioms that are always quoted: science fiction doesn't work; westerns aren't popular. Then along comes a film in one of these genres which is successful, but the axiom still holds; these are the exceptions that prove the rule.
Yes, it's always the same. I keep thinking I'm beginning to understand the place and can play on their terms. The exercise I committed to was to get Hollywood money for my kind of films, which may seem crazy, but it's necessary for the size of some of them. The first project wasn't even expensive. Dick has always been one of my favourite writers and I thought nobody has yet done one of his books properly, with the right sensibility, which I know I have. But, no. Nothing.

Then I was offered a lot of their projects. I became a victim of success.

Having a Hollywood agent, and having done a film that I didn't write, opened the floodgates to other scripts and they started pouring in. Some were interesting and I started getting distracted. I got involved in a project called *Loony Tunes*, which was about a guy who turns into a cartoon. It was a funny idea, because the hero was a smooth, cool but rather shallow character in real life, who became literally two-dimensional and developed all these gross cartoon attributes. When he saw a woman, his jaw would drop and his tongue would roll out, which was funny, but I was obsessed with trying to give it more weight. It had to be about more than just cheap tricks. We never quite solved that problem. Eventually, *The Mask* did much of what this was about.[2]

I have this repeating pattern: I get involved with a studio project and start taking it down a different path, making it darker or more intelligent or more about something; and since it always tends to be expensive, they don't want it. If it's going to be expensive, it's got to be mindless; and if it's going to be thought-provoking, it's got to be cheap. I keep getting caught in this trap of being neither fish nor fowl in their terms. They get nervous because they don't know what box to put my projects in.

How did your long-term pet project, The Defective Detective, *start?*
I don't remember the exact order of things but, at some point soon after *Fisher King*, it became the project I wanted to do. I had decided I've got to do something of my own. My ego is so desperate for attention that it's not enough to do someone else's script and make a good film from it. This ego, an ugly little thing, has to show it's got a few ideas that are totally its own, and they've got to be shown to be good and earth-shattering and world-changing. So I went through all my old notebooks from the period of *Time Bandits* and *Brazil* and started to put in order the ideas that had been accumulating over the years. How can I bring order to this chaos? This became the battle. Everything I write is autobiographical, in the sense that it's what I'm feeling at the moment, and I was feeling old and depressed; I could see nothing good in the world, just billions of people producing mountains of shit, with everything good dying. Suddenly, the idea took the shape of a middle-aged New York cop effectively having a nervous breakdown and being transported back into a kid's fantasy world where the rules are a child's rules, and he has to try to deal with this.

So I got Richard on board and we went round trying to flog this thing. But we got nowhere. Where would a middle-aged cop, a nervous breakdown, and a child's fantasy world fit in? Then Scott Ruden said, 'Come over to Paramount where Brandon Tartikoff is running the show, and I'm not going to allow him to let you leave the room until he says yes.' So we went to Paramount and he said yes. Bingo, we had a project. Then Brandon Tartikoff went the way of all executive flesh and Sherry Lansing came in. So now Richard and I have a script, but there's a new boss in place who is completely confused by the idea and doesn't get it at all.

It's the first time I've ever been involved in development hell – I had to wait until I was fifty-two years old, and have had a whole career as a film-maker before I get into what people experience at the start of their careers. The worst thing about development hell is that nobody says no: you're living on hope the whole time. You want to do it and they string you along. This went on for two or three years, and I thought I was strong enough to resist altering the script to appease the powers-that-be just to get it made. We worked away at it, but I didn't get on with Scott, who was trying to interfere creatively. He wanted to feel involved and I wasn't interested in that. His job was just to get us the money – end of story. We thought we'd got it to the point where it could be made; we had Nick Nolte and Danny De Vito lined up, we'd got the budget down, we had meetings and it seemed to be *yes* – then nothing. Once again, I found myself in the middle of the sale of a studio. Viacom were trying to buy Paramount and all their energies were being focused on that.

So I got totally disillusioned with that project and put it to one side. Strangely enough, I looked at it again after *Twelve Monkeys* and when I read what we'd done I realized it really wasn't good. It had been terribly affected by trying to deal with all those changes, thinking we weren't appeasing anybody, but in fact sliding in the wrong direction. Then, over Christmas 1996, I took an early version of the script from way down the pile, read it and discovered that it was fantastic. We were only a few steps away from a really good script, but we'd spent months in the wrong place; and it was disturbing to discover how influenced I'd been when I thought I wasn't influenceable.

This wasn't a process you'd ever been through before.
I'd always had an extraordinary amount of freedom on my other films. As an independent production, you'd have an idea, put the thing together and go and hunt for the money. This was the opposite way round. You're involved in dealing with the Hollywood executives from the start; and even though they don't want to make it, they also don't want to let it go in case someone else makes it, and it's successful. But if you're independent, there's always someone in town who's on your wavelength that day, and you get it done. With a studio, you realize that,

'The first time I've ever been involved in development hell – I had to wait until I was fifty-two.'

by altering it to get it through the system, you're destroying the very thing you set out to make. It nearly happened with *Fisher King*. Before I got involved it was at Disney. They felt it was a caper movie. So Richard LaGravenese – whose idea it had been – was writing scenes where Jack is stealing the Grail wearing roller-skates. Everyone is doing what seems best to get the film made, but they're destroying it in the process. And I was going through beginner's development hell during my mid-life crisis.

There were other projects during the early nineties. You were widely rumoured to be working on Don Quixote.
That's right – more classics illustrated, and by Doré again, no less.[3] I wrote the script with Charles McKeown and we were talking about it with Ciby 2000.

I remember you were also very close to starting A Tale of Two Cities *when I got you involved with* The Last Machine *in 1994.*

A Tale of Two Cities was a project with a script all ready to go. It's interesting that all three projects – *Tale of Two Cities*, *Defective Detective* and *Twelve Monkeys* – end with the hero committing suicide or sacrificing himself: I felt like a magnet for these stories. Anyway, Don Macpherson, a local boy, had written a wonderful script. It was like '*Gone With the Wind* by Charles Dickens'; it had great sweeping, cinematic, romantic, tragic elements, and I thought it was fantastic. Paula Weinstein, the producer, had been working on it for about two years, moulding it for Mel Gibson, and the only piece of the jigsaw not in place was the director. For whatever reason, I was the chosen one that day; I met Mel and we got on well. So Paula and Don and I started looking at how we were going to put it together.

One useful financial factor was that Roy Button, who was running Warner Bros in Britain and had briefly been a second assistant director on *Munchausen*, was trying to build a composite standing period set at Pinewood. The idea was to amortize the cost of it over several productions, because there was talk of other period films, and I thought it was a great idea because this country desperately needs a standing set.[4] So we were talking along these lines while waiting for Mel, who was finishing *Maverick* and couldn't make up his mind. The months started ticking past and you begin to realize you're in the hands of someone who has a lot of offers and doesn't know what he wants to do. In the end, it came down to us or *Braveheart*, and he decided he wanted to direct again, but several months had elapsed during which we were twiddling our thumbs. Once I'm committed to something and thinking about it, I find it very hard to do two things at once – I just commit myself and then go crazy waiting.

At this point, they would probably have done the film for $60 million with Mel Gibson, no problem; but without Mel we had to start scrabbling around for other actors. I went through a lot of people and finally settled on Liam Neeson, who had just been nominated for an Academy Award for *Schindler's List* and was therefore hot. Paula and I attacked the budget and somehow reduced it to about $31 million, having thrown in our own money and done everything we could to get it down while preserving the same production values as the Mel Gibson version. Then we went to meetings with the studio and they told us how much they respected us for getting the price down; however, they would only make the film with Liam Neeson for a budget of $26 million. So it's Mel at $60 million or Liam at $26 million – but the same film, same everything. There's a price tag on all of us. A bad joke.

That's when I got mad and decided there was no point in dealing with these people. It's their project, they want the same production values, but they won't give us a realistic budget. They took the view that Liam was fine in a Holocaust movie, backed up by 6 million dead Jews, but was he a true star? I tried to stay with the project and was given some new names that they would accept: one was Tom Cruise, another was Brad Pitt and then there was Matthew McConaughey. What's interesting about this is that you've got Tom, the big star, and whatever he's in is guaranteed; then Brad, who is the heir apparent, but hasn't totally proved himself yet; and finally the new boy, who they think is going to be the equivalent of one of those two and they're willing to gamble on him because at this point they can get him at a bargain-basement price. I think Johnny Depp is a far more interesting actor, but they wouldn't consider him because he'd made far too many films that were non-commercial.[5]

You did a commercial around that time for Nike. How did this come about?
Michael Kamen's brother runs a commercials house in New York. He's a very nice guy and there was a pile of money to come over and do it. It was a funny ad, easy to do, and I thought, 'Why not?' But it put me off doing commercials again, as they always do. I think what's so disgusting about them is that they're so easy. I actually feel corrupted because it's taking the money and doing rather minor work, although everybody does it. Even Scorsese has done Armani ads.[6] I have a funny feeling about commercials. It's some kind of puritanism that's floating around in the back of my head, because I worry about what they do to us and yet they're actually an art form in themselves. They shouldn't all be denigrated, because there are great commercials and I think the Brits have done some of the best ones. The most interesting are usually terrible at the job they're supposed to do – i.e. selling the product. I never know what the product is, I just know I've seen an amazing bit of imagery.

Do you think feature films involve a different attitude and skills?
Yes, they're very different: are you telling a story in thirty seconds or in two hours? For me, it's not so difficult because it's like doing a cartoon or a *Python* sketch: ads are short, succinct things that are easy to do. But I don't get any pleasure out of them – they're not worth the time, just the money.

You use the computer a lot for graphics as well as writing. What part did you play in the Python *CD-ROM* Monty Python's Complete Waste of Time?
I didn't spend a lot of time on it, although I sort of initiated the whole

thing. I met this guy Bob Ezrin, who's a man of many parts – he's a musician and he produces the Pink Floyd albums – and he was setting up a company to make interactive CD-ROMs. I was intrigued by them because I felt this could become a different way to tell tales. With CD-ROMs, stories don't have to be linear; they can be random, with instant access and unexpected juxtapositions. I still haven't done one, but I think there's something in that medium that nobody's dealing with: it's about how you put two things together and make something new.

I suppose that's influenced by your experience of collage animation, where you can juxtapose manually all kinds of images in space and time. But hearing you describe it this way reminds me again of Eisenstein and his efforts to understand the mystery of 'montage' in film. It wasn't just about cutting, he realized, but about how images 'overflow' into each other. I'm sure he'd have loved interactive media.
I keep playing with the idea and talking about it, but I've not actually achieved anything because I can't find many people who see the same potential for the medium that I do. These are things I get involved with and throw out ideas – like a kind of supervisor – but they're not from my heart.

That's pledged to regular cinema.
That's what I do, although it's very frustrating, because I waste a lot of my life. If I could be less monomaniacal, less intensely focused, I could do many more things; but I'll sit for months waiting for *The Defective Detective* and not really do anything else. It's a strange attitude, a bit like Charles de Gaulle going off and sitting in his little village until France calls him.[7] I've become the Charles de Gaulle of cinema: in fact, we were born on the same day, 22 November, as was Billie Jean King, so maybe I'm the Billie Jean King of cinema. One side of me has this extraordinary patience – I will out-wait them – and the other is just total frenzy, trying to make things happen immediately.

How did Twelve Monkeys *get started after the years of frustration?*
It was a guy named Barry Isaacson, a Brit working at Universal, who slipped me the *Twelve Monkeys* script and I thought it was terrific. Chuck Roven, the producer, started coming over to London, and was very enthusiastic and tenacious. And, of course, I loved David and Jan Peoples' writing. The irony in all this was that Chuck's wife was Dawn Steel, who had taken over at Columbia during *Munchausen*.[8]

It wasn't a case of saying, 'I have to make this at all costs.' But sometimes that's good, because having the overweening passion to do things isn't necessarily the best way to make them. I did Richard LaGravenese's film and now I was going to do David and Jan Peoples' film. In my own mind, I became a total servant of a project which was someone else's project. In the other cases, I'm a servant to the project and the project is really me. All the elements in *Twelve Monkeys* were things I understood and felt close to. I don't know how the script had been developed, but I've met people in the States who had read the script and then gone to see the finished film and thought I'd completely transformed it. I didn't think I had, and it may be that there are certain scripts people just don't know how to read, but which I can, and that's the difference.

How did the writers feel about your realization of their script?
I don't believe that what I imagined was very different from what David and Jan imagined, because all through the making of the film we maintained contact; we only had one fight, and that was just something silly that they were completely wrong about. It's when the thugs attack Railly and Cole and he kills one of them. In fact, I had him kill both, but in the end we left the bald guy alive: you couldn't tell if he was breathing or not, so on the soundtrack I put in a little moan, a breath, and, hey presto, he's alive – but, in fact, he was dead. We had a fight because David, or rather Jan in particular, thought that the fact he killed the black guy who was trying to rape Railly was politically questionable, and might imply that Railly would fall for Cole because he had saved her from the unspeakable act of rape. I said that I didn't think that's what you see in the scene: you don't get the feeling that she's been out there alone and he comes riding in on a white charger and saves her from the rapist and now she falls into his arms. I just didn't think that's what was in the scene at all, but when they saw rushes, they thought it was and we had a big fight about it. We put the moan in to keep David and Jan happy: they thought he would be too much of a killer otherwise and, to be honest, it didn't bother me enough to make a thing of it, considering how violent the scene is anyway.

When news of the casting of Twelve Monkeys *first broke, many thought Gilliam had indeed sold out to Hollywood. How did Bruce Willis and Brad Pitt come to be in it?*
The first names I came up with were Nick Nolte and Jeff Bridges, because both of them are great actors, but the studio wouldn't do it with them. So I pulled away from the whole project. I felt I could do it if we had control over it, but it was clear from the problems over casting that we didn't quite have the kind of control I wanted. So I walked. Then a

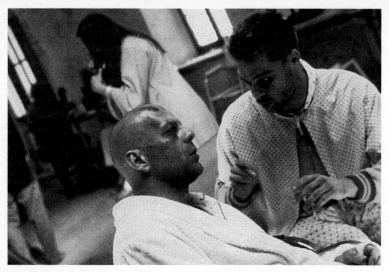

Two for the madhouse: both Bruce Willis and Brad Pitt wanted to expand their range and vied for roles in *Twelve Monkeys*.

few weeks later I got a call to say that Bruce Willis was interested. 'Uh-huh,' I thought. We talked to David and Jan a lot about whether we thought Bruce could do it. I had met him on *Fisher King*, when I was casting the part that Jeff played; he was really keen to work with me and we spent a very enjoyable afternoon together. Something that had intrigued me was the scene in *Die Hard* when he's picking glass out of his feet while on the phone to his wife and he's crying. He told me this wasn't in the script but was his idea, and I liked that, so when the prospect of Bruce doing *Twelve Monkeys* came up, I said let's talk to him.

Chuck and I went to New York and spent an evening with him. I'd been warned about his entourage, about people who interfered, and I told him that he couldn't bring any of them with him if he was going to do this; he'd have to isolate himself, to become a monk and lose himself in the role. It was a nice evening: he really wanted to do it and was determined to try. I thought it was perfect timing. We got Bruce when he had made enough money to feel secure, and was now trying to prove himself as an actor, so he was willing to place himself in the hands of a director. *Pulp Fiction* had opened this little door: he'd proved something and he wanted to go further with it.[9]

Had his performance in Pulp Fiction *convinced you?*
I thought *Pulp Fiction* was fine. He didn't blow me away like he blew a

Willis and Stowe as the last romantics: 'Was this not *Vertigo* remaking itself?'

lot of others away. But we agreed to have a go, on our terms. One of the reasons I've avoided working with stars in the past is that I don't want them dictating the terms of the movie. *I* want to be in control, or what I really mean is the movie's got to be in control. So Bruce was coming to us as a supplicant with the right frame of mind, willing to take a chance, and I thought that was great.

When it came to casting Dr Railly, we sat down and wrote names – as we always do – and the minute Madeleine Stowe was mentioned, that was it. I'd met her when we were trying to do *Tale of Two Cities*, and I liked her a lot. She's beautiful and funny and intelligent – and she has the most raucous horse laugh, totally at odds with her looks.

Next we started thinking about the Jeffrey part and Brad's name came up. At first I didn't think he could do it: I'd seen nothing that convinced me. The casting director thought he could; he'd seen something long ago that hinted he could do it. I wasn't certain, so we kept looking. Then I got a call saying that he wanted to meet and was coming to London. It turned out that what he was interested in was the Cole part, which would indeed make more sense – this laconic, poetic, brooding character. I told him that it was already taken and then – like all actors good at tap-dancing – he said it was *really* the other part he wanted. But I didn't buy that. Nevertheless, he came to London, we had dinner and I liked him. He was fast and funny, trying to prove he could do the part. I began to think maybe he could, but I still wasn't sure. There were a couple of other people available and I was vacillating, then we had another meeting with Brad and I said OK. He was so determined to prove something, like Bruce, and I thought that was great. I'm always a sucker for people trying to break out of the mould.

Then we went into a long period when I sent him to a voice coach and, after the first few sessions, Stephen Bridgewater – who'd worked with Jeff on *Fisher King* – was complaining, 'What have I ever done to you, Terry, to deserve this? He can't do it. He's got no breath control and a lazy tongue and he's just not working at it.'

What did you do? In the film, Pitt achieves an extraordinary rapid-fire delivery and physical mannerisms.

We just kept at him. We got him off smoking, and little by little he started improving, and eventually Stephen said, 'He can do it, I really think he can do it.' What was driving me crazy was that he was supposed to be sending me tapes of his progress, but he wasn't, so I was getting more and more nervous. I kept thinking I'd made a huge mistake and, right up to the moment of shooting, I was on edge, knowing I'd turned down other people who could have done it. The studio, of course, couldn't believe that I was hesitating about Brad Pitt. Most people probably thought that I had just gone for the big stars, whereas in fact I was taking a huge chance because both of them were trying to do the opposite of what they normally do, but that's what excited me. I mean, who would believe a film like this could get through the Hollywood system?

The problem was that, while we were trying to get our film off the ground, *Waterworld* was slowly sinking the studio.[10] That film was completely out of control; on the other hand, we had a firm budget of $29.5 million and two big stars, but we still couldn't get a green light. All their efforts were going on *Waterworld*; executives were flying out to Hawaii weekly, but of course it was too late – the train had left the station. Meanwhile, Chuck was very clever at prising little bits of money out of the studio to keep us alive, so we gradually accumulated momentum and suddenly the film was going. I don't think we were ever formally green-lit: it just happened.

It was frustrating because, compared with all that waste and profligacy on *Waterworld*, we had a budget which, below the line, was more like a low-budget film. But because we had big stars, the crew couldn't understand that we didn't have much money to work with. The fact is that Bruce worked for scale, which is almost nothing, and Brad did it for half a million. Yet you can't tell the crew these guys aren't getting paid much, because what's visible are the perks, like Bruce's big trailer and the huge gym that went along with us, pulled by an articulated lorry. We had a massive army of camp followers and security because of Bruce and Brad, yet we were making a comparatively low-budget film.

You were able to have at least a few familiar Brits in an otherwise all-American crew.
I had Roger Pratt as DP, Mick Audsley came over as editor and Ian Kelly looked after all the video equipment; but the rules of the game were that we had to use as many local people as possible. The heads of departments were from LA or New York or London, but the rest were local.

We went to Philadelphia and Baltimore because that's what the script said, only to discover that, having chosen to work there, neither David nor Jan had ever been to either city. That's what's so funny about the way films work. I'm very literal – the script says Baltimore and Philadelphia so we go to Baltimore and Philadelphia – then it turns out these were just two names the writers picked out of a hat. And when we get to the scene where Cole and Railly drive overnight from Baltimore to Philadelphia, it's only two hours so you don't have to drive overnight!

Have you read any of the *Dirk Gently, Holistic Detective* books?[11] Well, I've become a holistic director: I just walk around and eventually things start to fall into place. We went to this town by chance and several things started happening. The mayor of Philadelphia turns out to be keen on films, because he knows that putting his city on screen makes it famous. When we were shooting there, someone was always coming up to us and asking where were the steps that Rocky ran up – in fact, it's the art gallery.[12] So the Philadelphia Film Office offered us all sorts of help. We were able to use City Hall, the Convention Centre and many other extraordinary buildings that they controlled. All the decay we found in that city made it the right place to be.

The film is about a nostalgic sense of loss, a doomed civilization; and there's Philly, the former capital of the country, with two big power stations empty and redundant because all the industry moved west after the war. So there's all this stuff left over, waiting to be used by people like us, and that worked out really well.

This is essentially the same approach that you used in Brazil *– a mixture of real, mostly derelict, locations, and bold, architectural set-dressing.*
Yes, the found-art approach. You want to find real places to lock it down into some kind of reality, but even then it's not literal reality. For instance, our mental hospital was actually a penitentiary. Modern mental hospitals don't look like that, they look like office buildings, but

I wanted to use this place because I liked it and it felt right. I worked out a justification for it later, which is that it's Cole's point of view: he's probably schizophrenic, so he doesn't know what's real; and here's a room that is trifurcated, with three archways to escape by, but he doesn't know which way to go, which path to take, because he's lost in this world. Basically, it was an interesting room. I'm completely instinctive in the way I work and I don't want to have to justify why certain things feel right on any other level than *they just feel right*. But I do justify and explain to keep other people happy.

And if other people offer different justifications or interpretations?
When that happens, I just go along with it. It becomes their version of the film. I'm not proprietorial about the films; once they're done they belong to anyone who wants to watch them, and each person who watches creates a different film in their watching of it. But I also like throwing in things that don't quite add up, that aren't completely sensible, to create questions for which people can then supply their own answers. *Twelve Monkeys* has thrown up a lot of these. Somebody sent me a lot of the FAQs [frequently asked questions] from the Internet; there was a huge debate there about *Twelve Monkeys* and what each thing in it means. Now, I know exactly what everything means – or at least, what I intended it to mean. As I went along, it all made sense to me and I argued it through with David, but that doesn't mean there aren't a hundred different versions of the film out there. In this case, it was important to create a very tangible, real, tactile world, one that's solid and stacks up, with enough familiarity in the architecture of things so that you know this isn't just a complete fantasy. It was like that in the early Pasolini films: however magical they were, the baskets were woven by hand and the dirt was real. You could see this, so your feet are on the ground.

So how do you interpret Twelve Monkeys, *apart from its science-fiction aspect?*
For me, the film is very much about the twentieth century's inundation of information and about deciphering what among all this noise and imagery is useful and important to our lives. This is something we're all trying to sort out. Cole has been thrust from another world into ours and he's confronted by the confusion we live in, which most people somehow accept as normal. So he appears abnormal, and what's happening around him seems random and weird. Is he mad, or are we? Is our society mad? These are the aspects of it that I liked and wanted to preserve. Unlike what I think Peter Greenaway's doing – disguising his points and hiding the information, creating a riddle that only he has the

'Cole has been thrust from another world into ours: is he mad, or are we?'

answer to – I'm not trying to confuse or hide anything. But I'm also not trying to make it a totally defined and pinned-down affair.

There's a scene towards the end when they both discover from the telephone calls that Cole's not crazy: a police car goes by and they turn and see a bank of video monitors with their images on them. That wasn't in the script; I just wanted to do it because I loved the idea of them thinking they were hiding, yet being totally exposed by technology. It also related back to the video ball in the future, with all those faces and bits of faces. The video ball wasn't in the script either; it simply had people across a table doing the interrogation. So, although I think I'm not changing anything, I suppose I am. When you put a guy on a chair that slides up and down a wall – so that he's like a butterfly on display – with this ball of partial magnified images, that's different from you and me talking across the table. What I'm doing is taking the situation, an interrogation system, and making it highly subjective, but in an external, physical way. I know how vulnerable I would feel if my feet couldn't touch the floor.

In fact, there are two subjective points of view: the scientists are seeing their subject – a guy up there on a wall – in a clearly defined way; while, from his point of view, it's just chaos and confusion, and he can barely see who's there. His viewpoint is a more confused one, because his direct view of them is interfered with by the technology. So what's the statement here? That we use television and movies as mirrors that supposedly show us the world, but it's distorted; or that we communicate to each other through these things and less and less directly. But the possibility of all this was in the script; the characters actually say that their technology was a patchwork of all the things they'd been able to keep as they went underground – so that's, in effect, what we're showing.

But the showing of it, in all the extravagant detail you conjure up, adds extra layers of meaning or implication.
My concern was that this was what we had done in *Brazil* too, and I was trying to make it different, although essentially it's very similar.

Interrogation is very much at the heart of Twelve Monkeys. *There's an interesting contrast between Cole's interrogation by the scientists of the future and his questioning by the psychiatrists of the present, which is equally stylized.*
You would never do that in a psychiatric hospital, of course. The doctors wouldn't be lined up as severely as that, and Cole wouldn't be as isolated in that tiny chair with all the space around him. I set it in this

classical room, which is clean and reasonable, as a contrast to the darkness and messiness of the underground laboratory of the future. *Paths of Glory* was probably also at the back of my mind, with that great room where the court martial takes place, and I think there's the same tracking shot. But Kubrick tracks during the whole thing, while I just opened out the start of the scene with a great sweeping move – having cut from a very tight shot of Bruce's face. Interestingly, nobody complained about how the mentally ill were portrayed in *Twelve Monkeys*, whereas there had been a lot of discussion about the homeless in *Fisher King*, which seemed to be about where our group conscience was focused at that particular moment. In fact, there was very little said about the general social picture in *Twelve Monkeys*, except for the usual thing about Gilliam going over the top again.

The film only becomes stable towards the end when we realize that everything really is true: the future is there and they're all going to die. The script wasn't quite like that, but I wanted to delay that moment and keep open, as long as possible, the doubt about whether he's mad. This is a dangerous thing to do, but I was intrigued to see if I could keep an audience engaged all the way through without them just throwing up their hands. And I remember the first time my daughter Amy – who was nineteen – and a friend saw it at Technicolor. They wanted to go to the toilet but they couldn't because they thought they'd miss some vital piece of information. They were really engaged by the puzzle.

The core of the puzzle – the idea of someone haunted by an image of his own death – comes from Chris Marker's 1962 film, La Jetée. *Was he involved at all in* Twelve Monkeys *as a kind of adaptation of his short?*
Chris Marker was involved right at the beginning. One of Chuck Roven's associates had gone to him, and I think he knew David and Jan Peoples' work. Chris didn't want them to try to do a remake, nor did they want to, but his film was definitely a kernel. Actually, he wanted to be excluded from the process after that. They sent him a full-scale contract, but he sent it all back, saying, 'If you can't describe what we're doing here in one page, then forget it.'

But you hadn't seen La Jetée *when you signed up for* Twelve Monkeys?
No, I hadn't seen it. It was odd to have everyone writing about how I'd been inspired by Marker's film, but any inspiration came through what David and Jan had taken from it. In fact, I'd seen stills from it – well, the film consists of stills, but there's a book of the stills, with the voice-over text, which I didn't read. I remembered the image of the man being shot and the long jetty or pier, although I didn't really know what it

was. I also remembered a guy with a mask over his face and glasses, so our scientists had glasses. But I don't think our underground looks much like the underground of *La Jetée*.

The climax, the shooting, takes place at an airport in both films.
Yes, but in *La Jetée* it takes place outside – the images are all air and space – whereas in ours, he's shot running down a tunnel. Is that the medieval tunnel going to heaven? Is it death, or the birth canal? All these associations were present, which is why I liked that tunnel. But I didn't choose it, the tunnel sort of chose itself, because our location was a converted railway station in Philadelphia which had been turned into a convention centre that was just breathtaking to walk into. This was what we had to make into an airport, and all we did was put a big scrim at the end of the tunnel and pass light through it, making it an infinite passage into white. We kept that the brightest thing, while the rest was a of grey open space, with some post-modern marble and monolithic cenotaphs, which we made even taller, until it became like some kind of mausoleum.

Believe it or not, we couldn't get any of the airlines to give us free signage – because a man is killed at the airport. So we had to invent all those names – which cost us money – and be inventive in other ways. In the scene where Bruce and Madeleine arrive in a taxi and we track them inside, the first, exterior, part of the tracking shot is at Baltimore Airport, while the second, interior, is in Philly. We brought one piece of set with us, which became the cutting piece: they walk in, we go to black for two frames, then out the other side into Philly.

When did you finally see La Jetée *and what did you feel about it after all the build-up?*
At the Paris première of *Twelve Monkeys*: it was shown as the short. I thought it was fantastic. It wasn't translated and my French is terrible, but that didn't seem to matter, since the story is so simple. The girl isn't a real person, she's just a dream image, so David and Jan wrote a real woman. The play with all the animals is quite extraordinary – when we're in the zoo – and then the tree, which goes into *Vertigo*.[13] And that moment in *La Jetée*, when the girl moves – does she actually look at camera or did I just think she did?

Everyone's reaction first time is to wonder if she really moves. Before the days of video, people used to debate this. But you realized that various things in the script of Twelve Monkeys *related to it?*
The images from the book that I'd remembered were the underground, the guy with the glasses and the jetty itself, but I didn't really pay much

attention to the parts in between these images. What's fascinating is that it's all done with cutting, creating rhythms in the editing; it's pure cinema, with no dialogue, only voice-over. The interesting thing about *Vertigo* was how it started working its way into the film far more than originally planned. What was in the script from the start was the scene in *Vertigo* where Jimmy Stewart goes to the redwood trees – which, of course, comes from *La Jetée*. There were a couple of references to the original dialogue from *Vertigo*, but when we shot the scene we kept strictly to David and Jan's dialogue.

When Mick Audsley started cutting it together, he made a different scene from what was written because there was more on the actual *Vertigo* soundtrack that started working in a quite magical way. Mick created an extraordinary dialogue between the script and the film.

In the script Katherine was a blonde and she puts on a black wig as disguise. Since Madeleine has dark hair, we gave her a blond wig and put a trenchcoat on her, with the result that, when Bruce sees her in the lobby of the cinema, it's a totally Hitchcockian moment . . . with a Hitchcock blonde to boot.

You mean it recapitulates Stewart getting Kim Novak to dress up like the woman he thinks he's lost?
The music in the background is from *Vertigo* and Mick had grabbed a piece that seemed to work. Then we needed a better version of it, which involved going back to the film to find where exactly it came from. None of us had looked at the video while working on the film, and we discovered that this music came from the scene where Madeleine (Kim) has been remade as a blonde and appears before Jimmy – and the scene is cut exactly as we had cut ours, even up to the end where they embrace and the room starts spinning. I'd actually done a shot in the cinema foyer and, because it was circular, I'd put Madeleine and Bruce on a turntable so that they floated while the room spun around them. Was this not *Vertigo* remaking itself without us realizing it? We sat in the cutting room and couldn't believe it. It was spooky. If I had left in the spinning kiss, it would have been the exact *Vertigo* scene – and people would have said I was just stealing from it – but, since it was unnecessary, I left it out.

I suppose David and Jan had foreseen that these would begin to interact, even if you weren't mimicking Vertigo *consciously.*
No, they hadn't. *Vertigo* was purely and simply a reference in the script; and the fact that Katherine would be blonde wasn't predicted – it only happened because of casting Madeleine Stowe. You begin to think there

must be Platonic scenes already in existence, which just have to be remade.

Did you fine-tune the film as a result of test screenings?
At our first NRG screening in Washington, we discovered that we'd pushed the music too much. What emerged was that the audience didn't buy the relationship between Railly and Cole. They'd seen him kidnap her, then she took the bullet out of his leg, and the music we had put to the scene was definitely romantic. They said that she wouldn't fall for him like that; I realized the music was too definite, so we went back and changed it into something very ambivalent. That worked much better, letting the audience decide what's happening, instead of being Spielberg and telling them how to respond. The more ambiguous we kept things, the better it went: any time we made a definite statement, musically or otherwise, it didn't work.

You can see in *The Hamster Factor* how we were convinced we'd got them, until the numbers came in and it was, 'God, we've failed again!'[14] We made a few minor changes, apart from the music, and – surprise, surprise – we had a hit on our hands. Interestingly, the distribution and marketing people decided to release it on 27 December, after the pre-Christmas bloodbath. *Clockers* and *Casino* had come out and they'd killed each other. I thought no one would be paying attention by the time we appeared, but we got very good reviews and the audience came in numbers we didn't expect. Perhaps that was because of Bruce and Brad, but the point is that they came and kept coming. And the way distribution works now, if a film is wounded in the first week, the exhibitors get twitchy and are ready to sacrifice it. We did really well in the US – between $65 and $70 million – and abroad we did even better – a total of $175 million around the world. For a film that complex to do so well says something: it's here to keep telling Hollywood there's an intelligent audience out there. But a month or two after it was out, we had a meeting with Warners about *The Defective Detective*, which Bruce was interested in doing. They were congratulating me on the great success of *Twelve Monkeys* and I started to say, 'Yes, isn't it wonderful that an intelligent –' But they said it was all down to two words: Brad Pitt. It doesn't matter how many times you do a film with Harrison Ford or Brad Pitt that falls on its face, they still want to believe in those two words, whether it's Brad or Harrison or Bruce.

It was just before you started Twelve Monkeys *that our paths crossed when I persuaded you, very much against your better judgement, to present a TV series about early film that I was writing to mark the centenary of cinema,* The Last Machine.[15] *Dick Lester had just presented some*

Gilliam as the intrepid explorer of early cinema in *The Last Machine*, filmed at Pinewood Studios.

One in the eye for Méliès: getting back into make-up for *The Last Machine*.

programmes about British cinema rather hesitantly and you concluded that 'directors should direct and presenters should present'.

I warned everybody that I wasn't a good presenter, but one of my great weaknesses is not being able to say no to persistent, tenacious people.

We had to persuade you, but there's no doubt that the series going out mid-evening and its wide press coverage owed a lot to your presence.

I became your Bruce Willis! There's this desperate need to simplify and promote one person who's got it all together. If we're the best that society can throw up today, film stars and film directors, it's pathetic.

The reason we wanted you to do it was simply because you were the only practising film-maker I could think of who would be believable talking enthusiastically about pioneers like Méliès.

When I was a kid, I used to do magic shows and I still like magic tricks, so that's why I've always liked Méliès.[16] And I suppose I like to surprise, astound and even confound, so that's a parallel with early film-making. Cartooning is also a link: many of the first film-makers were cartoonists and 'lightning sketch artists' before this strange new profession opened up. In a way, I followed the same path when I moved from cartooning to animation, which I learned as I went along – again, very like the pioneers. But a lot of the material you showed in the series was completely new to me; it's just amazing how quickly you can see the language of cinema being discovered, invented, right before your eyes, all within less than ten years.

When you started sending me the tapes of early films, the thing that impressed me most was the film with the family, where the father leaves home, a burglar comes in, and the woman has to try to contact him by telephone to be rescued.[17] And in there – among all those wide shots which we think is what silent films mainly consisted of – there's a close-up. I remember watching that on the TV and being shocked by the power of that early close-up. I think that was what hooked me: it was like rediscovering film again, back at the beginning when the vocabulary and the grammar were in their most primitive form.

It reminded me of a TV documentary about a shaman who was teaching his apprentice all the tricks of the trade – out-of-body experiences, running with the jaguar, flying with the eagle and all that – and he took him into town for his first visit. He took him to the cinema and the apprentice came out ashen-faced and announced that he had seen the dream of death – he didn't understand any of the grammar of discontinuous shots of bits of people. We no longer see how strange it is. I'm beginning to think that genetic transformations must have occurred, because our children seem to understand it right from the beginning. Anyway, I was feeling like the apprentice shaman when I succumbed to your pressure.

'The Road to Monkey Heaven is a) Paved b) Littered c) Barricaded with Good Intentions': an interactive installation for the exhibition *Spellbound*.

The other cinema centenary project I got you involved with was contributing to the Hayward Gallery show Spellbound: Art and Film *early in 1996, just as* Twelve Monkeys *was being released.*[18]

The idea of *Spellbound* was interesting, getting film-makers to be serious artists and serious artists to be film-makers. It's like building a set. I've always been intrigued by expositions and the idea of a place that stands and is almost permanent, in which people can enter and experience something. It's another form of the darkroom – and my piece for *Spellbound* was just that.

You were very insistent that there had to be a turn in the corridor leading to the space where a wall of outsize filing-cabinet drawers towered over the spectators. And on both sides there were splashes of light leaking, as if from a hidden film screening.

Like a labyrinth, where you can't see what you're going into. It was designed so that the space gets smaller, then explodes. You're confronted by a space that your eyes have to get used to, and you can't work out what's going on. To me, the idea of a film that you can't see being projected, just squeezing out through the little gaps between the wall and the filing cabinets, seemed like a great metaphor. I was going to do a collage of famous films, but that became too complex, and the release was approaching, so the idea that the first screening of *Twelve Monkeys* in England would be one you couldn't see made me laugh.

Then the drawers – did I really have a hundred? A hundred years of cinema: a hundred drawers. The idea was that you could open a lot of these drawers and all the stages of film-making were parcelled up in them. I loved the idea that people had to participate; it was the only part of the exhibition where you could get your hands dirty. You had to climb up ladders, like children, and peer into drawers to find out what was in them – all the different stages of a film, from its embryonic start in an incubator, going through to meetings, telephone conversations, trying to get hold of your producer on a mobile phone. In this drawer, phones that don't communicate, and snakes. Another was a mortuary drawer, with a corpse in it. Through other drawers, you could see the screen, but only a tiny part of the image. If only I'd got it ready for the opening.

It was an extraordinarily complex installation, and you were away a lot promoting Twelve Monkeys. *We always knew it would be a close-run thing.*
It wasn't reviewed with the rest of the show, but people found their way to it. There's a side of me that likes that. I'll use the system to reach as many people as possible, but I also love having things that people find on their own, which they just stumble upon. Going to a cinema and finding a film for myself is still the most exciting experience – it's a moment of really possessing a film, but it's hard to do that now, since we live in an age where everyone is inundated with information. And I'm at the front of the queue, trying to inundate people. But when that fails – or I don't make the opening night and there's no review – that's fine. People still come up to me and say the exhibition was wonderful. But it no longer exists. That's like theatre. Ray Cooper is always saying I should do theatre, but I'm hooked on films because I can reach so many more people, and it's a more permanent artefact, or as permanent as any artefact can be.

I don't understand why you're still so determined to reach all those people, given the compromises and frustrations involved.

Because one of them might be me at the age of sixteen. As a kid coming from the country, cinema was the way to where I am now, and I like populist media, even though they've been taken over by all the wrong people, doing the wrong things and giving out the wrong message. That's what's so frustrating – I keep ending up as an élitist film-maker.

First sketch for the *Spellbound* 'filing cabinet' installation (1995).

NOTES

1 Science-fiction writer Philip K. Dick (1928–82) had a strong aversion to Hollywood, but since his death at least six stories and novels have been adapted for the screen, of which the best known is *Blade Runner* (based on the 1968 novella (*la Do Androids Dream of Electric Sheep?*).

2 Charles Russell's *The Mask* (1994) married computer animation to Jim Carrey's live action with sensational effect.

3 Doré's illustrations for *Don Quixote*, published in 1862, were among his most famous.

4 See ch.4, n.6, p 85.

5 This passage was recorded before Gilliam was offered *Fear and Loathing in Las Vegas* with Johnny Depp already signed up.

6 On Scorsese's Armani commercials, see *Scorsese on Scorsese*, p. 114.

7 De Gaulle spent over a decade after the war writing on his estate at Colombay les Deux Eglises before coming to power in 1958.

8 Dawn Steel (1946–97) became head of production at Paramount in 1984, then president of Columbia in 1987, after David Puttnam's departure, when *Munchausen* was in dispute.

9 After establishing his *Die Hard* tough-guy reputation, Bruce Willis sought to broaden his range in the early nineties, with cameo appearances (in Robert Altman's *The Player*) and untypical roles, including the washed-up boxer in Quentin Tarantino's *Pulp Fiction* (1994), followed immediately by *Twelve Monkeys*.

10 *Waterworld* (1995), starring and part-directed by Kevin Costner, eventually cost $175 million.

11 Douglas Adams, *Dirk Gently's Holistic Detective Agency* (1987) and its sequel, *The Long Dark Tea-time of the Soul* (1991).

12 Sylvester Stallone's fifteen-year five-part saga as Rocky began in Philadelphia in 1976.

13 The lovers from different times who meet in Marker's *La Jetée* (1962) are seen looking at the cross-section of a sequoia tree, in a reference to the scene in Hitchcock's *Vertigo* (1958) where James Stewart and Kim Novak contemplate a similar tree, showing the brevity of their lives compared with the tree's.

14 *The Hamster Factor and Other Tales of Twelve Monkeys* (1996) is a fly-on-the-wall documentary about the making of *Twelve Monkeys* by Keith Fulton and Louis Pepe.

15 *The Last Machine*, a five-part series on 'early cinema and the birth of the modern world', which Gilliam presents in a variety of cameo character appearances and projected images, was written and co-produced by Ian Christie, directed by Richard Curson Smith and produced by John Wyver through Illuminations and the British Film Institute for BBC TV (1995).

16 Georges Méliès (1861–1938) was a magician and illusionist in Paris before he began making trick films in 1896, becoming one of the leading producers for the following decade, before his business declined and collapsed in 1913. Gilliam pays tribute to Méliès in *The Last Machine*.

17 *The Physician of the Castle* (Pathé, 1908) includes an unexpected early close-up as the wife appeals to her husband by telephone.

18 *Spellbound: Art and Film* was an exhibition curated by Ian Christie and Philip Dodd for the British Film Institute and the Hayward Gallery in 1996, with installations and works by Fiona Banner, Terry Gilliam, Douglas Gordon, Peter Greenaway, Damien Hirst, Steve McQueen, Eduardo Paolozzi, Paula Rego, Ridley Scott and Boyd Webb.

On the road again: Gonzo film-making to match Hunter's Gonzo journalism.

10

An unexpected rendezvous with *Fear and Loathing in Las Vegas;* and still *The Defective Detective*

'. . . all the hallmarks of a dangerously innocent culture'
— HUNTER S. THOMPSON, *Fear and Loathing in Las Vegas*[1]

After finishing Twelve Monkeys, *did you want to go back to* The Defective Detective?
I wanted to work again with Chuck Roven, but we didn't seem able to convince anyone it was worth doing. We got Nick Cage involved, but there was a deadline to meet, otherwise we'd no longer be number one on his list. Getting the money was difficult: in the end Universal came in and the rest of it came from the same sources that did the foreign investment on *Twelve Monkeys*, which amounted to over 70 per cent. They were all very keen, but we'd missed the date with Nick by two weeks, and we had been shifted down his dance card. We still wanted him, so we spent a lot of time waiting to see if he was going to do *Superman* or *Snake Eyes*, but eventually it ground to a halt and I was in need of something to do.

So how did Fear and Loathing in Las Vegas *come to you?*
It was Cameron Diaz's manager, who was with her in London and mentioned that Johnny Depp was involved with *Fear and Loathing*. I told him that people had been trying to get me to do it for ten years. The last script that reached me must have been in 1989 or 1990 and I thought what a great way it would have been to start the decade, perfect timing – new broom sweeps clean: a cinematic enema for the nineties. Then Laila Nabulsi, who was producing it, called me to say that Alex Cox had been fired and they wanted me to direct it. Perfect timing again: I was keen to work with Johnny and *Fear and Loathing* was still intriguing.

So they sent the Alex Cox script over at Easter 1997 while I was in Italy. At first I didn't want to read it. Then one day I picked it up and just burst out laughing: it started exactly as the book starts, but later it fell apart. The characters become two rather boorish people senselessly crashing around the place, with no depth. I flew out to LA and met Laila, Hunter Thompson, and Johnny Depp and Benicio Del Toro, who were both already involved at that point. The budget they had was

Both the book and the film open with the same invocation of excess: 'Is it possible that we're talking metaphor here?'

about $7 million. Everyone got on well and I said that if I did it I'd want to write a new script and they'd better double the budget straight away.

Then I came back to England and called up Tony Grisoni, with whom I'd been working on *The Minotaur* during the *Defective Detective* lay-off, and asked him if he'd like to work on this. The extraordinary thing was that, when Alex Cox was first involved on *Fear and Loathing*, Tony had asked if he could write it with him. So we sat down at my computer and wrote a script in eight days. Then we read what we thought was a great script, realized it was crap and rewrote it in two days. You feel a heavy responsibility doing a book that was such a seminal work – and by a living writer who carries a gun!

So, to overcome that oppressive weight, our approach was to work fast and make very quick, instinctive decisions. We both felt we had a good sense of the spirit of the book and just went through it, picking everything we liked and ignoring what we didn't, cannibalizing lines from here and there, and making basic decisions about the structure. The book is really two adventures that Thompson thrusts together; the second half seems to go all over the place, which has always left me feeling unsatisfied. We felt we had to do something to make it tighter. Tony's idea was to use Adrenochrome as the drug that pushes Duke over the edge: he wakes up and the world is totally altered rather than changing in a steady progression.

The other crucial scene was the one in the North Star Café, with Ellen Barkin. Previous scripts had avoided it, but I remembered when I read the book again that this is the one scene which really jumps out; it has such a different tone. In all the others, nobody is really damaged or hurt, but this is truly ugly: two guys in the middle of the night in a café with a lone woman and a knife. This isn't funny. They've gone too far. I thought, 'We've got to use it, because everybody else has refused to,' and it became a linchpin for the second part. Duke wakes up not knowing what's happened; now we can throw in scenes that we like in any order we like as he tries to reconstruct events, building towards the point of some terrible crime.

When I went back to the book after seeing the film, it wasn't at all obvious how the café scene could be so important.
I could see the crazed games that Duke and Gonzo played up to this point, with people who were strong enough to handle them, like the DA from Georgia. You're in public spaces, crashing around or trashing hotel rooms. You may be endangering people's jobs, but it's all basically good fun. Even Alice, the maid who enters the devastated room, ends

up kind of jolly, with the promise of large sums of cash. But we felt we still had to make some kind of moral judgement in this whole thing: a lesson had to be learned somewhere, otherwise it's just rampaging around, with no point. The earlier script had no reflective element, but there's that central speech where Duke reflects back on the sixties which is vital. It seems to me that the book is about the despair of the American Dream never coming true. The sixties idea that we could change the world very quickly had all crumbled, and we'd slid into death, suicide, assassination and drugs, while the war went on and on. Hunter writes in this highly dramatic style: although often nothing is really happening, everything is dramatized. It's as if he's a war correspondent, but rather than going to Vietnam he stayed in America and carpet-bombed his psyche with drugs. So it's front-line writing, but set in this banal world.

There's a strange sexual innocence about the book, surprising perhaps amid the fleshpots of Las Vegas.
We're doing Dante's *Inferno* here, so basically our feeling was that Gonzo was Virgil – not the nice pagan poet, but a pagan primal force. He's Mexican, not Italian, so what do you expect? Mexicans are crazed and there's a passion and demonic energy there, while Duke is really the Christian, with a morality that he's testing, pushing to the limit. Hunter's writing is very Bible-based; after all, he comes from Kentucky, and he's mainly following and commenting.

Johnny Depp has cornered the market in bewildered innocents, from Edward Scissorhands *to* Arizona Dreaming *and* Ed Wood.
Johnny is a kind of innocent, no matter how he might appear. And, in a strange way, Hunter's an innocent too – maybe a very debauched innocent, but innocence can come in different forms. He has a moral structure he's trying to live within, although it seems to me Gonzo is beyond morality. We get to glimpse that he's a serious lawyer, dealing with Chicano rights and all that; and we know they're both against the Vietnam War. After the first public screening, the studio wanted us to contextualize it more, to explain that these are basically decent people, a hardworking journalist and a left-wing lawyer. But I didn't want to apologize. We spend too much time these days explaining everything into oblivion and justifying. I wanted the audience to have to work the meanings out for themselves. When the book was republished, Hunter had written presciently about America becoming a nation of panicky sheep, and how that was the last time anyone could drive round in a fire-red convertible and trash hotel rooms and live to tell the story. I felt that someone had to be *un*apologetic: it's got to be – boom – just what it is.

Johnny Depp's uncanny impersonation of Hunter Thompson as 'Raoul Duke':
'Maybe a very debauched innocent, but innocence can come in different forms.'

'We're talking Dante's *Inferno* here, with Gonzo as Virgil, a pagan primal
force.' Benicio del Toro as Duke's unreliable attorney and nemesis.

These are existential characters: we don't really have to know where they're coming from, but we should be able to understand them. Gonzo has the sexual energy that's lacking in Duke – who's caught up in his own paranoias – so everything about Gonzo is sex and frustrated sex.

Hence his infatuation with the juvenile artist Lucy.
He loves women, but he also seems to despise them. His behaviour with Lucy is quite extraordinary. I think it's one of Benicio's best scenes. Dressed in a bedspread, he looks like a degenerate pasha: he's with this tiny little girl surrounded by all those icons. Again, it was getting religious – is it a pasha's robe, or is it a priest's cope? – and Duke's not coping very well (there are a lot of puns you can make about copes). We were trying to build that whole sexual aspect that leads to the North Star Café; there's very little sex in the book, except that one moment near the end, after Duke's put Gonzo on the plane, when he's driving around the university and talking about girls with long legs.[2]

Apart from that passage, there's a wider current of repressed sexual fantasy on Thompson/Duke's part, such as when he imagines what Gonzo might do with Lucy. Given so much repression, did you feel you had to find other ways of restoring dynamism to the film – in the convulsive speed of the car chase, for instance?
We put Lucy in there again as they are trying to get Gonzo out of town. She doesn't reappear in the book, but in the film she's one of the demons, or forces – along with the highway-patrol man and hitch-hiker – who are waiting to block Duke's escape from the hell of Vegas. Ultimately, they do break out and the race to the airport became a kind of book-end to the beginning of the film, where we actually use the same music. First time round, the music is driving and intense as they're sweeping through the desert in the immaculate, sexy Red Shark, but at the end it comes as a raucous relief, jollier and funnier, once they see the airport and crash towards it in the trashed Cadillac – anything to get out of this place.

In a way, the book is pre-visualized, since Ralph Steadman's drawings have always been an integral part of it. Was that a problem for you?
From when Ralph illustrated it for *Rolling Stone* to when it was made into a book, the drawings have been essential, even though Ralph didn't go on the trip. I know them so well, because when I first came to England, as an illustrator, he was a big influence. But although they capture the energy and madness of the whole thing, I knew we couldn't translate them literally and make them three-dimensional. So I tried not to look at them, except for a few specific images, like the hitch-hiker.

And the reptiles in the hotel lobby when Duke and Gonzo check in under the influence of acid?

I wasn't totally happy with those. I was hoping for something a bit less literally lizardy – reptiles that Francis Bacon might have painted. We came out at the same time as *Godzilla*, so I used to say that we've got lizards, but ours fuck. Because we could only afford seven lizard heads, we had to rely on multiple costume changes and a set that was primarily mirrors. The establishing pull-back shot, with the room packed full of literal 'lounge lizards', was achieved with four separate passes, combined with a lot of work on computers. In the previous scene there is another computer-generated hallucination that was the result of my first recce for the film in Vegas – I'd only ever been there once before, during my escape from America in 1967. This time, walking around the casinos, I became obsessed with the carpet patterns: they were leafy, vegetal shapes, but bigger than you'd expect and more virulently coloured. Definitely dangerous. Were they moving? It was a small leap to imagine them crawling up the legs of the gamblers and dragging them down into beer-stained, woollen, tufted Venus fly-trap maws.

Was it a good experience to make a film so fast, after all the delays and disappointments you've had with your own projects recently? You already knew the book well, and someone else had lived with the torment of getting it up and running, and signing the actors.

Not at first. The preparation was truly a nightmarish time, a total act of faith. Johnny, Benicio and I were in there, but we didn't have all the money. When I said, 'Double it to $15 million,' they asked if I could do it for $12 million. I said I'd try, but it went the same distance in the opposite direction up to $19 million; and we discovered that Alex Cox's $7 million was a total lie: he could never have done it for that. The production company, Rhino Films, were idiots. We were making a film that would put them on the map as far as Hollywood was concerned, but they kept playing games, threatening to bring Alex Cox back and get other actors. All this time we were working without contracts and without being paid. I was originally promised a nice chunk of money and gross points, but, in the course of this nightmare preparation, that deal shrank down to getting paid less than I did on *Time Bandits*. However, it was the only way to keep the project afloat.

Rhino Films' Steve Nemeth, who managed to be credited as producer, only came to the production office once during the whole production. He was so despised that Johnny wanted it put in his contract that if Nemeth ever came on the set he would be required to drop his trousers and Johnny would whip him with a wire coat-hanger. His main contribution was to get in the way, make absurd threats and renege on his deals with us. He was incredibly inexperienced and, since we were doing everything so quickly, it took a lot of faith on many people's part.

Another Las Vegas film, Scorsese's Casino, *had similar problems of everything being done in a rush at the last moment.*
The difference is they had $40 million, and those extra millions buy you a lot. Johnny and I had to keep cutting and cutting our deals to keep the project moving forward. At the last moment, the British funding bank pulled out, and we were only saved by Universal coming in and picking it up.

Everything in the film had to be done in a very pragmatic way, on a very tight schedule of forty-eight days – which I think ended up as fifty-five. All the road stuff was expensive and time-consuming. We had to build Bazooko Circus – which is really Circus Circus but they wouldn't let us near their place – and that cost money. There's only one bit of Vegas left that looks like the Vegas of the seventies, where the old motels still have their signs. It's a street called North Fremont. It's the dead end of Vegas – in fact, when we were shooting there, they found a body in one of the motel rooms – and there were hypodermics all over the ground. My approach was: we're sharks here, so we just keep moving forward. If we stop, we die. No going back and reshooting things. Gonzo film-making to match Hunter's gonzo journalism.

How did you pick your team?
Patrick Cassavetti had been line producer on *Brazil*. He had managed to bring us in under budget on that one and I asked him to come out to LA to protect me and the project. Roger Pratt wasn't available to shoot the film, but we had a lot of A-list DPs coming forward who were interested. There was also this unknown guy pestering me, Nicola Peccorini. He had done one low-budget film in Budapest, but had been Vittorio Storaro's second camera for sixteen years and, most intriguingly, he only has one eye. Now, since I was pretending to be a young film-maker again, able to work fast and shedding the weight of huge budgets and big stars, I decided to hire the man who would kill to do the film and whose big break this would be. And he was wonderful. Nicola had been the best Steadicam operator in Europe and he was like a mountain, a sort of St Christopher carrying the baby Jesus on his shoulders.

Alex McDowell was the production designer. He had done *The Crow* and he's British, so that was a little bit of Britain for me to cling on to. Basically, he got the job because he brought in the right books – that's how I choose now, according to which book you bring. He brought a book by an American artist Robert Yarber, whose father used to build Holiday Inns, and who does paintings which look as if they're on black velvet, although they're not.[3] Fluorescent neon colours on black back-grounds, and strange dreamlike events which all take place in hotel rooms, like a couple lying in bed with the door bursting open and a very tiny bellboy leaping in with a flaming kebab. Another Brit, Lesley Walker, who had cut *The Fisher King*, came out, as did my eldest daughter Amy, who worked as a costume assistant under Julie Weiss. Julie did the costumes on *Twelve Monkeys* and also agreed to jump on board. She's American, of the right generation and politically very savvy. So the costumes became symbols for everything that was going on in America at that time, every political and social movement. We spent hours talking about colours and textures in a political context.

Can you give some examples, because I think people don't normally read costumes that way.
I'm sure they don't. Well, on the simplest level, at the DA's convention everyone is wearing red, white and blue. The Beverly Hills hotel crowd was dominated by Pucci designs – floral shapes and vivid colours – because that was our Garden of Eden, even guarded by an angel with a flaming sword, from which they're expelled into the desert wilderness. Nobody understands most of this stuff, but that's what I'm doing: there's a structure there, with biblical overtones. You keep hoping that some people will spot things and make connections – I mean, how many angels with flaming swords are there out there? But I don't mind if they don't, because these kind of references create a structure for me to work within, so that I think I know what I'm doing. Anyway, the Mint 400 race became the Vietnam War, all military fatigues and khaki. There are even people in Vietcong pyjamas at various points.

It looks like a cross between the Second World War North African cam-paign and Desert Storm – or The English Patient.
At the end of the film, when Duke's typing and the camera goes to the television, there's actually a shot from Desert Storm among all those images. I started with apocalyptic images from everywhere, from the seventies to the present, but most of the Desert Storm images didn't stay in, except one with a tank, which a trainspotter has noticed.

Was this a deliberate decision to use anachronisms to make the film relate to today?
That's the only time we did it. Everyone was asking how we could make

this relevant to the nineties, but I said I didn't want to – not because it isn't relevant, but I don't think we should spoonfeed the audience. In Bazooko Circus, we were aiming at the infantilization of Vegas that's taken place. Circus Circus was the forerunner of that – the first casino to allow in families – now Vegas is a family-oriented den of iniquity, but nice and safely sanitized. The booths in Bazooko Circus were a chance to do all sorts of jolly nightmarish things, from throwing hypodermics at the drug-addict hippie to the little girl firing her M-16. If you look closely you'll see the kosher butcher with his prayer curls throwing meat cleavers at pigs, and there's a Ku Klux Klansman whose robe partially covers up the fact that he's been tarred and feathered. Is he, perhaps, a black man underneath? Julie's references are very specific and I think they add up to a very intelligent approach to costume.

These are layers of the film that are hard to grasp at one viewing.
There's a lot going on. Television in the hotel rooms is the only way you get to see the real world outside, which is ironic, since that's the one thing television doesn't do – it's usually the medium of disinformation. But here television is a window on the world and shows there's a war going on. The sets all had a meaning too. Each of the casinos was like a different layer of hell, with different colours and different types of people. And the Mint Hotel room itself is the most hellish of all because we used purple and greens – basically German Expressionist colours; it's so dark and unpleasant. However, for the bathroom we went into pink, which actually foreshadows the second half, when Duke returns to Vegas and the Flamingo Hotel, and pink takes over the film. The Mint isn't the darkest scene, but it's the first disturbingly dark moment.

Some people thought that the film was ending when Duke escapes from Vegas. He's made it! But he's thrown back and some of the audience resent this. It takes them a while to accept that you don't get out that easily: there's a lot of pain still to be endured and, until we go back the second time, we haven't learned the real lessons. What's interesting is that this second version of hell is light and pink: is it the red of blood vessels, or is it a womb? Glenn Young, who published the screenplay, kept referring to all those 'amniotic moments', talking about birth and rebirth, and I love the idea that hell is all the colours you *think* you like – they're warm and caressing, but it's the worst hell.

There was a scene, the Hardware Barn, that I cut after the first screening in the States.[4] It comes in the middle of the book, but Alex Cox had put it at the end of the film. It was an interesting idea. It's after all the madness has finished and Duke is on his way home to LA; we did the same but with a different emphasis. He says, 'We went in search of the American Dream and we failed to find it, but sometimes life gives you a second chance.' Then he sees a sign for 'Cold Beer' and drives up to a little country-store bar where a nice old man serves him. It's like a commercial for the Dream, pure Norman Rockwell, and they start talking: 'Where you from?' 'Vegas.' Then a pretty girl walks in smiling at him and Duke looks at her. He can't believe his luck: he's got a great drink, everything's perfect and it's going to be his day. But then she kisses the old man, who says, 'My granddaughter.' And Johnny says, 'Sure, and I'm the district attorney from Ignoto County. Just another good American like yourself, sir.'

The old man looks at him and walks away in disgust, and the girl pays him no attention. He has fucked up. Now he has to stand there, ignored and embarrassed, and has to pull his money out to pay; guiltily, he leaves a bit more, and walks out chastened. He walked into 'what the American Dream would be' and he sullied it with his smart-arse comment. As he's getting into his car, a bus pulls up and two marines get off: he looks at them and there's a brief flash of stretcher-bearers in Vietnam, then he pops his amyl nitrate and drives off shouting, 'God's mercy on you, swine!'

Which is actually his last line of dialogue in the book, delivered there in the airport.

I really liked the scene. But Lesley Walker, the editor, and I were the only ones who seemed to get it; everybody else saw something more in it. Because everything in the film is so twisted, when we finally did something simple and straight, they thought maybe the old man was pimping for the girl, or something like that. They were so disoriented that they couldn't accept something normal. There are a lot of endings in the film and this was one too many. I talked to a lot of people, and they'd clearly got the sense of him knowing they'd gone too far in the North Star Café, so we chopped the scene out.

We also took out the DA from Georgia, a very funny scene from the book, which takes place at the convention. Duke and Gonzo terrorize a cop by describing the most outrageous nonsense, about people in LA having their blood sucked out by Satanists. It's a good scene, but it was unnecessary. In the book you can take these individual tales at your own pace, but film makes different demands on the audience. At some point we realized we were giving them too much stuff. It's sad, because I and a lot of people I know just want *more* – we want to go in and wallow in cinema. But audiences have been corrupted by simplistic film-making and storytelling, to the point where they can't handle complexity or different lengths. I bet they could have taken it twenty or thirty years ago.

But the audience for that kind of cinema was always a relative minority. For Easy Rider and a lot of other films like that, there was a bigger audience available. After all, we had a baby boom. I'm sure forty-year-old couples weren't going to see Easy Rider, but there were all of those kids – and I was one of them – so we could provide this huge market for off-beat films. Now we're all middle-aged, with mortgages, and don't go to the movies any more.

You think today's audience is corrupted by simple storylines, structured in three acts with strong motivation, just like the screenwriting manuals teach?
Exactly.

Whereas your natural instinct is to construct a Chinese box of as much complexity as you can get away with ...
I no longer know who does and doesn't like my work. I'm confused. I know almost everybody who loves movies loves *Fear and Loathing*. I know people on the technical side and musicians love it, and people from a generation that isn't in denial love it, and there are these fourteen-year-old kids from high school who love it. I'm trying to corrupt youth in my own way, not in Spielberg's: mine is a Socratic corruption. It's been interesting to see kids write on the Web, 'This is the best movie I've ever seen.'

Kids who didn't previously know the book?
Yes, and now the book is back in the bestseller lists. I seem to make movies to get people to read books. I was hoping they would do this with Raspe and *Munchausen*, but I think I've finally succeeded on this one. There must be a new generation who need to see that you can do these things. I met a really bright fourteen-year-old girl in New York who said that all her friends in high school were sneaking in to see it, even though it's R-rated, and loving it. One fifteen-year-old said, when asked why he rated it so highly, 'Because it's honest.' Perhaps the kids can see through the hypocrisy that currently clothes the American empire. In the end, I think it'll be a grass-roots thing, but the way it was first released – going into 1,100 cinemas and sold as a romp – was just wrong.

Each sequence is an attempt to simulate the sense of derangement of the senses.
Of all my work, this is the hardest for me to know whether I've made a

good or a bad film. For me, it was a juggling act, trying to keep all the plates in the air and to keep it entertaining and involving, because the audience can't rely on normal dramatic structure, suspense or romance. You don't have a narrative of any real strength, you're not gripped by the normal tools of film-making. Richard LaGravenese said he laughed hysterically for the first hour, then suddenly we pulled him inside out, with nerves and tissue exposed, but he couldn't look away. He thought it was some of the best work I've done. Some people think that in five years we'll look back and realize what a watershed the film was. Others are just appalled by it. I think there's a secondary language embedded in the film that people either grasp or don't.

Many of the same problems would apply to a film that was made in parallel with yours, Scorsese's Kundun, *where again we pretty much know the story in advance and the film-maker has to rely on a filmic structure, for want of a better phrase, and on all sorts of devices that are normally suppressed by a strong narrative.*
It's the director's tightrope walk, where you're really showing off your skills. I thought the Tibetans in *Kundun* were mesmerizing. In ours, I thought Johnny and Benicio were totally watchable characters. From the moment I saw the rough cut, which ran two hours and forty-three minutes, I was intrigued by these guys, so when reviews say we don't care about them, I feel they're just making a moral judgement. For me, Johnny is so watchable and sympathetic you want to see what's going to happen to him; and Benicio is so unpredictable that it's a case of 'What's he going to do next?'

He's terrifying because there's no sense of limit or boundary.
When I talked to Ralph Steadman, his only criticism was that he doesn't think Benicio is Gonzo because he has no real charm, no twinkle, he's just a demonic force. And I understand that, because when we were shooting I often thought, 'That's really funny, but he's missing some of the humour because he's so into the intensity of the character.'

They were both on board as a team when you came to the film?
Yes, but they're quite antithetical in the way they work. Benicio is very slow and steady; he spends a huge amount of time going over it again and again, rehearsing, discussing this word and that move – totally Method. Johnny's approach is different: effectively he spent months with Hunter Thompson, digging into his archives, stealing his clothes and objects as talismans. In fact, the Red Shark we use in the film is Hunter's: Johnny drove it from Aspen to Vegas. But when Johnny's on

set he's very quick, almost like Jonathan Pryce in *Brazil*, just one or two takes, and very relaxed. We're laughing before the take, during the take tears flow, then we're laughing after it. Benicio was more like De Niro in *Brazil*: it was rough because I couldn't get a tempo. I'm sure it was frustrating for Benicio because he wasn't getting enough takes, but it was also frustrating for Johnny because we were doing too many for him. I had to keep things moving: 'We've done seven takes and that's it.' So I ended up having to shoot in a very different way. Benicio doesn't repeat himself: in the wide shot he'd do one thing and in the close-up something else, so there's no continuity. Johnny, on the other hand, was perfect, hitting marks within millimetres. Technically, he's the most superb actor, fast and inventive. Cutting the film, Lesley said that while a normal scene would take one day, if Benicio was in it, it would be four days minimum, because nothing matched. So I shot wider than usual.

The wide-angle lenses are the most immediately striking aspect of the film.
I was watching *Face/Off* the other day, where you're right in tight with huge close-ups.[5] But although I was using a 16mm or 14mm lens as our standard, I didn't want to distort, so I only pushed in tight sometimes. A lot of the wide-shot style was to encompass whatever Benicio might do and also to see more of Johnny, because he's so physical and uses his whole body. Shall we go in closer? No, we'll just stay back so the environment is ever present. We were also doing things with the horizon – there must be more Dutched shots in this film than any ever made.

What are Dutched shots?
It's when you put the horizon off-level. I don't know why it's called Dutching; perhaps something to do with Holland being so flat – trying to make it more dramatic? We do it so much in the first part of the film that, when things get really weird later and we level the horizon, it's even more disturbing. The world is always moving, often within shots, where we go from the horizon tilted one way to then another all in one movement. It was fun to do and part of the whole idea of working fast and forcing myself to take chances.

The interiors are shot very wide too, so there's a constant sense of distorted space.
They're disturbing spaces that people either want to get out of or hang on in there. Many people clearly see the whole film as a drug trip, a complete drug experience that starts on speed and the fun of being free, then sags a bit and turns ugly; then, when the knife appears, you want to get out, but that passes. In the middle of the film, you escape to the open

spaces of the desert, but then it starts all over again, and the disorienta-
tion and relentlessness are worse. Some people react really strongly
against that.

'Like being the only sober person in a room full of drunks or druggies'
was a common verdict at Cannes. But there is a general problem about
simulating derangement of the senses, isn't there? How does it work for
the sober/sane/non-drug-taking spectator?
Well, there are obviously some people who never get into the film and so
hate it. Those who start by liking the characters and go with them
become immersed, and they're the ones who come out saying this is the
best thing they've ever seen. I haven't got to grips yet with how the sheep
and the goats separate on this. What triggers these reactions? Some people think that, if we cut this or that, it would improve responses, but I'm
sure it wouldn't, although one recurrent issue has been the vomiting.
The editor of the *LA Times* calendar section walked out of the film and
refused to do a piece on it, then her staff called up a week later to ask if
I'd comment for a survey they were doing on vomiting in current films.
A perfect example of the American media in action.

I think in the end we've made an anti-drug movie, although not
everyone agrees with me. But even if it's not anti, at least it's an honest
film about drugs in the sense that you get the ups and downs, the goods
and bads – the whole thing; you're put through the intensity of what
drugs are about. The actor who played the stockbroker who comes into
the toilet when the guy's sucking acid off Johnny's sleeve e-mailed me
and said something like: 'I was in there and I was loving it and then hating it. I wanted out but I couldn't get out, then I was back in and loving
it.' So he took the ride, and I think it's about being brave enough to take
the ride properly.

I didn't know what Maggie, my wife, was going to make of it,
because she's not a wild person and has never taken a drug in her life.
But she came out beaming and saying, 'Buy the ticket: take the ride.' I
was surprised by how much she liked it. And Lesley Walker doesn't take
drugs, but she's not frightened by these trips.

The inevitable question: how much is it influenced by your own experi-
ence of drugs?
From the beginning, with *Python*, people have always thought I was on
drugs, but I'm not. That stuff is all inside me and I guess I'm just sensitive to it, whereas most people block these things out. I've never taken
acid in my life; in fact, I've never tried any of these drugs, except marijuana and, once or twice, cocaine. Perhaps I'm able to make a film like

this because I sense I know what the drugs are about without having done them. I know that cocaine just speeds me up and leaves me with a terrible hangover, and that marijuana or hash make me implode. But I find that people are intimidated by certain words and ideas – like the latent paedophilia in the Lucy scenes – when they hear specific buzz-words they blank, but one of the reasons for making this film was to push people into those extreme situations and experiences, hopefully to get them thinking.

Which is short-circuited if they have a literal response to the drugs or the vomiting.

Right from the beginning, they should wonder: how can that drug collection be real? Is it possible that we're talking metaphor here? There's no way you can take the book literally: it's bigger than literal, just like Vegas, with those noises and colours and lights, all designed to disorient you. The old Caesar's Palace, built in the fifties, has a kind of Deco look, all black and red with crystal lights. It's beautiful and essentially quite abstract. In the new Caesar's Palace, they've re-created the streets of Ancient Rome, with an arched, sky-painted ceiling, and the lighting changes as you go through the day. So the new Vegas is literal, while the old Vegas was more abstract, and that's very much what has happened to films. People's ability to read a film in something other than a literal way seems to be lost.

So how do you think we should be reading all those recent films set in Las Vegas? Apart from Casino *and* Fear and Loathing, *there have been* One From the Heart, Indecent Proposal, Leaving Las Vegas *and* Bugsy.[6] *Do they point to something?*

Vegas is the peak of American society. All of America is there, or comes there. I'm sitting in the Tropicana Hotel and right across the street is New York, New York – the entire island of Manhattan compressed into one city block and girdled by a roller coaster. Next to that is Excalibur, where you've got those silly medieval-style buildings with turrets stuck on top that look like gigantic ice-cream cones painted blue and with red on top – awful. By contrast, New York, New York is beautifully done: you walk through Grand Central Station and descend into Central Park. It's permanently night, with neon lights flashing, and there's a good Italian restaurant where we ate most nights. There are artificial trees, so you can dine in or out — except it's all indoors. Watching the people there, they've taken on these new American shapes and they walk the way people at Disneyland walk: they waddle, very slowly, because everything's being done for them. They have become spoonfed infants feeding on predigested pap. And now they're building Venice and Paris in Vegas.

The whole world is being sucked in . . .
Vegas is a black hole – a strange attractor in chaos theory. It's also the fastest-growing city in America.

This reminds me of your interest in Baudrillard and his view of America.
Yes, his idea of the simulacrum, that everything now is a copy of something else and there's no reality.[7] That's what I found with Vegas. Architecturally, it makes no sense, in a most disturbing way. There are arches that should be supported, but they're not; they put a Byzantine dome on to an ante-bellum façade and then serve Polynesian-style food. 'Nothing has any meaning' is what Vegas says. All that's left, all that means anything, is winning or losing, which is America today. It's all about money and materialism.

When you were growing up in LA, you had a great admiration for the craftsmanship and, in a way, the integrity of Disneyland, until you felt it became something tacky and fraudulent. Do you see Vegas as Disney's destination?
Disneyland has certainly arrived in Vegas. It's like Bad Boy's Island in *Pinocchio*: it's beautiful and it's got everything, yet there's a rot at the centre which is actually destroying something. *Fear and Loathing* is about an anarchic quality, a sense of madness, of pushing things – including yourself – to the limit, like the Dr Johnson quote that Hunter uses as an epigraph to *Fear and Loathing*: 'He who makes a beast of himself gets rid of the pain of being a man.'[8] In a sense, this is an anti-material film: everything material in it, like rooms and cars, is destroyed, so it's attacking the very heart of modern America. Nobody wins, nobody walks out with a clear moral message. The wisdom at the end is a kind of sadness. It isn't necessarily offering any help for the future.

It's also a kind of fusion of the archetypal pilgrimage and trickster stories, with the innocent and his worldly wise or tempting accomplice.
Hopefully, there is a kind of knowledge at the end. The book doesn't offer this as clearly as the film, so perhaps my moral sense is stronger than Hunter's, although I doubt it. A lot of people seem to think that the speech about Tim Leary and a whole generation of acid-heads is a cop-out, that we've had this wild ride and then we just take a moral stance at the end. But they're missing the point. It's about *not* being able to buy peace and understanding – or experience or knowledge, or, for that matter, anything of real value – and it's ultimately about individual

responsibility: there is no one tending the light at the end of the tunnel except us. The film asks: is it possible to deal with our responsibility by becoming totally irresponsible?

One aspect of Gonzo in the film, as distinct from the book, is that he keeps disappearing on Duke. In the book, in the first half he takes the lawyer to the airport. In the film, he's just gone; he somehow has the right to abandon Duke, who doesn't have the corresponding right to leave him, which results in him encouraging Duke to try the Adrenochrome. It's as if Gonzo is punishing him: 'You tried to leave, but I'm the free one; you're doomed and you've got to go through this process.' He's the tempter with the Adrenochrome and, when he walks up with the tray; it reminded me of Dirk Bogarde in *The Servant*, he's so oily and smooth, using the gun and the knife to serve cocaine.[9] He has Duke totally in his clutches, toying with him, taking him to crazed, demonic heights, then dropping him in the most dismissive way.

The film also coexists with the myth of Hunter Thompson, who's written a lot of other books all about his battles with bureaucracy and official-dom. He's turning into a familiar American figure, the cranky, backwoods sage – somewhere between Mark Twain and Edmund Wilson.
. . . Fighting for truth, justice and the American way. That's what he is: a great writer, but one who works too hard at being an outrageous icon. Yet when the conditions are right, he's incredibly gentle, solicitous and generous. We had a falling out after I was quoted out of context in the *New York Times*, saying that I thought he died in 1974 and there's a mummified effigy of him sitting on this hill in Aspen, where everyone goes to worship. It wasn't meant malevolently, but he took great offence at this. He's like Baron Munchausen: he's the only one who gets to write his lies. Nevertheless, he described the finished film as possibly a master-piece, and called it 'an eerie trumpet call over a lost battlefield'. Like I said, a great writer.

Where did you start from on the music for the film, given that there are a lot of quite definite references and cues in the book?
We started from the book, which is full of songs like 'One Toke Over the Line', which is what Gonzo is singing in the car. Then I thought about having some good Vegas stuff: Tom Jones was the first choice; then what could be better than Debbie Reynolds? 'Tammy' has never been used like that before. I started with what was in the book, then began to throw them out for various reasons. For instance, 'Sympathy for the Devil' is the anthem of the book to many people, but we couldn't afford it – they wanted $600,000 – and the tempo was wrong for the beginning of the

film. We had to get in with a bang, so I finally got out an old Big Brother and the Holding Company album with Janis Joplin, and there it was: the right energy, speed, raw wild madness, and the title, 'Combination of the Two', couldn't be better, although I don't know if anyone notices these things. I just love those magic moments – ah, Perry Como! That made me howl, so we stuck 'Magic Moments' in as Duke leaves another distraught group of people in his wake, and Wayne Newton with 'Strangers in the Night'. It seemed to me that the more bizarre things were getting, the more these reassuring songs worked.

Three Dog Night's 'Mama Told Me Not to Come' has always been a song I liked, and Jefferson Airplane is in the book, of course. The song that's playing under the 'wave' speech is one that Johnny was actually playing on set in his earwig, a tiny radio receiver stuck in his ear with an assistant off-stage giving him his lines. This is a trick he learned from Marlon Brando, but he uses it more often to play music and sound effects. He started out as a musician and having music in his head while on set helps him a lot.

When I started this whole project, I thought there would be five or six songs and I was going to convince Ray Cooper to compose the rest, which would basically be rhythmic. But, in the end, I used more songs and Ray did the music for the Adrenochrome and post-Adrenochrome sequences. They're amazing sequences, not composed as such, with Ray laying down lots of different tracks and then bringing in a famous Japanese guitarist, Tomoyasu Hotei, who did a great Hendrix imitation. Originally, we wanted to use several Hendrix songs, but the Hendrix family won't allow his music to be used in any film about drugs. More denial?

So who was really controlling the music and sound decisions, the overall layering process?
Ray and I work together. He can respond like a performer to what he sees, but probably most of the final song choices are mine. Ray is constantly introducing me to new musical material and he originally had the idea of using lounge music, but ironic counterpoint seemed to be the better way to go and the Robert Goulet 'Amore Scusami' – which is over the Lizard Lounge, is so big and inflated that it's much crazier than anything cool. The very last song that went in was when they get rid of Lucy at the wedding chapel, and I was going to be very obvious and have 'Going to the Chapel', but it was expensive and we were already over the music budget. So Harry Garfield at Universal music sent us some 'cheap' music and there was 'Yummy, Yummy, Yummy', which just cracked me up.

The intro is perfect for Johnny running out of the room – it doesn't sound like it's going to be a song – then it goes into this silly bubblegum music, and ends with Gonzo's violent vomiting after 'Yummy, yummy, yummy, I've got love in my tummy'. That's the way it works: you keep digging and eventually things find their place. Even the Stones made it. Since everyone expected them at the beginning, perversely we decided to put them at the end: we finish where Hunter began, musically, and I think the lyrics of 'Jumping Jack Flash' work in a different way than you've ever heard them before. You're coming out of this painful experience and it's all right; in fact, it's a gas, it's reassuring.

Yes, reassuring. There were some knowing smiles around me when the lights went up in a downtown Washington cinema, where I first saw it. Send 'em out feeling warm and loved. The most ridiculous thing about this project is that I set out to be totally politically incorrect and badly behaved, and after spending a year on it I wanted everyone to love it. Well, how can I expect that? The best you can hope is that you plant a seed so that there'll be enough people who think, 'Yes, I can do a bit more,' or 'I want something more.' I kept saying at Cannes that perhaps *Godzilla* was the end of the Jurassic age of the big predictable corporate product films, so that the little furry mammals could crawl out, and I hoped we were the first of these.

Instead you took a broadside of outrage.
Yes. The press at Cannes hated it. It was awful. What was surprising was that it had gone incredibly well at the screenings here, and I can usually tell from these. In the States, the studio people loved it; the French distributor loved it; and Gilles Jacob even thought it might win the Palme d'Or before the whole Cannes mess began. I don't know what they thought Terry Gilliam and Johnny Depp were going to do. Obviously, they didn't know the book; they *thought* they knew it, because 'fear and loathing' has entered the language. Wild and funny, yes, but it's also really dark and disturbing and emetic. I was stunned, but I had to keep doing these interviews and talking to people who obviously hated it. I remember babbling all through an interview with Barry Norman and I think he was terrified we were going to talk about the film properly. At the main press conference, I kept trying to be combative, trying to push the press to ask me some ugly questions, but they wouldn't do it. The problem is that politeness has taken over: some journalists didn't want to interview us because they didn't like the film – how pathetic.

There is a culture of stardom which demands, and gets, anodyne adulation.

When we were making the film, Johnny and I kept joking about what a disgusting, dangerous film we were producing and that, luckily, I lived outside the US, so they would come looking for him; about how the decent people of this great country had spent twenty-five years dredging themselves up from those appalling times, and then along comes this shit which undermines everything that's good and true in America.

I thought they were going to say either 'great' or get very angry, but the angry just went quiet. It was a case of 'ignore the nightmare in the bathroom: ignore the nightmare in the cinema'. Unfortunately, as I said, the wide release was a big mistake; it should have been built more slowly.

It needed to be released more like an art movie, however big its budget. The marketing people really thought it would go big. However, the tracking wasn't good and awareness wasn't what it should have been before it opened. There were problems with key reviews not coming out in time; even, ironically, *Rolling Stone*. Add to that the fact that most of the colleges weren't in session and you have the makings of something less than a box-office smash. Then people started saying it's going to be huge on video; I heard someone describe it as a 'seminal' film. Great, maybe I've finally made my art film, the one that'll be recognized after my death and that changed the course of cinema! This is my desperately megalomaniac side coming out. At least Duke learns something in the film, but have I learned anything? I'm still trying to work it out: wisdom takes longer than it takes to see a film.

People also need ideas to help them respond to a film, so it depends what verdicts are in circulation. The now-notorious case of Peeping Tom *is a good example. It's still the same film, but now people have a whole range of ideas about it to draw upon.*
You need a John the Baptist. I was still hoping that people would get into discussions about *Fear and Loathing*, but they don't seem to be.[10] Those who like it aren't sure which of their friends will like it; they're not sure what to say. Other people just don't like it and don't want to talk about it. Then there's the American obsession with success: it's perceived not to have been a success, so why should I want to go and see it? Sometimes I feel my films are a litmus test of society. What I fear is that America has returned to a kind of conservatism that's reminiscent of the fifties. Only this time it's more hypocritical and unfocused. As Hunter predicted, America has become a nation of panicky sheep.

What's going to happen next?

I don't know. We're still trying to get *The Defective Detective* free. The script of *Minotaur* isn't right, nor is *Don Quixote*. I got excited about *A Tale of Two Cities* again and I've been reading other scripts and books. There's even another Philip K. Dick book that I've been looking at. It's about society becoming polite and decent. Relativism is in the ascendant and absolutism is outlawed. Then a character comes along who can see the future, so he can be definite about things. Absolutism and the mob take over, because people are so desperate for something to believe in. That book was trying to get people to think about things in the fifties, and *Fear and Loathing* is trying to get them to think again.

I'm sure I did the right thing, originally: getting away from America, coming to England and working completely outside the Hollywood system. But now that I've allowed myself to put one foot back in, I'm really torn between these two worlds. And it's the English or European side that's flagging, because I'm so determined to prove to Hollywood that things they don't believe in are possible. In a strange way, I don't think I should still be trying to do *The Defective Detective*, because I've already done it: it's like trying to get *Munchausen* right. Or perhaps it's my *Fanny and Alexander*, a compendium of everything I've ever tried to do on a large scale, so that I can finally get the epic stuff out of my system and go back to doing smaller, more delicate pieces.[11]

There are certain things I can do, like creating images or worlds that nobody else thinks of, and I feel a responsibility to do that. I've always had this problem of talent – or whatever it is that I've got: I'm the caretaker who's supposed to look after this gift or mutation and use it wisely. And when I feel time is getting wasted, I kick myself for not using it in another way, but I still tend to commit to one thing and say, 'None shall pass but that.'

NOTES

1 Hunter S. Thompson, with illustrations by Ralph Steadman, *Fear and Loathing in Las Vegas: A Savage Journey to the Heart of the American Dream* (1972).

2 *Fear and Loathing*, p. 172.

3 Robert Yarber (b. 1948) an American figurative painter who studied at the Cooper Union in New York and has exhibited widely throughout the US and occasionally in Europe. His characteristic scenarios were described by critic Joanne Burstein as 'macabre plastic cartoon people love and/or hate and simultaneously fall through neon-lit space' (quoted in Sanford Sivitz Shaman, *Robert Yarber Paintings: 1980–88*, Palmer Museum of Art, The Pennsylvania State University, 1989).

4 *Fear and Loathing*, p. 95–6.

5 *Face/Off* (1997), directed by John Woo.

6 *Casino* (Martin Scorsese, 1995), *Indecent Proposal* (Adrian Lyne, 1993), *Leaving Las Vegas* (Mike Figgis, 1995), *Bugsy* (Barry Levinson, 1991).

7 See, for instance, Jean Baudrillard, *Simulacra and Simulation (The Body, in Theory: Histories of Cultural Materialism)* (1995); or Baudrillard's notorious *The Gulf War Did Not Take Place* (1995).

8 This epigraph also appears at the beginning of the film.

9 *The Servant* (1963), screenplay by Harold Pinter, directed by Joseph Losey.

10 Recorded in June 1998, before the film's UK release.

11 *Fanny and Alexander* (1982) was announced as Ingmar Bergman's farewell to cinema, a complex family drama that alludes to many of his films and includes elements of autobiography.

Filmography

No filmography can be definitive, but should be regarded as a stage reached of work-inevitably-in-progress. This aims to include all of Terry Gilliam's work as a director or main creative contributor, although it does not attempt to identify his individual contribution to the television series of *Monty Python's Flying Circus*. It has been compiled from a variety of sources, but has benefited especially from information kindly supplied by Max Schaefer and Markku Salmi of the Filmographic Unit in the the British Film Institute's National Library. The detail of credits listings has increased massively during the period covered by the filmography, hence much more information is available for later films (and more may become available eventually for earlier ones). To prevent major creative credits becoming lost in a mass of names, the *Sight and Sound* convention of listing these first has been followed.

1968
Jimmy Young Puns
The History of the Whoopee Cushion
Beware the Elephants
Animations for *We Have Ways of Making You Laugh*, London Weekend
  Television

Animated Sequences for *Marty*, BBC Television

The Christmas Card
Animation for *Do Not Adjust Your Stocking*, Thames Television,
  Christmas 1968

1969
Animation Sequences (including **Elephants**) for *Do Not Adjust Your Set*,
  Thames Television

1969–70
Monty Python's Flying Circus

First series: 5 October 1969–11 January 1970
Second series: 15 September–22 December 1970

1970
Title sequnce for *Cry of the Banshee,* American International Pictures

1971
And Now for Something Completely Different
Director: Ian Macnaughton
Producer: Patricia Casey
Screenplay: Graham Chapman, John Cleese, Terry Gilliam, Eric Idle, Terry
    Jones, Michael Palin
Director of Photography: David Muir
Editor: Thom Noble
Art Director: Colin Grimes
Animation: Terry Gilliam
Production company: Kettledrum Productions/Python (Monty) Pictures
Production Manager: Kevin Francis
Assistant Director: Douglas Hermes
Animation Photographer: Bob Godfrey
Special Effects: John Horton
Sound Recording: John Brommage
Sound Editor: Terry Poulton
Cast: Graham Chapman, John Cleese, Terry Gilliam, Eric Idle, Terry Jones,
    Michael Palin, Carol Cleveland
88 mins

Titles and **Animated Sequences,** including **The Miracle of Flight** (5 mins) for
    The Marty Feldman Comedy Machine, ABC

1972
The Great Gas Gala
Two commercials for British Gas

1972–3
Monty Python's Flying Circus
Third series: 19 October 1972–18 January 1973
The German programmes:
Monty Python in Deutschland (1972)
Monty Python Blodeln für Deutschland (1973)

1973
Title Sequence for *William,* ABC Television back to school special

1974
Monty Python and the Holy Grail
Directors: Terry Gilliam, Terry Jones
Producer: Mark Forstater
Screenplay: Graham Chapman, John Cleese, Terry Gilliam, Eric Idle, Terry
    Jones, Michael Palin
Director of Photography: Terry Bedford
Editor: John Hackney
Production Designer: Roy Smith
Animation: Terry Gilliam
Production company: Python (Monty) Pictures
Executive Producer: John Goldstone
Assistant Director: Gerry Harrison
Special Photographic Effects: Julian Doyle
Special Effects: John Horton
Costumes: Hazel Pethig, Charles Knode
Title Design: Lucinda Cowell, Kate Hepburn, Francine Lawrence
Music and Songs: Neil Innes
Additional Music: De Wolfe
Choreography: Leo Kharibian
Sound Recording: Garth Marshall
Boom Operator: Godfrey Kirby
Fight Director/Period Consultant: John Walker
Cast: Graham Chapman (King Arthur), John Cleese (Black Knight/Sir
    Lancelot the Brave/French Knight/Tim the Enchanter), Terry Gilliam
    (Patsy/Soothsayer), Eric Idle (Sir Robin the-Not-Quite-So-
    Brave/Concorde/Roger the Shrubber/Brother Maynard), Terry Jones (Bede-
    vere the Wise/Herbert), Michael Palin and others (Knights of NI), Eric Idle
    and Graham Chapman (Guards of Swamp Castle), John Young (famous his-
    torian), Carol Cleveland (Zoot/Dingo)
90 mins

Monty Python
Fourth series (without John Cleese): 31 October–5 December 1974

1977
Jabberwocky
Director: Terry Gilliam
Producer: Sandy Lieberson
Screenplay: Charles Alverson, Terry Gilliam
Director of Photography: Terry Bedford
Editor: Michael Bradsell
Production Designer: Roy Smith
Music: De Wolfe

Production company: Umbrella Entertainment
Executive Producer: John Goldstone
Associate Producer: Julian Doyle
Production Supervisor: Joyce Herlihy
Production Manager: Bill Camp
Assistant Director: Bob Howard
Additional Photography: Julian Doyle
Special Effects: John F. Brown, Effects Associates
Monster creation: Valerie Charlton, Clinton Cavers, Jen Effects
Art Director: Millie Burns
Costumes: Hazel Pethig, Charles Knode
Sound Recording: Garth Marshall
Boom operator: Godfrey Kirby
Sound Re-recording: Bob Jones, Bill Rowe
Sound Editor: Alan Bell
Armourer: Terry English, Peter Leight
Cast: Michael Palin (Dennis Cooper), Max Wall (King Bruno the Question-
   able), Deborah Fallender (Princess), John le Mesurier (Passelewe), Annette
   Badland (Griselda Fishfinger), Warren Mitchell (Mr Fishfinger), Brenda
   Cowling (Mrs Fishfinger), Harry H. Corbett (squire), Rodney Bewes (Other
   Squire), Dave Prowse (Good Knight/Black Knight), Bernard Bresslaw (land-
   lord), Derek Francis (Bishop), Alexandra Dane (Betsy), Peter Cellier (1st
   merchant), Frank Williams (2nd merchant), Anthony Carrick (3rd mer-
   chant), Kenneth Thornett (merchant's steward), John Bird (1st herald), Neil
   Innes (2nd herald/drummer), Paul Curran (Mr Cooper), Graham Crowden
   (fanatics' leader), Kenneth Colley (1st fanatic), Christopher Logue (2nd
   fanatic), JanineDuvitski (3rd fanatic), Tony Aitkin (flagellant), Peggyann
   Clifford (merchant's nurse), John Blain (foreman), Ted Milton (puppeteer),
   John Hughman (King's valet), John Gorman (guard with aunt), Glenn
   Williams (1st gate guard), Bryan Pringle (2nd gate guard), Terry Jones
   (poacher), Anne Way (merchant's wife), Brian Glover (armourer), Desmond
   Jones (1st door opener/servant), Eric Chitty (2nd door opener/servant),
   Julian Hough (1st peasant/4th fanatic), Harold Goodwin (2nd peasant),
   Tony Sympson (3rd peasant), Bill Gavin (old man with petition), Willoughby
   Goddard (eggman), Sarah Grazebrook (serving wench), Bob Raymond
   (mason), Anita Sharp-Bolster (old crone/woman with stone), George Silver
   (bandit chief), Peter Casillas (3rd squire), Simon Williams (prince), John
   Sharp (sergeant), Jerrold Wells (Wat Dabney), Gordon Rollings (Sister Jes-
   sica), Mollie Maureen (head nun), Peter Salmon (monster man).
101 mins

1979
Monty Python's Life of Brian
Director: Terry Jones

Producer: John Goldstone
Screenplay: Graham Chapman, John Cleese, Terry Gilliam, Eric Idle, Terry
    Jones, Michael Palin
Director of Photography: Peter Biziou
Editor: Julian Doyle
Music: Geoffrey Burgon
Animation: Terry Gilliam
Production company: HandMade Films
Executive Producers: George Harrison, Dennis O'Brien, Tarak ben Ammar
Associate Producer: Tim Hampton
Assistant Director: Roger Christian
Songs: 'Brian' by Andre Jacquemin, David Howman performed by Sonia
    Jones; 'Bright Side of Life' by and performed by Eric Idle
Costumes: Hazel Pethig, Charles Knode
Make-up: Maggie Weston, Elaine Carew
Sound Recording: Garth Marshall
Sound Re-recording: Hugh Strain
Sound Editor: John Foster
Cast: Terry Jones (Mandy, mother of Brian/Colin, a passer-by/Simon the Holy
    Man/Bob Hoskins/saintly passer-by), Graham Chapman (1st Wise
    Man/Brian called Brian/Biggus Dickus), Michael Palin (2nd Wise Man/Mr
    Big Nose/Francis, a revolutionary/Mrs A, who casts second stone/ex-
    leper/Ben, an ancient prisoner/Pontius Pilate, Roman governor/boring
    prophet/Eddie, a passer-by/Nisus Wettus), John Cleese (3rd Wise Man/Dirk
    Reg, Leader of Judean People's Front/Jewish official at stoning/Centurion of
    the Yard/Arthur, a passer-by), Eric Idle (Mr Cheeky/Stan, called Loretta, a
    confused revolutionary/Harry the Haggler, a bread-and-stone salesman/cul-
    prit woman, who casts the first stone/intensely dull youth, a passer-by/Otto,
    Leader of the Judean People's Front/jailer's assistant/Mr Frisbee III), Terry
    Gilliam (another person further forward/revolutionary/masked com-
    mando/blood-and-thunder prophet/Geoffrey, a passer-by/jailer), Ken Colley
    (Jesus), Gwen Taylor (Mrs Big Nose/woman with sick donkey/young girl, a
    passer-by), Terence Bayler (Gregory/revolutionary/masked commando/Den-
    nis, a passer-by), Carol Cleveland (Mrs Gregory/Elsie, a passer-by), Charles
    McKeown (man further forward/revolutionary/masked commando/Roman
    soldier/giggling guard/blind man/false prophet), Sue Jones-Davies (Judith, a
    beautiful revolutionary), John Young (stonee/passer-by in crowd), Bernard
    McKenna (official Ssoner's helper/revolutionary/masked commando/giggling
    guard/passer-by in crowd), Neil Innes (weedy Samaritan at amphitheatre),
    John Case (gladiator), Chris Langham (revolutionary/masked commando/
    giggling guard/Alfonso), Charles Knode (passer-by), Spike Milligan (Spike),
    George Harrison (Mr Papadopoulis).
93 mins

Story Time
Animation compilation of earlier material
Director: Terry Gilliam
9 mins

1981
Time Bandits
Director: Terry Gilliam
Producer: Terry Gilliam
Screenplay: Michael Palin, Terry Gilliam
Director of Photography: Peter Biziou
Editor: Julian Doyle
Production Designer: Millie Burns
Music: Mike Moran
Production company: HandMade Films
Executive Producers: George Harrison, Dennis O'Brien
Associate Producer: Neville C Thompson
Production Manager: Graham Ford
Location Manager: Patrick Cassavetti
Production Assistant: Linda Bruce
2nd Unit Director: Julian Doyle
Assistant Directors: Simon Hinkley, Guy Travers, Mark Cooper, Chris Thompson
Camera Operator: David Garfath
Model Photography: Julian Doyle
Optical effects: Kent Houston, Paul Whitbread
Optical effects assistants: Tim Ollive, Dennis De Groot, Peerless Camera Company
Matte Artist: Ray Caple
Special effects supervisor: John Bunker
Special effects technician: Ross King
Special effects consultants: Chris Verner, Andy Thompson
Special effects modeller: Christine Overs, Lewis Coleman
Special effects runner: Chris Ostwald
Trolls: Ray Scott
Models: Valerie Charlton
Models assistant: Carol Dejong, Jean Ramsey, Alix Harwood, Behira Thraves
Puppet show: John Styles
Art Director: Norman Garwood
Draughtsperson: Steve Cooper
Sculptures: Geoff Rivers Bland, Laurie Warburton
Costumes: Jim Acheson, Hazel Coté
Make-up: Maggie Weston, Elaine Carew
Wigs and beards: Kenneth Lintott
Greek dance music: Trevor Jones
Additional music: De Wolfe, Ready Music

Songs/additional material: George Harrison
Music producer/percussion performer: Ray Cooper
Music Director: Harry Rabinowitz
Greek dance choreography: Tom Jobe
Sound Recording: Garth Marshall
Sound Re-recording: Paul Carr, Brian Paxton, Roger Cherrill
Sound Editor: Roger Cherrill
Dialogue editor: Mike Hokins
Footstep editor: Dino di Campo
Sound effects: André Jacquemin
Stunt Co-ordinators: Peter Brayham, Terry Yorke
Stunt knight: Brian Bowes
Og the Pig supplied: Mike Hearst
Benson the Dog supplied: Joan Woodgate
Cast: John Cleese (Robin Hood), Sean Connery (King Agamemnon), Shelley
Duvall (Pansy), Katherine Helmond (Mrs Ogre), Ian Holm (Napoleon),
Michael Palin (Vincent), Ralph Richardson (Supreme Being), Peter Vaughan
(Ogre), David Warner (Evil Genius), David Rappaport (Randall), Kenny
Daker (Fidgit), Jack Purvis (Wally), Mike Edmonds (Og), Malcolm Dixon
(Strutter), Tiny Ross (Vermin), Craig Warnock (Kevin), David Baker (Kevin's
father), Sheila Fearn (Kevin's mother), Jim Broadbent (compere), John Young
(Reginald), Myrtle Devenish (Beryl), Brian Bowes (Hussar), Leon Lissek (1st
refugee), Terence Bayler (Lucien), Preston Lockwood (Neguy), Charles McK-
eown (theatre manager), David Leland (puppeteer), John Hughman (The
Great Rumbozo), Derrick O'Connor (Robert Leader), Declan Mulholland
(2nd Robber), Neil McCarthy (3rd Robber), Peter Jonfield (Arm Wrestler),
Derek deadman (Robert), Jerold Wells (Benson), Roger Frost (Cartwright),
Martin Carroll (Baxi Brazilia III), Marcus Powell (Horsefish), Winston Dennis (bull-headed warrior), Del Baker (Greek fighting warrior), Juliette James
(Greek queen), Ian Muir (Giant), Mark Holmes (Troll father), Andrew
MacLachlan (fireman), Chris Grant (voice of TV announcer), Tony Jay
(voice of Supreme Being), Edwin Finn (Supreme Being's face)
113 mins

1982
Monty Python Live at the Hollywood Bowl
Director: Terry Hughes, Ian Macnaughton
Producer: Terry Hughes
Screenplay: Monty Python
Director of Photography: (not credited)
Editor: Julian Doyle
Music: John Duprez, Ray Cooper
Production company: HandMade Films
Executive Producer: Dennis O'Brien

Sound: Stan Miller
Cast: Graham Chapman, John Cleese, Terry Gilliam, Eric Idle, Terry Jones,
    Michael Palin, Pamela Stephenson, Carol Cleveland, Neil Innes
80 mins

1983
Monty Python's The Meaning of Life
Director: Terry Jones
Special sequence and animation director: Terry Gilliam
Producer: John Goldstone
Screenplay: Graham Chapman, John Cleese, Terry Gilliam, Eric Idle, Terry
    Jones, Michael Palin
Director of Photography: Peter Hannan
Editor: Julian Doyle
Production Designer: Harry Lange
Production company: Celandine Films/The Monty Python Partnership
Production Manager: David Wimbury
Location Manager: Peter Kohn
Production Assistant: Valerie Craig
Assistant Director: Ray Corbett
Camera Operator: Dewi Humphreys
Optical effects: Kent Houston, Paul Whitbread, Roy Fields, Tim Spence
Special Effects Supervisor: Richard Conway
Special Effects: Bob Hollow, David Watson, Ray Hanson
Model makers: Valerie Charlton, Carole De Yong
Animators: Tim Ollive, Richard Ollive, Kate Hepburn, Mike Stuart, Jill Brooks
Art Director: Richard Dawking
Set Decorator: Simon Wakefield
Costume Designer: Jim Acheson
Costume makers: Ray Scott, Vin Burnham, Shirley Denny, Jill Thraves,
    William Baboo, Lizzie Willey
Make-up: Maggie Weston
Choreography: Arlene Phillips
Sound Recording: Garth Marshall
Sound Re-recording: Paul Carr, Brian Paxton
Sound Editor: Rodney Glenn
Cast: : Graham Chapman, John Cleese, Terry Gilliam, Eric Idle, Terry Jones,
    Michael Palin, Carol Cleveland, Simon Jones, Patricia Quinn, Judy Loe,
    Andrew MacLachlan, Mark Holmes, Valerie Whittington, Jennifer Franks,
    Imogen Bickford-Smith, Angela Mann, Peter Lovstrom, Victoria Plum, Ann
    Rosenfeld, George Silver
90 mins

The Crimson Permanent Assurance (special sequence)

Director: Terry Gilliam
Producer: John Goldstone
Screenplay: Terry Gilliam
Director of Photography : Roger Pratt
Editor: Julian Doyle
Production Designer: John Beard
Music: John Duprez
Production company: The Monty Python Partnership
Costumes: Joyce Stoneman
Make-up: Elaine Carew
Hair: Maureen Stephenson, Sallie Evans
Cast: Sydney Arnold, Ross Davidson, Eric Francis, Russell Kilminster, Peter
    Merrill, Larry Noble, John Scott Martin, Guy Bertrand, Myrtle Devenish,
    Matt Frewer, Peter Mantle, Cameron Miller, Paddy Ryan, Eric Stovell,
    Andrew Bicknell, Tim Doublas, Billy John, Len Marten, Gareth Milne,
    Leslie Sarony, Wally Thomas.
16mins

1985
Brazil
Director: Terry Gilliam
Producer: Arnon Milchan
Screenplay: Terry Gilliam, Tom Stoppard, Charles McKeown
Director of Photography: Roger Pratt
Editor: Julian Doyle
Production Designer: Norman Garwood
Music: Michael Kamen
Production company: Brazil Productions
Co-Producer: Patrick Cassavetti
Production Accountant: Terry Connors
Assistant Accountant: Lesley Broderick
Cashier: Judith May
Production Co-ordinator: Margaret Adams
Production Manager (French Unit): Chantal Perrin-Cluzet
Unit Manager: Linda Bruce
Location Manager (French Unit): Yves Duteil
Production Manager: Matthew Scudamore
Post-production Assistant: Sally Kinnes
Production Runner: Laurence Bodini
Producer's/Director's Secretary: Katy Radford
Location Research: Hamish Scott
2nd Unit Director: Julian Doyle
Assistant Director: Guy Travers
2nd Assistant Director: Chris Thompson

3rd Assistant Director: Richard Coleman
Assistant Directors (additional): Christopher Newman, Terence Fitch, Kevin
  Westley
Script Supervisor: Penny Eyles
Trainee Continuity: Melanie Matthews
Casting Director: Irene Lamb
Casting Director (US): Margery Simkin
Camera Operator: David Garfath
Follow Focus: Bob Stilwell
Camera Assistant: John Ignatius
Clapper Loader: Mark Cridlin
Additional Camera Assistants: Brian Herlihy, Steve Parker
Camera Grip: Rosie Straker
Grips: Porky Rivers
Grips (French Unit): Jean-Yves Freess
Gaffer Electrician: Roy Rodhouse
Best Boys: Chuck Finch, Brian Martin
Electricians: George White, Perry Evans, Toby Tyler, Brian Sullivan, Alan
  Crosch, Les Rodhouse
Chief Electrician (French Unit): Jean-Claude Lebras
Video Consultant: Ira Curtis Coleman
Stills Photography: David Appleby
Model/Effects Photography: Roger Pratt, Julian Doyle, Tim Spence
Matte Artist: Ray Caple
Blue Screen Consultant: Stanley Sayer
Special Effects Supervisor: George Gibbs
Special Effects technicians: Robert Hollow, Martin Gant, Dave McCall, Ray
  Hanson
Special Effects Assistants: Terence Cox, Dale Knowles, Ernest Hill
Special Effects Buyer: Ron Burton
Special Effects Runners: Tim Willis, Darrell Guyon
Model Maker: Valerie Charlton
Modeller: Keith Short
Graphic Artists: Dave Scutt, Bernard Allum
Editing Assistants: Keith Lowes, Peter Compton, Margarita Doyle, Cilla
  Beirne, Roya Salari
Art Directors: John Beard, Keith Pain
Assistant Art Director: Dennis Bosher
Assistant Art Director (French Unit): Françoise Benôit
Art Department Assistant: John Frankish
Art Department Research: Christine Vincent
Set Dressing Designer: Maggie Gray
Draughtsmen: Tony Rimmington, Stephen Bream
Scenic Artist: Andrew Lawson

Construction Manager: Peter Verard
Construction Manager (Assistant): Craig Hillier
Dream/Models Construction Manager: Bill McMinimee
Costume Designer: James Acheson
Costumes: Ray Scott, Martin Adams, Vin Burnham, Jamie Courtier, Martin Adams, Annie Hadley
Assistant Costume Designer: Gilly Hebden
Wardrobe Assistants: Colin Wilson, Anthony Black
Wardrobe Supervisor: Joyce Stoneman
Wardrobe Master: Frank Vinall
Wardrobe Mistress: Jean Fairlie
Hair/Make-up Design: Maggie Weston
Prosthetics Make-up: Aaron Sherman
Make-up/Hairdressing: Elaine Carew, Sallie Evans, Sandra Shepherd, Meinir Brock
Titles and Opticals: Peerless Camera Company, Nick Dunlop, Neil Sharop, Kent Houston, Tim Ollive, Richard Morrison
Music Performer on Soundtrack: National Philharmonic Orchestra
Music Co-ordinator: Ray Cooper
Music Recording: Eric Tomlinson
Additional Music Recording: Andy Jackson
Choreography: Heather Seymour
Sound Recording: Bob Doyle
Re-recording Mixer: Paul Carr
Sound Editor: Rodney Glenn
Footsteps Editor: Barry McCormick
Stunt Arranger: Bill Weston
Samurai Fight Arranger: Bill Hobbs
Stunts: Vic Armstrong, Tim Condren, George Cooper, Clive Curtis, Perry Davey, Jim Dowdall, Terry Forrestal, Tex Fuller, Martin Grance, Frank Henson, Nick Hobbs, Bill Horrigan, Wayne Michaels, Dinny Powell, Greg Powell, Terry Richards, Tip Tipping, Chris Webb
Cast: Jonathan Pryce (Sam Lowry), Robert De Niro (Archibald 'Harry' Tuttle), Katherine Helmond (Mrs Ida Lowry), Ian Holm (Mr Kurtzman), Bob Hoskins (Spoor), Michael Palin (Jack Lint), Ian Richardson (Mr Warrenn), Peter Vaughan (Mr Eugene Helpmann), Kim Griest (Jill Layton), Jim Broadbent (Dr Jaffe), Barbara Hicks (Mrs Terrain), Charles McKeown (Lime), Derrick O'Connor (Dowser), Kathryn Pogson (Shirley), Bryan Pringle (Spiro), Sheila Reid (Mrs Buttle), John Flanagan (TV Interviewer/Salesman), Ray Cooper (technician), Brian Miller (Mrs Buttle), Simon Nash (Boy Buttle), Prudence Oliver (Girl Buttle), Simon Jones (arrest official), Derek Deadman (Bill, Department of Works), Nigel Planer (Charlie, Department of Works), Terence Bayler (TV commercial presenter), Gordon Kaye (MOI lobby porter), Tony Portacio (neighbour in clerks' pool), Bill Wallis (bespec-

tacled lurker), Winston Dennis (samurai warrior), Toby Clark (Small Sam Double), Diana Martin (telegram girl), Jack Purvis (Dr Chapman), Elizabeth Spender (Alison/'Barbara' Lint), Antony Brown (porter, Information Retrieval), Myrtle Devenish (typist, Jack's office), Holly Gilliam (Holly), John Pierce Jones (basement guard), Ann Way (old lady with dog), Don Henderson (1st Black Maria guard), Howard Lew Lewis (2nd Black Maria guard), Oscar Quitak, Harold Innocent, John Grillo, Ralph Nossek, David Grant and James Coyle (interview officials), Patrick Connor (cell guard), Roger Ashton-Griffiths (priest), Russel Keith Grant (young gallant at funeral)
142 mins

1989
Orangina commercial

The Adventures of Baron Munchausen
Director: Terry Gilliam
Producer: Thomas Schühly
Screenplay: Charles McKeown, Terry Gilliam
Director of Photography: Giuseppe Rotunno
Editor: Peter Hollywood
Production Designer: Dante Ferretti
Music composed/orchestrated/conducted by: Michael Kamen
Production companies: Prominent Features (London), Laura Films (Munich)
Executive Producer: Jake Eberts
Co-producer: Ray Cooper
Line Producer: David Tomblin
Supervising Producer: Stratton Leopold
Production Executive: Joyce Herlihy
Executive in Charge of Production: Robert Gordon Edwards
Production Supervisor: Mario Pisani
Production Co-ordinators: Nancy Rubin Levin, Susana Prieto, Gail Samuelson
Production Manager (Spain): Francisco Molero
Production Manager (Italy): Pino Buti
Production Manager (2nd unit): Giorgio Russo
Unit Manager (Italy): Vittorio Fornasiero
Unit Manager (Spain) Fernando Marquerie
Location Manager (2nd unit, Spain): Pepe Panero
Production Assistants (Italy): Riccardo Spada, Claudio Corbucci
Production Assistants (Spain): Manolo Garcia, Gonzalo Jimenez
2nd Unit Director: Michele Soavi
Assistant Directors: Gianni Cozzo, Lee Cleary
Assistant Director (Italy): Luca Lachin
Assistant Director (Spain): José Luis Escolar
2nd Unit Assistant Director (Italy): Catherine Ventura

2nd Unit Assistant Directors (Spain): Javier Chincilla, Javier Balaguer, Mañuel Zarzo
Casting: Irene Lamb, Margery Simkin, Francesco Cinieri
2nd unit Photographer: Gianni Fiore Coltellacci
Model Photography: Roger Pratt
Optical Photography: Nick Dunlop, Doug Forrest, Tim Ollive, Andrew Jeffery, Steve Cutmore, Les Broughton, Michael Ferriter
Matte Photography: John Grant
Matte Photography consultants: Dennis Bartlett, Stanley Sayer
Camera Operator: Franco Bruni
Video Operator: Ian Kelly
2nd unit video operator: Giovanni Piperno
Matte Painters: Doug Ferris, Joy Cuff, Bob Cuff, Leigh Took
Special Effects: Richard Conway
Special Effects (Italy): Adriano Pischiutta
Special Effects (Spain): Antonio Parra
Special Effects Technicians (Italy): Fausto Baldinelli, Luigi Battestelli, Michele Borea, Baniamino Carozza, Marcello Coccia, Marino Erca, Gianni Indovino, Giancarlo Mancini, Massimo Nespoli, Duilio Olmi, Claudio Savassi, Simon Weisse
Special Effects Technicians (GB): Normal Baillie, Christopher Cobould, Peter Davey, Jamie Courtier, Martin Gant, Stephen Hamilton, Bob Hollow, Brian Lince, Dave McCall, Tim Willis
Special Effects Technician (2nd unit Spain): Manolo Gomez
Models Supervisor: Martin Gant
Animatronics Design: Stephen Onions, Jamie Courtier, Ian Whittaker, Alan Croucher
Model Makers: James Machin, Brian Cole
Modellers: Valerie Charlton, Christine Overs
Wireman: Bob Wiesinger, Kevin Matthews, Billy Howe
Puppeteers: David Barclay, Jeff Felix
Computer Animation: Digital Pictures
Rotoscope Artists: Janice Body, Rashid Khares
Motion Control: Peter Tyler, Kenneth Gray
Associate Editor: Chris Blunden
Special Effects Associate Editor: Brian Mann
Supervising Art Director: Maria Teresa Barbasso
Art Directors: Giorgio Giovannini, Nazzareno Piana
Model Unit Art Directors: Michael Lamont, Ken Court
Set Decorator: Francesca Lo Schiavo
Model Unit Set Decorator: Gillian Noyes-Court
Model Unit Decor Artist: Robert Walker
Model Unit Draughtsmen: Dennis Bosher, Neil Lamont
Sculptures Supervisor: Filomeno Crisaro

Sculptures: Giovanni Gianese, Salvatore Placenti
Model Unit Sculptures: Keith Short, John Blakely
Costume Designer: Gabriella Pescucci
Wardrobe Mistress: Irene Santarelli
Wardrobe Master: Gregorio Simili
Wardrobe Supervisor (2nd unit, Spain): Martin Diaz
Wardrobe Master (2nd unit, Spain): Monolo Gomez
Make-up Design: Maggie Weston
Make-up: Fabrizio Sforza, Pam Meager
Make-up artists: Antonio Maltempo, Enrico Iacoponi, Alfredo Tiberi, Gino
    Tamagnini, Christina De Rossi
Make-up chief (2nd unit Spain): Fernando Perez
Make-up (2nd unit Spain): José Perez, Manual Martin Gonsalez
Title Graphics: Chris Allies
Titles and Opticals: Peerless Camera Company
Optical Effects Supervisor: Kent Houston
Optical Effects Co-ordinator: Martin Body, Peerless Camera Company
Music Performed by: Symphony Orchestra Graunke, Chamber Choir 'Pro
    Musika Seria'
Additional Orchestration: Fiachra Trench, John Fiddy, Alan Arnold, Edward
    Shearmur, Rick Wentworth
Orchestra Manager: Paul Talkington
Music Producers: Michael Kamen, Ray Cooper
Music Editor: Chris Brooks
Music Preparation: Vic Fraser
Music recorded and mixed: Stephen McLaughlin
Choreography: Pino Penesse, Giorgio Rossi
Sound Recording: Frank Jahn
Chief Dubbing Mixer: Graham V. Hartsone
Dubbing Mixer: Nocilas le Messurier, Michael A. Carter
Supervising Sound Editor: Peter Pennell
Sound Editors: Colin Miller, Peter Horrocks, Bob Risk
Stunt Co-ordinator: Tony Smart
Stunt Co-ordinator (Italy): Ricardo Cruz Moral
Stunts: Billy Horrigan, Les Maryon, Ricardo Cruz Moral, Dinny Powell,
    Angelo Ragusa, Kiran Shah, Jesus Riaran Torres
Stunts (2nd unit Spain): Eduardo Garcia, José Garcia, Paquito Gomez, Luis
    Gutiérrez, Salvador Marios, Camilo Vila Novoa
Horsemaster: Tony Smart
Cast: John Neville (Baron Munchausen), Sarah Polley (Sally Salt), Eric Idle
    (Desmond/Berthold), Charles McKeown (Rupert/Adolphus), Winston Den-
    nis (Bill Albrecht), Jack Purvis (Jeremy/Gustavus), Valentina Cortese (Queen
    Ariadne/Violet), Uma Thurman (Venus/Rose), Oliver Reed (Vulcan),
    Jonathan Pryce (Horatio Jackson), Bill Paterson (Henry Salt), Peter Jeffrey

(Sultan), Alison Steadman (Daisy), Ray Cooper (functionary), Don Henderson (Commander), Andrew MacLachlan (colonel), Sting (heroic officer), Jose Lifante (Dr Death), Mohamed Badrsalem (executioner), Ray D. Tutto [Robin Williams] (King of the Moon), Kiran Shah (executioner's assistant), Franco Adducci (treasurer), Ettore Martini (1st general), Antonio Pistillo (2nd general), Michael Polley and Tony Smart (gunners)
126 mins

1991
The Fisher King
Director: Terry Gilliam
Producers: Debra Hill, Lynda Obst
Screenplay: Richard LaGravenese
Director of Photography: Roger Pratt
Editor: Lesley Walker
Production Designer: Mel Bourne
Music: George Fenton
Production Company: TriStar Pictures
Associate Producers: Stacey Sher, Anthony Mark
Production Co-ordinator: Pam Cornfeld
Production Office Co-ordinator (NY Unit): Jackie Martin
Unit Production Manager: Anthony Mark
Location Manager: Bill Bowling
Location Managers (NY Unit): Mark Baker, Mark Rhodes
Post-production Supervisor: Sharre Jacoby
1st Assistant Directors: David McGiffert, Joe Napolitano
2nd Assistant Director: Carla Corwin
2nd 2nd Assistant Director: Cynthia Potthast
2nd 2nd Assistant Director (NY Unit): Cyd Adams
Script Supervisor: Marion Tumen
Casting: Howard Feuer
Camera Operator: Craig Haagensen
1st Assistant Camera: Nicholas Musuraca
Special Effects (Creative Consultant): Robert McCarthy
Special Effects (Supervisor): Dennis Dion
Special Effects: Dan Sudick
Special Effects Supervisor (NY Unit): Edward Drohan
Art Director: P. Michael Johnston
Set Designers: Jason Weil, Rick Heinrichs
Set Decorator: Cindy Carr
Set Decorators (NY Unit): Kevin McCarthy, Joseph Bird
Costume Designer: Beatrix Pasztor
Red Knight Costume Design: Keith Greco, Vincent Jefferds
Costume Supervisor: Joie Hutchinson

Key Make-up Artist: Zoltan Elek
Make-up Artist (NY Unit): Craig Lyman
Key Hairstylist: Lisa Joy Meyers
Titles: Chris Allies
Optical/Special Effects: Peerless Camera Company
Synth Programming: Adrian Thomas
Additional Orchestrations: Jeff Atmajian
Music Editor: Kevin Lane
Music Scoring Mixers: Keith Grant, Simon Smart, Gerry O'Riorden
Music Consultant: Ray Cooper
Choreography: Robin Horness
Sound Mixer: Thomas Causey
Sound Mixer (NY Unit): Dennis Maitland II
Re-recording Mixers: Paul Carr, Robert Farr
Sound Editor: Peter Pennell
Dialogue Editor: Alan Paley
Foley Editor: Bob Risk
Stunt Co-ordinator: Chris Howell
Stunts: Janet Brady, Greg Brickman, Jophery Brown, Loyd Catlett, Gilbert
    Combs, Peter Corby, Jeff Dashnaw, Andy Duppin, J.B. Getzwiller, Bonnie
    Hock, Rikke Kesten, Harry Madsen, Bennie Moore, Julie Stone
Horses Owned/trained by: James Zoppe
Cast: Robin Williams (Parry), Jeff Bridges (Jack Lucas), Amanda Plummer
    (Lydia), Adam Bryant (radio engineer), Paul Lombardi (radio engineer),
    David Pierce (Lou Rosen), Ted Ross (limo bum), Lara Harris (Sondra), War-
    ren Olney (TV anchorman), Frazer Smith (news reporter), Mercedes Ruehl
    (Anne Napolitano), Kathy Najimy (crazed video customer), Harry Shearer
    (sitcom actor Ben Starr), Melinda Culea (sitcom wife), James Remini (bum
    at hotel), Mark Bowden (doorman), John Ottavino (father at hotel), Brian
    Michaels (little boy), Jayce Bartok (first punk), Dan Futterman (second
    punk), Bradley Gregg (hippie bum), William Jay Marshall (Jamaican bum),
    William Preston (John the bum), Al Fann (superintendent), Stephen Wesley
    Bridgewater (porno customer), John Heffernan (stockbroker bum), Chris
    Howell (Red Knight), Michael Jeter (homeless cabaret singer), Richard
    LaGravenese (straight jacket yuppie), Anita Dangler (bag lady), Mark
    Bringelson (drooler), Johnny Paganelli (pizza boy), Diane Robin (reception-
    ist), John Benjamin Red (motorcyclist), Lisa Blades (Parry's wife), Christian
    Clemenson (Edwin), Carlos Carrasco (doctor), Joe Jamrog (guard), John
    deLancie TV executive), Lou Hancock (nurse), Caroline Cromelin, Kathleen
    Bridget Kelly, Patrick Fraley (radio show call-ins).
137 mins

1995
Nike commercial

1996
Twelve Monkeys
Director: Terry Gilliam
Producer: Charles Roven
Screenplay: David Peoples, Janet Peoples, Inspired by the film *La Jetée* by
  Chris Marker
Director of Photography: Roger Pratt
Editor: Mick Audsley
Production Designer: Jeffrey Beecroft
Music composer and conductor: Paul Buckmaster
Production company: Polygram Filmed Entertainment in association with Universal Pictures and Atlas/Classico present an Atlas Entertainment Production
Executive Producers: Robert Cavallo, Gary Levinsohn, Robert Kosberg
Co-Producer: Lloyd Phillips
Associate Producers: Kelley Smith-Wait, Mark Egerton
Atlas Production Executive: Richard Suckle
Production Co-ordinator: Elizabeth J. Nevin
2nd Unit Co-ordinator: Ellen Hillers
Unit Production Manager: Lloyd Phillips
Location Manager: Scott Elias
Post-production Co-ordinator: Lucy Darwin
Assistant Directors: Mark Egerton, Phillip A. Patterson, Andrew Bernstein,
  John Rusk
Script Supervisor: Marilyn Bailey
Casting: Margery Simkin, Mike Lemon, Mikie Heilbrun
Camera Operators: Craig Haagensen, Kyle Rudolph, Peter Norman
Computer Graphics Digital and Optical Effects: Peerless Camera Company
Visual Effects Supervisor: Kent Houston
Visual Effects Co-ordinator: Susi Roper
Computer Graphics Supervisor: Manfred-Dean Yurke
Computer Graphics Animators: Richard Doy, Tim Ollive,
Digital Compositing: Richard Bain, Martin Body, Steve Cutmore, Doug Forrest, Chris Panton
Additional Digital Compositing: The Mill
Optical Effects: David Smith
Digital Snow Effects: Emily Goodman, Jim Goodman, Josh Pines
Graphic Artist: R. Scott Purcell
Art Director: Wm Ladd Skinner
Set Decorator: Crispian Sallis
Production Illystrator: Matt Codd
Special Effects Mechanical and Pyrotechnic Engineer: Vincent Montefusco
Special Effects Project Manager: Shirley Montecusco
Special Effects On-set Supervisor: Anthony Simonaitas
Costume Design: Julie Weiss

Wardrobe Supervisor: Melissa Stanton
Costume Supervisor: Eric Sandberg
Make-up/Hair Design: Christina Beveridge
Title Design: Penny Causer
Music Editor: Robin Clarke
Supervising Sound Editor: Peter Joly
Sound Editor: Imogen Pollard
Digital Sound Editor: Jennie Evans
Digital Sound Adviser: Nick Church
Dialogue Editor: Danny Longhurst
ADR Editor: Budge Tremlett
Foley Editor: Ian Wilson
Sound Mixer: Jay Meagher
ADR Mixers: Thomas J. O'Connell, Dominick Tavella
Foley Recordist: Ted Swanscott
Sound Re-recording Mixers: Peter Maxwell, Mick Boggis, Clive Pendry
Foley Artists: Jack Stew, Diane Greaves, Jason Swanscott
Stunt Co-ordinator: Phil Neilson
Animal Co-ordinators: Ernie Karpeles, (London) Jim Clubb
Film Extracts: *Swing Shift Cinderella* (1945), *Little Tinker* (1948), *Who Killed Who?* (1943), *Vertigo* (1958)
Cast: Bruce Willis (James Cole), Madeleine Stowe (Kathryn Railly), Brad Pitt (Jeffrey Goines), Christopher Plummer (Dr Goines), Joseph Melito (Young Cole), Jon Seda (Jose), Michael Chance (Scarface), Vernon Campbell (Tiny), H. Michael Walls (Botanist), Bob Adrian (Geologist), Simon Jones (Zoologist), Carol Florence (Astrophysicist), Bill Raymond (Microbiologist), Ernest Abuba (Engineer), Irma St Paule (Poet), Joey Perillo (Detective Franki), Bruce Kirkpatrick, Wilfred Williams (policemen), Rozwill Young (Billings), Nell Johnson (ward nurse), Fred Strother (L.J. Washington), Rick Warner (Dick Casey), Frank Gorshin (Dr Fletcher), Anthony 'Chip' Brienza (Dr Goodin), Joilet Harris (harassed mother), Drucie McDaniel (waltzing woman patient), John Blaisse (old man patient), Louis Lippa (patient at gate), Stan Kang (X-ray doctor), Pat Dias (WW1 captain), Aaron Michael Lacey (WW1 sergeant), David Morse (Dr Peters), Charles Techman (Professor), Jann Ellis (Marilou), Johnnie Hobbs Jnr (Officer no. 1), Janet L Zappala (anchorwoman), Thomas Roy (evangelist), Harry O'Toole (Louie/Raspy Voice), Korchenko, Chuck Jeffreys (thugs), Lisa Gay Hamilton (Teddy), Felix A Pirie (Fale), Matthew Ross (Bee), Barry Price, John Panzarella, Larry Daly (agents), Arthur Fennell (anchorwoman), Karl Warren (pompous man), Christopher Meloni (Lt Halperin), Paul Meshejian (Detective Dalva), Robert O'Neill (Wayne), Kevin Thigpen (Kweskin), Lee Golden (hotel clerk), Joseph McKenna (Wallace), Jeff Tanner (plain clothes cop), Faith Potts (store clerk), Michael Ryan Segal (Weller), Annie Golden (woman cabbie), Lisa Talerico (ticket agent), Stephen Bridgewater (airport

detective), Franklin Huffman (plump businesswoman), JoAnn A Dawson (gift Ssore clerk), Jack Doughery, Lenny Daniels, Herbert C. Hauls Jnr (airport security), Charley Scalies (impatient traveller), Carolyn Walker (terrified traveller)

129 mins

1998
Fear and Loathing in Las Vegas
Director: Terry Gilliam
Producers: Laila Nabulsi, Patrick Cassavetti, Stephen Nemeth
Screenplay: Terry Gilliam, Tony Grisoni, Tod Davies, Alex Cox
Based on the book by: Hunter S. Thompson
Director of Photography: Nicola Pecorini
Editor: Lesley Walker
Production designer: Alex McDowell
Music: Ray Cooper
Production companies: Summit Entertainment and Universal Pictures present a Rhino Films/Laila Nabulsi production,
Executive producers: Harold Bronson, Richard Foos, Patrick Wachsberger
Co-producer: Elliot Lewis Rosenblatt
Associate producer: John Jergens
Unit production managers: Elliot Lewis Rosenblatt, Mark Indig
Location manager: Molly Allen
First assistant director: Philip Patterson
Second assistant director: Christina Fong
Assistant Directors: Jamie Marshall, Seth Edelson (Las Vegas); Doug Aarniokoski, Ingrid Behrens (2nd unit)
Script supervisors: Karon May, Brenda Wachsel; Patricia Gordon (2nd unit)
Casting: Margery Simkin
Camera Operator: Frank Perl
First Assistant Camera: Steve Itano
Second Assistant Camera: Hilton Goring
First Assistant 'B' Camera: Lucas Biclan
Loaders: Forrest Thurman, Lila Bayall, Peter Dacey
Steadicam Operator: Nicola Pecorini
Visual Effects Supervisor: Kent Houston, Peerless Camera Company
US Effects Co-ordinator: Michael Cooper
UK Effects Producer: Susi Roper
Digital Effects: Andrea Adams, Steve Cutmore, Ditch Doy, Tim Olive, John Swinnerton, Kitty Veevers
Special Effects Co-ordinator: Steve Galich
Special Effects Supervisor: Ray Svedin
Graphic Design: Martin Charles, michael Marcus
Lizard Puppeteers: Melissa Chang, Michael Colton, Amanda Forman, Julie

Forman, Motoyoshi Hata, Chris heeter, Lisa Nelson, Vince Niebla, Art
Pimental, Bradley Ross, Sam Sainz, Terry Sandin, David Weigand
Art Directors: Chris Gorak; Steve Arnold (Las Vegas)
Set Designer: Lynn Christopher
Set Decorator: Nancy Haigh
Costume Designer: Julie Weiss
Costume Supervisor: Eden C. Coblenz
2nd Unit Wardrobe: Jacky Ward
Make-up: Patty York, Cheryl Nick, Bob Scribner
Lounge Lizard Designer: Rob Bottin
Additional Make-up Effects: Matthew Mungle
Demon Effects Make-up: Rob Bottin
Demon Effects: Fernando Favilia, Russ Shinkle, Dawn Sverdia
Hair: Bridget Cook
Hair Stylists: Lynn Del Kail, Eileen Powell, Cindy Rose
Title Design: Chris Allies
Optical Effects: David Smith, Trevor Withers
Digital Scanning: Pete Williams, Cinesite (Europe) Ltd
Music Performed by: Ray Cooper, Tomoyasu Hotei
Electronic Music Treatments: Stephen McLaughlin
Music Editor: Kevin Lane
Sound Engineer: Rupert Coulson
Soundtrack: 'My Favourite Things' by Rodgers and Hammerstein, performed
by The Lennon Sisters; 'Combination of the Two' by Sam Andrew, per-
formed by Big Brother and the Holding Company; 'One Toke Over the
Line' by Michael Brewer, Tom Shipley, performed by Brewer and Shipley;
'Thinking of Baby' by/performed by Elmer Bernstein; 'Spy v. Spy' by Eliza-
beth Cox, Michael Cudahy, Nicholas Codahy, performed by Combustible
Edison; 'Moon Mist' by Mercer Ellington, performed by The Out-Islanders;
'Lady' by Jeff Beck, Tim Bogert, Carmine Appice, Duane Hitchings, performed by Beck, Bogert, Appice; 'She's a Lady' by Paul Anka, performed by
Tom Jones; 'My Love, Forgive me' by Vita Pallavicini, Sydney Lee, performed by Robert Goulet; 'It's Not Unusual' by Gordon Mills, Les Reed,
performed by Tom Jones; 'Strangers in the Night' by Bert Kaempfert,
Charles Singleton, Eddie Snyder, performed by Wayne Newton; 'Sgt Pep-
per's Lonely Hearts Club Band' by Lennon and McCartney, performed by
the Hollyridge Strings; 'For Your Love' by Graham Gouldman, performed
by The Yardbirds; 'White Rabbit' by Grace Slick, performed by Jefferson
Airplane; 'Stuck Inside of Mobile with the Memphis Blues Again' by/per-
formed by Bob Dylan; 'Somebody to Love' by Darby Slick, performed by
Jefferson Airplane; 'Let's Get Together' by Chet Powers, performed by The
Youngbloods; 'Mama Told me Not to Come' by Randy Newman, performed by Three Dog Night; 'Time is Tight' by Stephen Cropper, Donald
'Duck' Dunn etc, performed by Booker T. & the MGs; 'You're getting to Be

a Habit with Me ' by Harry Warren, Al Dubin, performed by Frank Sinatra; 'Magic Moments' by Burt Bacharach, Hal David, performed by Perry Como; 'Yummy, Yummy' by Hal Levine, performed by Ohio Express; 'Tammy' by Jay Livingstone, performed by Debbie Reynolds; 'Ball and Chain' by Willie Mae Thornton, performed by Big Brother and the Holding Company; 'Expecting to Fly' by Neil Young, performed by Buffalo Spring-field; 'Jumpin' Jack Flash' by Mick Jagger, Keith Richards, performed by The Rolling Stones; 'Viva Las Vegas' by Doc Pomus, Mort Shuman, per-formed by Dead Kennedys.

Choreography: JoAnn Pregaletto Jansen
Production Sound Mixer: Jay Meagher
Sound Editor: Peter Pennell
Dialogue Editor: Alan Paley
ADR: Stephen Bridgewater, J. R. Westen, Lia Sargent, Paul Carr, Mike Prest-wood Smith, Joe Gallaher
Foley Editor: Bob Risk
Stunt Co-ordinator: Noon Orsatti
Aerial Co-ordinator: Danny Castle
Film Extract: *Death of the Red Planet* (1973)
Cast: Johnny Depp (Raoul Duke), Benicio Del Toro (Dr Gonzo), Christina Ricci (Lucy), Gary Busey (highway patrolman), Ellen Barkin (North Star waitress), Michael Jeter (L. Ron Bumquist), Harry Dean Stanton (judge), Katherine Helmond (reservations clerk), Tobey Maguire (hitchhiker), Craig Bierko (Laceda), Cameron Diaz (blonde TV reporter), Jenete Goldstein (maid), Michael Lee Gogin (uniformed dwarf), Larry Cedar (car rental agent, LA), Brian LeBaron (parking attendant), Michael Warwick (bell boy), Mark Harmon (magazine reporter), Tyde Kierney (reporter), Tim Thomer-son (hoodlum), Richard Riehle (dune buggy driver), Ransom Gates (buggy passenger), Frank Romano (buggy passenger), Gil Boccaccio, Gary Bruno (Desert Room doormen), Richard Portnow (wine coloured tuxedo), Steve Schirripa (goon), Verne J. Troya (wee waiter), Will Blount (black guy), Ben Yeager (clown barker), Penn Jillette (carnie talker), Christopher Callen (Bazooko Circus waitress), Ben Van der Veen (TV crew man), Lyle Lovett (road person), Flea (musician), Alex Craig Mann (stockbroker), Gregory Itzin (clerk at Mint Hotel), Troy Evans (police chief), Gale Baker (police chief's wife), Chris Meloni (clerk at Flamingo Hotel), Chris Hendrie (execu-tive director), Larry Brandenburg (cop in black), Stephen Bridgewater (human cannonball), Robert Allen (car rental agent, Las Vegas), David Bris-bin (man in car), James O'Sullivan, Milt Tarver (TV newsmen), Donald Morrow (voice of film narrator), Debbie Reynolds (voice of Debbie Reynolds).

118 mins

Index